Maximum Influence

Maximum Influence

The 12 Universal Laws of Power Persuasion

Kurt W. Mortensen

American Management Association
New York • Atlanta • Brussels • Chicago • Mexico City • San Francisco
Shanghai • Tokyo • Toronto • Washington, D.C.

10/05
20.00
MATT

Special discounts on bulk quantities of AMACOM books are
available to corporations, professional associations, and other
organizations. For details, contact Special Sales Department,
AMACOM, a division of American Management Association,
1601 Broadway, New York, NY 10019.
Tel.: 212-903-8316. Fax: 212-903-8083.
Web site: www.amacombooks.org

This publication is designed to provide accurate and authoritative
information in regard to the subject matter covered. It is sold with the
understanding that the publisher is not engaged in rendering legal,
accounting, or other professional service. If legal advice or other expert
assistance is required, the services of a competent professional person
should be sought.

Library of Congress Cataloging-in-Publication Data

Mortensen, Kurt W.
      Maximum influence : the 12 universal laws of power persuasion /
   Kurt W. Mortensen.—1st ed.
         p.   cm.
      Includes bibliographical references and index.
      ISBN 0-8144-7258-3
      1. Persuasion (Psychology)   2. Influence (Psychology)   3. Success—Psychological
   aspects.   I. Title.

   BF637.P4M67 2004
   153.8'52—dc22

                                                              2004000847

Printing Hole Number

10   9   8   7   6   5

Contents

Foreword

Napoleon Hill said, "Persuasion is the magic ingredient that will help you to forge ahead in your profession or business—and to achieve happy and lasting personal relationships." As we all know, persuasion is the skill of the ultra-prosperous. It is how people gain power and influence. It is how people create staggering wealth—how businesses thrive, how books are published, how properties are purchased, and how Web sites sell millions of dollars worth of product. Persuasion is the life-blood of powerful and effective day-to-day living. The art of persuasion is what makes the world turn.

I have known Kurt Mortensen for years. A master of persuasion himself, he exudes every quality and possesses every skill set forth in this book. Through this book, Kurt has provided the most complete, comprehensive work on persuasion and influence I have ever read. Nowhere in persuasion literature have I ever seen the art broken down into such thorough and easy-to-understand concepts, covering every aspect of persuasion imaginable. Never before has it been so easy to understand human behavior and how to use it to your advantage. Based on true-life examples and exhaustive psychological and sociological research, Kurt imparts of his wisdom, knowledge, and experience with insight, wit, and enthusiasm.

The powerful, time-tested, and proven techniques in the following pages will equip the reader with the tools necessary to make profound life changes. These very laws of persuasion have made me millions of dollars and have helped thousands of others apply them in both their business and personal lives to strengthen relationships, to create wealth, to transform careers, to influence lives for the better. Each one of the laws discussed will improve your success dramatically, even doubling and tripling your income. I only wish I had had this kind of information earlier in my career! It would have limited the number of lessons I had to learn through the school of hard knocks.

Kurt's message embodies the mission of my Latest Challenge: to create a million *enlightened* millionaires by the year 2020. Together with my partner Mark Victor Hansen, we will create millionaires who are enlightened and who give back to their communities. One of the number one skills our students must learn in building their financial empires is persuasion. Reading this book will truly be a life-changing influence for anyone who applies the principles so thoroughly and carefully outlined. *Maximum Influence* is a must for the library of anyone who wants to be in control of all aspects of his or her life. Reading this book will not only make you a student of persuasion, but also a learned scholar.

Robert G. Allen
Author of *Nothing Down, Creating Wealth, Multiple Streams of Income,* and Coauthor of *One-Minute Millionaire.*

Acknowledgments

Grateful acknowledgments to all of the people who helped make *Maximum Influence* a reality. I want to express my love and appreciation to my loving wife Denita and my children, for their love and support throughout this project. I also want to express special thanks to Emily Spencer, Beth Davis, Kathy Kehrli, Mike Ray, Robert Allen, and all my friends and family for their time and support during the creation of *Maximum Influence*.

Maximum Influence

Introduction

I LOVE TO FIX PEOPLE! I draw genuine pleasure in helping others achieve success and fulfill their dreams. I have committed many years of my life to studying the path to success, and have trained, coached, and mentored thousands of people. Early on, I learned that persuasion is one of the most important skills to develop if you truly want to be in control and achieve all you can in life. After learning this profound lesson, I decided to dedicate my life even more specifically to the study of persuasion and influence because I knew it was the only way I would realize my loftiest dreams.

I now see that persuasion permeates day-to-day life, influencing hundreds of decisions large and small. I can't even imagine carrying on my daily routine without my sharply honed persuasion skills! For example, how can someone be an effective manager or parent without persuasion skills? I have worked for many corporations and have seen time and time again the old style of management: Do it or you're fired. Sure, this results in short-term compliance, but it also results in long-term resentment, mistrust, and anger. And it definitely does *not* result in effective, win-win persuasion, either in the short or long term. So, I dedicated my life to finding the true, honorable, win-win forms of persuasion, motivation, and influence.

Here, within these pages, lie some of the gems I've learned about helping others become better people and achieve more in their lives—while they in turn improve the lives of others. Why go through life doing things you hate to do? Why lose spark and energy as life progresses? Life should be full of excitement, enthusiasm, and vitality! These traits are not reserved just for children. When you find your passion, your calling in life, then you will once again possess these traits. The missing ingredients for most people are contained in *Maximum Influence*. Learn them, use them, and you'll change your world.

Maximum Influence contains thousands of hours' worth of academic and scientific research with hands-on models and examples. Over the years, I have read countless books and taken just as many training sessions and seminars. They all offered excellent key points on persuasion, motivation, and influence, but I could never find a source that combined the hundreds of scientific studies of persuasion and influence into a single, comprehensive catalog of persuasive principles, strategies, and techniques. They all had a few nuggets of wisdom, but I was looking for the gold mine. The principles of Maximum Influence are designed for anybody who relies on the power of persuasion in his or her career. It is an absolute must for sales professionals, business managers, marketers, advertisers, lawyers, fundraisers, politicians, nonprofit enterprises, or anyone who wants more control over their income, their job, and their life. Applying these skills makes the difference between *hoping* for a better future and *having* a better future. As you effectively apply the principles taught in this book, the results you desire will come with greater speed and less effort.

Persuasion and influence have changed a great deal in the past twenty years. If you are involved in any kind of persuasion, your consumer, your prospects, and your customers have changed. They are bombarded with more than five thousand persuasive messages a day. Your prospect is better educated and more skeptical than ever before. If you use only the same tactics that you learned years ago, you'll lose sales. Have you ever had a potential customer that you knew needed your product or service? They wanted your product or service, they could afford it, but they still didn't buy from you? What happened? It was a perfect fit for both parties. As a master of persuasion and influence, you will understand your prospects' mindset, their decision-making process, and how to close the sale so both of you win.

I have never met anyone who knows all the laws of Power Persuasion. What we have found through research is that most people actually use only two or three persuasive techniques. Even the most successful salespeople typically use only seven or eight persuasive tools. This is like playing "Chopsticks" when you could be equipped to play Mozart. Many top producers stop learning when they start making a comfortable living. If you follow the steps I outline in the following chapters, you will be equipped with countless techniques, strategies, insights, and tools to manage any situation. You will find yourself starting to wield Maximum Influence.

Pay the price to become a professional in your field. Don't settle for mediocrity; become the best you can be at what you do. Who is the best in basketball? Michael Jordan. He knew he could not become the best without daily practice of fundamental skills along with the addition of new skills. He also knew he could not excel without a team, and especially not without a coach. True excellence comes from knowledge, continuing education, and consistent practice.

To help you as you learn the techniques and strategies of Maximum Influence, let me outline what I call the "Five P's of Success." The first "P" is *psyche*. That's the mental aspect of the game. It's a critical skill for all successful salespeople, but it works equally well in all fields. You will not be able to achieve your goals until you *believe* you can achieve your goals. All the best techniques and tools will not help you until you first believe in yourself. Unfortunately, most of the people we know tend to bring us down. When you tell them about your dreams and the things you want to accomplish in life, they can be very discouraging. Do you know people like that? When you have the right psyche, you know where you're going and what you want to accomplish, and anything that people say is not going to matter. The right psyche involves knowing what you want and having a plan to get it. When your psyche is in its proper place, you will always follow your heart.

The second "P" is *persistence*. Persistence is the number one reason why people are successful in life. It's also the driving force that determines why certain people are wealthy. Their success is not due to financial backing or education. They owe their achievements to persistence. There's an old sales adage: "Some will; some won't. So what? Who's next?" It's a numbers game. Most sales are closed after the fifth attempt. Never let obstacles in life take your eyes off your goals.

The next "P" is *personal development*. All top producers have a personal development program. There is a direct relationship between your personal development program and your income. Personal success expert Brian Tracy says, "If you can get yourself to read thirty minutes a day, you're going to double your income every year," and I know from personal experience that this technique works! Most homes valued at over a quarter of a million dollars have a library. Studies consistently demonstrate that those who are learning and growing every day are more optimistic about life. They are more enthusiastic about where they're going and what they hope to accomplish. Those who aren't learning and growing every day become negative, pessimistic, and doubtful about themselves and their future. Turn your car into a university on wheels by listening to motivational tapes and CDs. When you're at home, turn off the TV and read a book. There are two ways to learn in life: You can learn by trial and error, attempting to figure things out on your own, or you can learn from somebody else, who's already been there and done it before. Somebody has already figured out everything you need to learn about life, and written a book about it or put it on disk or tape. So invest in your future by investing in your personal development.

Do you know the number one thing that will change someone's mind? It's the fourth "P"—*passion*. More than anything, passion will allow you to recruit the hearts and minds of your prospects. Do you have passion and heartfelt conviction for your product or service? We love people who are excited, animated, and full of passion. When you have passion for something you're excited about, you have zeal and you want to share it with the world. You're excited to convert as many people to your cause as possible. Passion alone can be effective in swaying opinion and getting people to support your product or service. Passion springs from a combination of belief, enthusiasm, and emotion. Find passion for your product and find joy in helping others enjoy it.

The fifth and final "P"—and the one that comprises most of this book—is *persuasion*. Spend a little time each day learning and mastering the world of persuasion and influence. The basic premise of Maximum Influence is to get what you want when you want it, and in the process to win friends and to help people love doing what you want them to do. There is a big difference between presenting and persuading. Anyone can spit out a list of features and benefits, showing off their product or service and pushing their products on people. By using Maximum Influence you draw people to you, and thus attract more customers—and more sales. We want you to get customers to beg for your product or service and win customers for life. And that's exactly what *Maximum Influence* strives to do.

For further information on any of the topics covered in this book, or to master the art of persuasion and influence, go to www.maximuminfluence .com, click on free reports and use the following keywords:

Keywords

Chapter 1. Power of Persuasion	Test Your Persuasion IQ
Chapter 2. Twelve Laws of Persuasion	Free Persuasion Newsletter
Chapter 3. Law of Dissonance	What Is Dissonance (audio)
Chapter 4. Law of Obligation	Universal Laws of Success

1

The Power of Persuasion

The most important persuasion tool you have
in your entire arsenal is integrity.
—ZIG ZIGLAR

UNDERSTANDING THE THEORIES OF PERSUASION, motivation, and influence will put you in life's driver's seat. Why? Because everything you want, or will want, in life comes from these three simple concepts. Did you know that less than 1 percent of the world's population understand and can actually apply the twelve Laws of Persuasion? Therefore, as I reveal the secrets of influence and science of persuasion, you will be able to persuade and influence with complete accuracy. You will gain instant influence over others and inspire others to take action, all while getting exactly what you want from life. You will win people to your way of thinking and will empower yourself with an unshakable confidence. You will triple your prosperity in sales and marketing. You will become a captivating magnet of success.

As you develop what I call Maximum Influence, others will be drawn to you as metal filings are drawn to a powerful magnet. Financial, social, and personal success will come to you. Gateways previously closed to you will swing wide open and the world of opportunity will beat a path to your door. The life-changing skills and techniques described in this book are based on timeless, *proven* principles. They have been developed from countless hours of persuasion research and exhaustive studies into human nature. And now, for the first time, they are being unveiled to you.

This book teaches the twelve critical Laws of Persuasion and instructs you on how to utilize these cutting-edge persuasion strategies so you can gain the influence you need NOW. You'll learn how to make people instinctively like and trust you, something that might otherwise take you years to accomplish. No longer will you face the unexpected with fear or intimidation. Rather, you will confront it head on with credibility, control, and confidence. Day in and day out, you will turn each challenge facing you into a winning situation. In short, you will be a master of your own destiny.

Persuasion: The Heartbeat of Our Economy

The power of persuasion is of extraordinary and critical importance in today's world. Nearly every human encounter includes an attempt to gain influence or to persuade others to our way of thinking. Regardless of age, profession, religion, or philosophical beliefs, people are always trying to persuade each other. We all want to be able to persuade and influence so others will listen to, trust, and follow us. A recent study by economists found that a whopping 26 percent of gross domestic product was directly attributable to the use of persuasion skills in the marketplace.[1] Persuasion is the gas to our economy's engine. Think about it—$2.3 trillion of our gross domestic product comes from the skills of persuasion and influence. You rarely see large corporations downsizing their sales forces. Sales professionals are assets to the company, not liabilities. Master Persuaders will always find employment, even in the slowest of economies.

The ability to persuade is power, for good or for bad. Think of all the people in your life who have persuaded you to reach higher and achieve greatness. Persuasive people keep kids off drugs, prevent wars, and improve lives. Of course, persuasive people also get kids on drugs, stir up wars, and destroy lives. We want to focus on the power of persuasion for the improvement and betterment of ourselves, our friends and families, and our communities. Let's face it, though: Most of us are not born persuaders. For the majority of us, the arts of persuasion and influence are not gifts we inherently possess. Sure, there are the stereotypical persuaders who are naturally friendly, outgoing, and sometimes loud. Research reveals, however, that some of the best persuaders are actually introverts.

For many, the notion of becoming a Master Persuader means being forceful, manipulative, or pushy. Such an assumption is dead wrong. Tactics like these might get results for the short term, but Maximum Influence is about getting results for the long term. Lasting influence isn't derived from calculated maneuvers, deliberate tactics, or intimidation. Rather, proper implementation of the latest persuasion strategies will allow you to influence with the utmost integrity. People will naturally and automatically trust you, have confidence in you, and want to be persuaded by you. In short, they will want to do what you want them to do.

It is a common misconception that only individuals involved in sales, marketing, or leadership positions need to learn the laws of persuasion. This is simply not true! Sales professionals, business managers, parents, negotiators, lawyers, coaches, speakers, advertisers, and doctors can all use these skills. Everyone needs persuasion skills, no matter their occupation. What people don't realize is that everyone uses the techniques and tactics of persuasion each day. People constantly study one another, trying to figure out how to get someone to do what they want them to do. Needless to say, mastering communication and understanding human nature are essential life lessons if we want to effectively persuade and influence people. We can't get anywhere in life unless we are able to work with other human beings. It is through our dealings with others that we achieve success. No one is self-sufficient. Everything of any value that we accomplish in life is achieved through the support and help of the people around us. As a society, we are interconnected, and the ability to make those connections is vital to our success.

Used for You or Against You

Advertisers spend billions of dollars researching and analyzing our psychographics and demographics to figure out how to subtly persuade us. Roselli, Skelly, and Mackie point out that "even by conservative estimates, the average person is exposed to 300 to 400 persuasive media messages a day from the mass media alone."[2] We are bombarded with thousands of persuasive messages each day through a myriad of sources, including newspapers, magazines, billboards, signs, packaging, the Internet, direct mail, radio, TV, mail order, catalogs, coworkers, management, sales professionals, and even parents or children. The question is: Are these tactics being used for you or against you? Thousands, even millions, are persuaded against their better judgment every day, simply because they are unequipped to accurately interpret and effectively respond to the advertising barrage we perpetually face. In this case, what you don't know *will* hurt you. Persuasive influences flood our daily existence and are inescapable. It is without question in our best interest to master Maximum Influence, know how it works, and learn how to implement its proven techniques so we are empowered *today*.

When You Have the Right Tools You Will Succeed

Let's be honest: We all want and need things from other people. We want people to follow, trust, and accept us. We want to influence others to our way of thinking. We want to get what we want—when we want it. Possessing the right tools and knowing how to use them is the secret to success.

Maximum Influence supplies a complete toolbox of effective persuasion techniques. Most people use the same limited persuasion tools over and over, achieving only temporary, limited, or even undesired results. You can do only so many things with a hammer, right? We need to open our minds to the whole toolbox of persuasion and influence. We have all heard the maxim: "If the only tool you have is a hammer, you tend to see every problem as a nail." The problem is, everyone is not a nail. The art of persuasion must be customized to every group or individual, to every situation or event. It's like playing the piano with only two or three notes: You're playing "Chopsticks" when you should be playing Mozart. When you play with all the keys of persuasion and influence, you can create a masterpiece with your life.

Definitions

■ **Persuasion** is the process of changing or reforming attitudes, beliefs, opinions, or behaviors toward a predetermined outcome through voluntary compliance. If you properly implement the strategies of Maximum Influence, you'll persuade others not only to *want* what you want, but also to be eager to *do* what you want. Note that persuasion is not the same as negotiation, a term that suggests some degree of backing down or meeting in the middle. Rather than compromising, as in negotiation, effective persuasion will actually convince the opposing party to abandon their previous position and embrace yours.

■ **Influence** is who you are and how you, as a person, will impact the message. This includes whether you are viewed as trustworthy and credible, for example.

■ **Power** increases your ability to persuade and influence. This power can be seen with people who possess knowledge, have authority, or use coercion during a persuasion process.

■ **Motivation** is the ability to incite others to act in accordance with the suggestions and ideals you have posed. Motivation is your "call to action," or what you want your audience to *do*.

Persuasion and Rhetoric

One's ability to persuade meant great social prestige in the ancient Greek world. Homer regarded the rhetorical skills of Nestor and Odysseus as tremendous inborn gifts. It was Aristotle who first introduced persuasion as a skill that could be learned. At that time, rhetorical training became the craze for the citizens of Athens, especially the politically elite. The first book ever written on persuasion was Aristotle's *The Art of Rhetoric.* The book's basic principles established a foundation for persuasion that still holds true today.[3]

Aristotle taught that rhetoric was an art form that could be approached systematically by a formula for all persuasive attempts. Aristotle's most famous contribution to persuasion was his three means of persuasion: ethos, pathos, and logos. He argued that the most effective persuasive attempts contain all three concepts, setting an unshakable foundation for success. Let's briefly review Aristotle's three basic means of persuasion.

Ethos

Ethos refers to the personal character of the speaker. Aristotle believed that audiences could be persuaded if they perceived a speaker as credible. In his own estimation: "We believe good men more fully and readily than others." Aristotle also stated that "ethos is not a thing or a quality but an interpretation that is the product of the speaker-audience interaction."[4] Ethos includes such things as body type, height, movement, dress, grooming, reputation, vocal quality, word choice, eye contact, sincerity, trust, expertise, charisma . . . well, you get the idea. It is the audience's perception of the credibility of the speaker.

Aristotle taught that ethos was the most powerful of the three persuasive means. Indeed, scientific research has proven the power of individual ethos. A study by Hovland and Weiss gave students messages that were identical in all respects except for their source. High-credibility sources yielded large opinion changes in the students while low-credibility sources produced small opinion changes.[5]

Pathos

Pathos is the psychological state of the audience. The psychological or emotional state of the listener can affect persuasion because "our judgment when we are pleased and friendly [is] not the same as when we are pained and hostile."[6] When considering pathos, it is important to know both the individual's actual state of mind and his desired state of mind. When you determine the difference between the two, you can use that knowledge to your advantage. By helping them see how they can get from their current state to their desired state, you can persuade people to do just about anything.

Logos

Logos is the substance of a message, or the logic presented to provide proof to the listener. Aristotle believed that humans are fundamentally reasonable people who make decisions based on what makes sense. This manner of reasoning is what enables the audience to find the message persuasive and convincing.

Aristotle's three concepts are central to understanding modern-day persuasion. The principles and laws described in *Maximum Influence* are founded upon the principles presented by Aristotle and the ancient Greeks. Admittedly, however, the times and the means of persuasion have changed over the years. It is more difficult now than in any other time in history to persuade and influence those around us. In Aristotle's time, the people had limited access to information and most could not read. That gave Aristotle an advantage we no longer have today.

Modern-day Master Persuaders run into three major factors that make persuasion a greater challenge than it was in the past. First, people are better educated and have access to more information than they did in any other time in history. With the explosion of the Internet, information is instantly available. We can now find out the cost of a car before we even enter the dealership. The second roadblock to persuasion is that today's consumers are increasingly doubtful and skeptical. The number of persuasive arguments we see and hear every day is growing at an alarming rate, and it takes more and more effort to sort out the valid offers from the scams. The third barrier to persuasion is choice. Now, via the Internet, the consumer has access to the world market. In the past, if you had the only bookstore in town, that is where people had to shop. Now, one bookstore owner has to compete with hundreds of bookstores around the globe and with Amazon for the same business.

Persuasion, Communication, and Knowledge Breed Confidence

The greatest common denominator of the ultra-prosperous is that wealthy people are master communicators. There is a direct correlation between your ability to persuade others and the level of your income. Impeccable and masterful communication unarguably leads to wealth. The highest paid and most powerful people on the planet are all master communicators. These individuals put themselves at stake in front of large groups, communicating and persuading in such a way that people are inspired to support them. Your financial success in life will be largely determined by your ability to communicate with other people. Everything you want, but don't currently have, you will have to get from others. Your ability to effectively communicate and persuade will be your key to riches.

Persuasion is also your golden ticket to promotion. Communication skills rank number one of all the personal qualities employers seek in college graduates.[7] While most people shy away from overtly persuasive situations, master communicators welcome such opportunities. Master communicators feel in control of challenging situations because they understand the art of persuasion and they know how to recognize and use persuasive strategies.

The Foundational Principles of Persuasion

The Laws of Persuasion Are Neutral

Central to understanding persuasion is the concept of neutrality. The laws of persuasion are neither good nor evil. They simply exist. Just as nuclear energy can be used to create electricity or an atomic bomb, persuasion can be used to create unity or to force compliance. Whether the outcome is good or bad depends on the person using the laws and how that person applies the techniques of persuasion. Some people desire to win at any cost, using any available tactics including misusing the laws of persuasion. These individuals are willing to use guilt, violence, intimidation, temptation, bribery, and blackmail to get the desired result.

However, when used properly, persuasion is our best friend. Through persuasion we create peace agreements, promote fund-raising efforts, and convince motorists to buckle up. Persuasion is the means by which the coach of an underdog team inspires players to win. It is also the method employed by the Surgeon General to convince people to have regular mammograms and prostate examinations, by managers to increase employee performance and morale, and by hostage negotiators to convince criminals to free their captives.

This book focuses on using Maximum Influence in positive ways. Misuse of the laws will only come back to haunt you in the long run. You might get short-term instant results, but your long-term future will be bleak. The tools outlined in this book are powerful and are not to be used selfishly. They should not be considered a means of gaining a desired result at any cost. Rather, you should use these tools to get your desired outcome only when it is a win-win situation for all involved.

The fable of the sun and the wind provides an excellent example of properly implemented persuasion. The sun and the wind were always arguing about which of them was the strongest. The wind believed he was stronger because of his destructive power in tornados and hurricanes. He wanted the sun to admit he was stronger, but the sun held fast to his own opinion and could not be convinced. One day the sun decided he wanted the matter settled once and for all, so he invited the wind to compete with him in a contest. The sun chose the contest carefully. He pointed out an old man taking a walk, and challenged the wind to use his power to blow the man's jacket off. The wind felt this would be an easy contest to win and began to blow. To his surprise, each gust of wind only made the man cling more tightly to his jacket. The wind blew harder, and the man held on tighter. The harder the wind blew, the more the man resisted. The powerful blows of wind even knocked the man down, but he would not let go of his jacket. Finally, the wind gave up and challenged the sun to succeed in getting the man to take off his jacket. The sun smiled and shone radiantly upon the man. The man felt the warmth of the sun, and sweat began to appear on his forehead. The sun continued pouring out warmth and sunshine upon the man and, at last, the man took off his jacket. The sun had won the contest. This is an example of Maximum Influence at its best. If your attempt to persuade is a win-win, others will be eager to do what you want them to do. As you perform the exercises and techniques outlined in this book, you will notice powerful changes in your ability to persuade and influence others.

Persuasion Must Have an Audience

The art of persuading and influencing others always requires an audience, whether it's a single person, a small group of ten, or a much larger assembly of listeners. This component is constant, so it is critical to know how to adapt quickly to your audience's needs, wants, fears, and desires. Knowing how to research and read your audience will help you determine which tools or techniques will be the most effective in any given situation. Using the wrong techniques and tools, on the other hand, will automatically create barriers between you and your audience, which in turn will diminish your potential to persuade them. When you effectively integrate the principles and laws of persuasion with the characteristics of influence, power, and motivation, your audience will always be friendly, and desirable results will be the outcome. In Chapter 15, Your Pre-Persuasion Checklist, I will spend more time on how to analyze, adapt to, and read your audience.

Effective Persuasion Requires Adaptation

Have you ever tried the same approach with a customer that your boss uses on you and had it bomb miserably? Becoming a Master Persuader requires more than mimicking other persuaders. You must not only fully understand the wide variety of persuasive techniques available, but you must also be ready to use the techniques best suited for any given situation. Acquiring this level of skill demands a commitment to watch, analyze, study, and apply the concepts of Maximum Influence.

Human nature is as varied as the colors of the rainbow. Human actions and thoughts are never perfectly predictable because each of us has different emotions, attitudes, beliefs, personalities, and traits. A beginner's tendency is to find one persuasive technique that works and stick with that. Unfortunately, you cannot use the same persuasion tool on everyone. Depending on the situation and the techniques you use, people will agree with you, refuse to listen, or be indifferent to your efforts. The Master Persuader has many tools and can therefore adapt and customize them to suit any situation or personality.

Effective Persuasion Has Lasting Impact

Do you want short-term temporary results or long-term permanent results? Effective persuasion has lasting impact, but it requires dedicated study and long-term commitment on the part of the persuader. The Hierarchy of Persuasion (Figure 1-1) sheds light on how the world uses different levels of persuasion, ranging from control at the most short-term level to genuine commitment at the long-term level.

The qualities listed at the base of the pyramid are the most easily and commonly used, but they achieve only temporary results. Such results are temporary because they do not address a person's genuine wants or desires. Persuasion based on the qualities listed at the top of the pyramid is effective whether pressure is perceived or not. Such a method creates lasting results because it taps into and involves a person's true interests. Determining whether you want short or long-term results dictates which area on the pyramid should be the focus of your efforts.

Imagine the CEO of a large corporation calling one of his vice presidents to a meeting. At the meeting, the vice president is informed that he must raise $20,000 in employee contributions for a charity the company is going to sponsor. The CEO is not concerned with the means the vice president

Figure 1-1. Hierarchy of Persuasion.

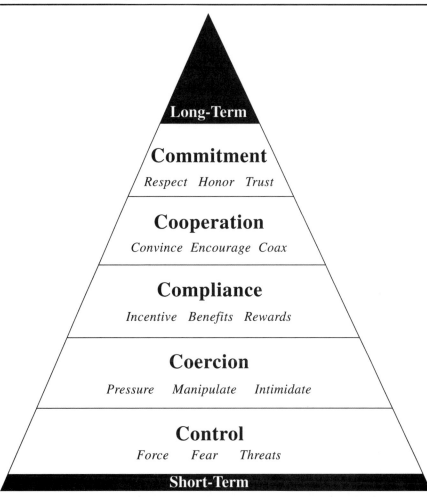

uses as long as they result in a check for $20,000. Raising such a sum requires getting $100 from each employee—a daunting endeavor! The vice president considers the various ways he could accomplish this task. It would be both easy and quick to approach the employees using control. He could use fear or threats to obtain the money. This do-it-or-else mentality would get immediate results. The long-term impact, however, would likely involve rebellion, revenge, and resentment. What about coercion? Surely the employees would provide the requested donation if they were told doing otherwise would negatively affect their next job evaluation. Would this tactic get immediate results? Sure. Again, however, the long-term effects would be resentment, rebellion, and revenge.

The vice president decides control and/or coercion do not provide the best outcomes. Next he considers compliance. If he offered incentives, benefits, or rewards, it would be a win-win situation, right? Suppose each employee who donates $100 gets an extra two weeks of paid vacation. The problem is, once the incentive is gone, compliance will also disappear. He might get the $100 this time, but what about the next time he asks for a donation? This method is still only a temporary fix because the employees will be conditioned to always expect a reward for their compliance.

The vice president next considers cooperation. He could spend time with the employees explaining why this charity is so important and how it would be a great honor for them to participate. He could convince, encourage, or "sell" with logic, emotion, and information to donate to this worthy cause. Now, armed with the tools of effective persuasion, he's onto an approach that will have lasting, positive results. As long as the employees feel he is telling the truth and acting in their best interest, they will be open to his proposal.

Finally, the vice president considers the top form of persuasion: commitment. If he has a great reputation and relationship with his employees, there will be mutual respect, honor, and trust. These conditions will enable the employees to comfortably make out their $100 checks. They know the vice president is a man of honor who would never ask them to do anything that would not be in their best interest. They can commit to him because they feel he is committed to them.

Commitment is the highest ideal of Maximum Influence because its impact is the most permanent and far-reaching. Your reputation as one possessing integrity, honor, trust, and respect will continuously inspire commitment from everyone you seek to persuade.

The Formula: Twelve Laws of Maximum Influence

Getting people to do what you want and, at the same time, to enjoy it is not an accident or coincidence. You must use techniques based on the proven laws of persuasion and influence to achieve such results. As you master these techniques, you'll experience predictable control and influence over others.

Professional negotiators, sales professionals, and upper management professionals around the world use these twelve laws. They are the same principles that help thousands of people gain control of their lives and their financial futures. Mastery of all the twelve laws is crucial for Maximum Influence. I *promise* that if you read this book and act upon your newly acquired knowledge, it will not be long before you find yourself in a completely different position than you are today. You will act instead of being acted upon. You will speak and be heard. You will lead and be followed.

2

The Twelve Universal Laws of Power Persuasion

Thinking is the hardest work there is, which is probably the reason why so few engage in it.

—HENRY FORD

AS THE SPECIES WHOSE THINKING ABILITY supposedly separates us from the animals, we really don't spend much of our life reasoning. Most of the time our minds get stuck on cruise control. Thinking takes up too much time and requires too much energy. Imagine having to think about every decision we make. It wouldn't leave us much time to accomplish anything else, would it? Most of us have a systematic way of looking at the world. When this mode is operating, our minds are perfectly primed to automatically respond to persuasion triggers. I call these triggers the Laws of Persuasion.

Twelve Automatic Triggers of Persuasion

The Laws of Persuasion operate below our conscious thoughts. When employed properly, your prospects don't even realize you're using them. On the other hand, if you blunder your way through a persuasion situation, your audience will be totally aware of what you're doing. It's like seeing a police car on the side of the road—it jars us back to reality. If the persuader is skilled, he or she will use the Laws of Persuasion so the message is delivered below the radar.

Understanding the Laws of Persuasion involves understanding the human psyche. Such knowledge empowers you to improve your persuasive abilities. It magnifies your effectiveness in relationships, improves your parenting skills, enhances your leadership ability, and helps you sell yourself and your ideas. In short, it maximizes your influence.

Thinking About Not Thinking

In his book *Triggers*, best-selling author Joseph Sugarman estimates that 95 percent of the reasoning behind a consumer's purchase is associated with a subconscious decision. In other words, most buying is done for reasons a person hasn't even fully formulated. Professor of psychology Gregory Neidert estimates that our brains actually run on idle 90 to 95 percent of the time. Let's face it, thinking is hard work. It is human nature to conserve cognitive energy. Thinking burns three times as many calories as watching TV. Those who use their brains for a living have traditionally been among the highest paid professionals. Consider the incomes for doctors, lawyers, and engineers, just to name a few. Most of us feel we don't have the time or even the desire to think on the level that these professionals do each day.

What are the main reasons we choose not to think? First, sometimes the amount of information available is so overwhelming we don't even attempt to digest any of it. Sometimes our decisions simply aren't weighty enough to warrant the effort of researching all the available information. Consciously and subconsciously, from the bombardment of information we receive, we selectively choose what we will acknowledge and what we will ignore.

Whether we realize it or not, we love shortcuts to thinking. When we buy an item, we don't always take the time to research the product or read the latest consumer guide's ratings on the product. Instead, we often rely on the salesperson's advice. We might just buy the most popular brand, or we might bring a friend along for his opinion. Although we would never admit it, we sometimes even buy an item just because of its color or packaging. Certainly we know this is not the best way to make decisions, but we all do it anyway, even when we know we might make a mistake or feel regretful afterwards. If we thoroughly considered every single decision, we would constantly be overwhelmed and we'd never get anything done.

The Laws of Persuasion are so powerful because they capitalize on two very predictable things: one, what we expect from human nature, and two, how people will respond in certain situations. People react predictably under a given set of circumstances. If we learn to recognize how the Laws of Persuasion work, we will know how to use them in our interactions with others.

We will also become more aware of how others will attempt to use them on us.

The Twelve Laws of Persuasion

This book explores and categorizes the twelve essential Laws of Persuasion. These laws form the basis of the art and science of persuasion and influence. Adherence to these laws can help you understand and gain control of any situation involving persuasion. Our minds are programmed with automatic persuasion triggers. Most of us experience persuasive situations without realizing or thinking about it. Master Persuaders know what these triggers are and how to utilize them to their advantage. Understanding the Laws of Persuasion helps us become aware of how we are influenced without having conscious knowledge of it.

Learning to influence and persuade takes time, skill, and experience. What most people don't realize is that we already instinctively use many of these laws in our daily communications. The same Laws of Persuasion that we unknowingly use every day are the very same ones Master Persuaders use deliberately, consciously, and consistently. Master Persuaders make persuasion a habit. Think about how conscientious you were when you first started driving. Now, after years of practice, driving a car doesn't require as much thought or focus. Master Persuaders understand the rules of persuasion and practice them constantly. They can apply the techniques subconsciously, without even thinking about them. For them, the application of persuasion has become second nature.

Two Paths of Persuasion

There are two paths to persuasion: the conscious and the subconscious. Both paths can persuade others to your way of thinking, but each path uses a very different means of processing information.

In the *conscious path*, both you and your audience make an active or conscious attempt to understand, define, and process an argument. A person who is interested in your persuasive attempts will be highly motivated to listen. As such, she will also be able to consciously evaluate your message by carefully weighing the pros and cons of the evidence you present.

On the *subconscious path*, the listener spends little or no time processing the information. This approach results in those automatic triggers we previously talked about. These knee-jerk reactions happen when you follow your intuition or use a mental shortcut. Your mind reaches a decision without doing any logical processing. These subconscious decisions are largely driven by instinct and emotion. Individuals who spend lots of time on the subconscious path do so because they lack the time, motivation, desire, or ability to really listen to your message. They're not really involved in the subject. They use their instinct or emotions instead of their intellect. Passive processing and automatic decision triggers rule their decision making.

The key is knowing when to use which method. Successful application of all the laws and techniques taught in this book requires that you become skilled at quickly identifying which ones will be the most effective in which situations. In his book *Multiple Streams of Income*, influential investment advisor Robert G. Allen relates a story of a factory owner whose machine broke down:

It was a major and necessary piece of equipment, and so a repairman was quickly summoned to fix it. The repairman studied the machine in order to assess the problem. After a just a few moments, he pulled out his hammer, tapped the machine twice, and stood back to survey the results. The machine started up immediately. The repairman turned to the factory owner and said, "That will be $500, please." Furious that the repairman would dare charge such an outrageous amount for so little work, the factory owner demanded an itemized statement. The repairman left and sent the itemized bill the next day, which read:

Tapping with hammer:	$ 1
Knowing where to tap:	$499
Total:	$500

As you study and acquire knowledge about Maximum Influence, you too will know where to tap. Learn, implement, and make the twelve Laws of Persuasion, a part of your life.

3

The Law of Dissonance
Internal Pressure Is the Secret

There is only one way . . . to get anybody to do anything. And that is by making the other person want to do it.

—DALE CARNEGIE

MOST OF US FEEL MORE HARMONY in our lives when everything is consistent: our jobs, our homes, our habits, even our soft drinks. Consistency is the glue that holds everything in our lives together, thereby allowing us to cope with the world. Think of all the people you admire. I'll bet, by and large, most of them are consistent, congruent people. What they believe, what they say, and what they do (even when no one is watching) flow together seamlessly. Typically, a high degree of such consistency in one's life is indicative of personal and intellectual strength.

People are naturally more inclined—even subconsciously—to gravitate toward and follow individuals who are consistent in their behavior. The converse is also true: Inconsistency in one's personal and professional life is generally considered undesirable. The person whose beliefs, words, and deeds don't consistently match up is seen as hypocritical, two-faced, confused, or even mentally ill.

The Theory of Cognitive Dissonance

Leon Festinger formulated the cognitive dissonance theory in 1957 at Stanford University. He asserted, "When attitudes conflict with actions, attitudes or beliefs, we are uncomfortable and motivated to try to change." Festinger's theory sets the foundation for the Law of Dissonance, one of the twelve laws of Maximum Influence.

The Law of Dissonance states that people will naturally act in a manner that is consistent with their cognitions (beliefs, attitudes, and values). Therefore, when people behave in a manner that is inconsistent with these cogni-tions, they find themselves in a state of discomfort. In such an uncomfortable state, they will naturally be inclined to adjust their behaviors or attitudes to regain mental and emotional consistency. When our beliefs, attitudes, and actions mesh, we live harmoniously. When they don't, we feel dissonance at some level—that is, we feel awkward, uncomfortable, unset-tled, disturbed, upset, nervous, or confused. In order to eliminate or reduce such tension, we will do everything possible to change our attitudes and behavior, even if it means doing something we don't want to do.

Imagine that there is a big rubber band inside you. When dissonance is present, the rubber band begins to stretch. As long as the dissonance exists, the band stretches tighter and tighter. You've got to take action before it reaches a breaking point and snaps. The motivation to reduce the tension is what causes us to change; we will do everything in our power to get back in balance. We seek psycho-emotional stasis at all times, much like we experi-ence the ever-present, driving need for food and water to satisfy our physical being.

Methods of Protecting Mental Consistency

When we feel cognitive dissonance, we have to find a way to deal with the psychological tension. We have an arsenal of tools at our disposal to help us return to cognitive consistency. The following list outlines different ways people seek to reduce dissonance.

■ *Denial*—To shut out the dissonance, you deny there is a problem. You do this either by ignoring or demeaning the source of the information. You might also deliberately misperceive the confronting position.

■ *Modification*—You change your existing cognitions to achieve consis-tency. Most of the time this involves admitting you were wrong and making changes to remedy your errors.

■ *Reframing*—You change your understanding or interpretation of the meaning. This leads you to either modify your own thinking or devalue the importance of the whole matter, considering it unimportant altogether.

■ *Search*—You are determined to find a flaw in the other side's position, to discredit the source, and to seek social or evidentiary support for your own viewpoint. You might attempt to convince the source (if available) of his error. You might also try to convince others you did the right thing.

■ *Separation*—You separate the attitudes that are in conflict. This compartmentalizes your cognitions, making it easier for you to ignore or even forget the discrepancy. In your mind, what happens in one area of your life (or someone else's) should not affect the other areas of your life.

■ *Rationalization*—You find excuses for why the inconsistency is acceptable. You change your expectations or try to alter what really happened. You also find reasons to justify your behavior or your opinions.

Consider how each of the above strategies could apply if the following experience actually happened in your own life: Your favorite politician, the local mayor, for whom you campaigned and voted, is in trouble. You spent your own time and money convincing family, friends, and neighbors to vote for this candidate. You thought he was a family man, a man of values, somebody who could be trusted. Now, after two years in office, he's been caught red-handed having an affair with an office staff member, who is barely older than his daughter. The news creates dissonance inside you. To alleviate the dissonance, you might react in any one or combination of the following ways:

■ *Denial*—"This is just the media going after him. He is doing a great job, so the opposing party is trying to smear his good name. This will all blow over when the facts come out. It's all just a big misunderstanding."

■ *Modification*—"I can't believe I voted for this guy. I feel swindled and taken advantage of. I really mistook him for a man of character. I need to apologize to my family and friends. I cannot support a man who does not honor his wedding vows."

■ *Reframing*—"The media said *affair*. Well, I'm sure he didn't actually sleep with her. Maybe they're just good friends. I'm sure his wife knew all about the whole thing. Even if they did have an affair, who doesn't? Is it that big of a deal?"

■ *Search*—"I've heard about the reporter breaking this story. He's blown things out of proportion before. All the friends I've talked to don't think the story is true. In fact, this reporter has been against the mayor from the time he became a candidate. I'm going to call that reporter right now."

■ *Separation*—"I voted for him and he is doing a great job. Inflation is low, unemployment is not a problem, and crime has been reduced. He is doing everything he said he would. It does not matter what he does in his private life. What matters is how he is doing his job. There is no connection between an affair and his job performance."

■ *Rationalization*—"Well, his wife is cold to him and she's never around when he needs her. She's never really supported him since he took office. After all, she still has her own business. Maybe this is just a marriage of convenience and this relationship is part of their agreement."

Everyday Examples of Dissonance
Listed below are some situations that might create dissonance.

- You are a strict vegetarian but you see a stylish leather jacket on sale and want to buy it.
- You made a New Year's resolution to exercise every day. It is now halfway through February, and you have not yet been to the gym once.
- You are on a stringent diet when you see Ben and Jerry's ice cream on sale at the grocery store.

"Buyer's remorse" is also a form of dissonance. When we purchase a product or service, we tend to look for ways to convince ourselves that we made the right decision. If the people around us or other factors make us question our decision, we experience buyer's remorse. On feeling this inconsistency, we'll look for anything—facts, peer validation, expert opinion—to reduce the dissonance in our minds concerning the purchase. Some of us even use selective exposure to minimize the risk of seeing or hearing something that could cause dissonance. Often people won't even tell family or friends about their purchase or decision because they know it will create dissonance.

Maintaining Psychological Consistency
We find what we seek. If we can't find it, we make it up. In politics, members of different parties will refuse to peaceably or tolerantly listen to opposing party commercials. Smokers won't read articles about the dangers of smoking. Drug users don't spend much time at clinics. We don't want to find information that might oppose our current points of view.

A study by Knox and Inkster found interesting results at a racetrack.

They interviewed people waiting in line to place a bet, and then questioned them again after they'd placed a bet. They found people were much more confident with their decisions after they had placed their bet than before the bet was made. They exuded greater confidence in their decisions and their chosen horses after their decisions were final and their bets were firmly in place.[1]

Younger, Walker, and Arrowood decided to conduct a similar experiment at the midway of the Canadian National Exposition. They interviewed people who had already placed bets on a variety of different games (bingo, wheel of fortune, etc.) as well as people who were still on their way to place bets. They asked each of the people if they felt confident they were going to win. Paralleling the findings of Knox and Inkster's study, the people who had already made their bets felt luckier and more confident than those who had not yet placed their wagers.[2]

These studies show that to reduce dissonance, we often simply convince ourselves that we have made the right decision. Once we place a bet or purchase a product or service, we feel more confident with ourselves and the choice we've made. This concept also holds true in persuasion and sales. Once the payment is given for your product or service, your prospects will usually feel more confident with their decisions. Have them make the payment or finalize the choice as soon as possible! This will increase their confidence in their decision and they will look for reasons to justify that decision.

Many times, even when we have made a bad decision, we become so entrenched in our belief that it was right that we will fight to the bitter end to prove it. We can't handle the dissonance in our minds, so we find anything to prove our decision was right. We become so embroiled in justifying our actions that we are willing to go down with the burning ship.

When buying and selling shares of stock, investors commonly stick with stocks that have recently slumped in price, with no prospects of recovery. Rationally, the best decision is to cut their losses and invest elsewhere. Irrationally, however, investors often hang on, ensnared by their initial decision.

McDonald's sued five London activists for libeling them in a leaflet entitled "What's Wrong with McDonald's?" The pamphlets asserted many claims, including that the franchise's food was unhealthy and that the company exploited its workers, contributed to the destruction of rain forests through cattle ranching, produced litter, and sought to target children through its advertising. While three of the activists backed down, two of them went on to fight McDonald's in court. The case evolved into the longest court proceeding in the legal history of Britain. It came to be considered "the most expensive and disastrous public relations exercise ever mounted by a multinational company."[3]

Spreading negative publicity across the globe, two million copies of "What's Wrong with McDonald's?" went into circulation. An Internet site following the case received seven million hits in its first year. Having publicly asserted its stance that the company would challenge its antagonists, McDonald's was trapped. Forced to remain consistent to its position, McDonald's fought to the bitter end. This case took two-and-a-half years and cost McDonald's over $10 million to fight before the company finally won the case. Given the ramifications, perhaps it would have been better if the company had just cut their losses and moved on.

Using Dissonance to Create Action

Dissonance is a powerful tool in helping others make and keep commitments. In one study, researchers staged thefts to test the reactions of onlookers. On a beach in New York City, the researchers randomly selected an accomplice to place his beach towel and portable radio five feet away. After relaxing there for a while, the accomplice got up and left. After the accomplice had departed, one of the researchers, pretending to be a thief, stole the radio. As you might imagine, hardly anyone reacted to the stage theft. Very few people were willing to put themselves at risk by confronting the thief. In fact, over the course of twenty staged thefts, only four people (20 percent) made any attempt to hinder the thief.

The researchers staged the same theft twenty more times, only this time with one slight difference repeated in each scenario. The minor alteration brought drastically different results. This time, before leaving, the accomplice asked each person sitting next to him, "Could you please watch my things?" Each person consented. This time, with the Law of Dissonance at work, nineteen out of twenty (95 percent) individuals sought to stop the thief by chasing, grabbing back the radio, and in some cases, even physically restraining him.

Most people try to follow through when they promise they will do something—especially if it is in writing. This is why corporations sponsor writing contests about social issues or their products. They really don't care about your writing style. What they're really looking for is consumer endorsement. The writer puts down, in her own words, what she thinks the company wants to hear about its issue or product. Having made a written commitment to supporting and endorsing a product or issue, the consumer will now support the sponsoring company in their cause or will willingly buy their product.

In one particular study, 100 high school students were asked to write an essay on whether or not the voting age should be lowered. Half the students were told the speeches would be published in the school newspaper, while the other half were told the essays would be kept confidential. After completing the essays, researchers exposed the students to a persuasive speech arguing that the voting age should not be lowered. Of the students assuming their papers were going to be published, very few of them changed their original position. Of the students who believed their papers were confidential, most altered their stance on the issue to agree with the persuasive speech.

The Law of Dissonance in Marketing

The Bait and Switch

If you can get someone to mentally commit to a product or a decision, he is likely to remain committed even after the terms and conditions change. This is why when stores, for example, advertise very low prices on a television set, they include in small print, "Quantities Limited." By the time you get to the store, all the bargain televisions are sold, but you are mentally committed to buying a new TV. Luckily for you, there are more expensive models available. So, you go home having spent $300 more on a television set than you originally planned, just because you needed to maintain a consistency between your desire for a new TV and your action of being in the store.

This tactic is also often used when goods and products go on sale. For example, a customer may be lured to a store by an incredible deal on a pair of nice dress shoes. Upon inquiring, the disappointed customer learns from the salesperson that her size is not in stock. Just as the customer is about to leave, the salesperson miraculously displays another strikingly similar pair—but this pair is not on sale.

Think of a time when you purchased a new car. Have you ever noticed that when you're about to sign the contract the price is $200 more than you expected? Well, someone conveniently forgot to tell you about the advanced suspension or some other feature found in your car. You pay the extra $200 anyway because you're mentally committed to that car, and you don't want to go through the whole hassle and headache of trying to renegotiate the deal.

Often car dealers promise an incredible price, even a few hundred dollars below a competitor's price, all the while knowing it's not actually going to go through. The deal is offered only to motivate the buyer to purchase from their dealership. Once the customer decides to buy, the dealer sets up several conditions, each of them causing the customer to feel increasingly committed before finding out the real price: lengthy forms are filled out, great lengths are taken to set up specific financing terms, the customer is encouraged to take the car home and drive it to work, to run errands, to cruise the neighborhood. The dealer knows that while the customer is out joy riding, she is thinking of all the many reasons her purchase is justified.[4]

These tactics are even used when high school students and their parents are narrowing down the colleges they should attend. Just like car dealers, colleges often give a low estimate on your costs, and it's not until after you've signed up and registered that you discover your *actual* costs.

Brand Loyalty

It's a challenge getting consumers to remain loyal to a particular brand. Unlike the good old days when brand loyalty was a given, times have changed. As a society, we no longer feel compelled to stick with a certain company or product. I grew up with Crest, Cheerios, and Tide being staples in my home. Now I change brands much more easily. I'm not likely to remain loyal to a brand unless they reward me for my commitment to them, for example, with frequent flyer miles, with the little cars you can buy for your kids at Chevron, or with a Unocal 76 ball to swing from your car antennae. Acquiring consumer loyalty is the reason the tobacco industry spends over $600 million giving away paraphernalia with tobacco logos.[5] We constantly see companies putting their logos on coffee mugs, T-shirts, pens, and mouse pads, to name just a few promotional items. Even though you might not have paid for these items, owning them creates loyalty to the product advertised on them. Most people who wear a Budweiser T-shirt don't drink Coors beer.

Cognitive Dissonance and Public Commitment

Public commitments and dissonance go hand in hand. Even when we feel an action is not right, we still go through with it if we have publicly committed to such a course of action.

For example, when you ask that young lady to marry you and she says yes, there's a commitment. The announcement of the engagement is a second commitment. All the other actions that follow suit increase your public commitment: telling your friends, getting the rings, asking the parents, setting the date, taking the pictures, sending announcements, paying the deposit for the reception location, etc. Each step closer to "I do" results in a greater level of commitment. Even if one or both of you decide you want to call it off, it actually feels easier to go through with the wedding than to stop the whole procession created by so much public commitment.

The more public our stand, the more reluctant we are to change it. A now famous experiment conducted in 1955 by social psychologists Morton Deutsch and Harold Gerard demonstrates this principle. A group of students were divided into three groups. Each group viewed some lines and had to estimate their length. The students in the first group had to privately write down estimates, sign their names to it, and hand it in. The second group of students also had to privately write down their estimates, but they did so on a Magic Writing Pad. They could lift the plastic cover on their notepad and their figures would instantaneously disappear. The third group of students did not write down their estimates but just kept them privately in their minds. Not surprisingly, even when new information was presented contradicting their estimates, the students who had written down their estimates, signed their names to them, and handed them in remained the most committed to their choices, while those who had never committed anything to writing were the most readily swayed to change their responses.[6]

Procedures, customs, and traditions are often specifically established for the purposes of creating psychological commitment. Consider fraternity initiations, military boot camps, political rallies, protest marches, and demonstrations. When we make our vows, beliefs, statements, or endeavors public, we feel bound to them. We can back out on commitments and claims we've made public, but we will pay a psychological and emotional price. What's more, the more public we made those commitments, the greater the emotional price tag will be.

A pair of researchers, Elliot Aronson and Judson Mills, claimed that "persons who go through a great deal of trouble or pain to attain something tend to value it more highly than persons who attain the same thing with a minimum of effort."[7] Additional research confirmed their assertion when coeds who were required to endure pain rather than embarrassment to get into a group desired membership more than their counterparts. In one particular case, the more pain one young woman endured as part of her initiation, the more she later tried to convince herself that "her new group and its activities were interesting, intelligent, and desirable."[8]

Another study of 54 tribal cultures found that those with the most dramatic initiation rituals also have the most unity and commitment,[9] and these groups oppose any attempts to undermine or destroy these customs, which render so much strength to their tribe and their culture.

Understanding the psychology of commitment through publicity can be used to bring about good societal changes. Many organizations exist to help individuals conquer bad habits, patterns, or abuses. For example, weight-loss centers commonly encourage clients to share their goals with as many friends, relatives, and neighbors as they can, understanding that this public commitment and pressure often works when other methods don't.

An experiment conducted by Pallak, Cook, and Sullivan in Iowa City used an interviewer who offered free energy-saving hints to natural gas users. Those residents who agreed to try to conserve energy would have their names publicized in newspaper articles as public-spirited, fuel-conserving citizens. The effect was immediate. One month later, when the utility companies checked their meters, the homeowners in the publication sample had each saved an average of 422 cubic feet of natural gas, a decrease of 12.2 percent. The chance to have their names in the paper had motivated these residents to put forth substantial conservation efforts for a period of one month.

Even during the months when their names weren't in the paper, the families continued to conserve gas. When a letter went out stating that their names would no longer be printed in the paper, the families did not return to their previous wasteful energy usage, as was expected; rather, they continued to conserve energy.[10]

Getting Your Foot in the Door

One aspect of the law of dissonance is the urge to remain consistent with our commitments. Even if someone begins with a small request then follows it up with a larger request, we still tend to remain consistent in our behavior and answers. This technique of capitalizing on such a principle has been called by several names, including "foot-in-the-door" (FITD), self-perception theory, or the "sequential request." Basically, it is a means of using a person's self-perception to motivate her to partake of the desired action. When an individual complies a first time, she perceives herself to be helpful.

If she is asked to comply a second time in an even greater way, she is likely to consent. In an effort to maintain consistency with the first impression and with her own self-perception, she agrees to give even more of themselves.

The following outline highlights three key principles in learning how to use this technique:

1. *Small commitments* often later lead to large commitments. For example, salespeople often focus first on securing an initial order, even if it's a small one. Once this is accomplished, the customer will be more likely to commit to buying from them again.

2. *Written commitments* are usually more powerful than verbal commitments. We know the power of the written word. When contracts are signed and promises put into writing, the commitment level correspondingly increases tenfold.

3. *Public commitments* are stronger than private commitments. Taking a public stand that is witnessed by others compels us to continually endorse that commitment. Otherwise, we risk being seen as inconsistent, weak, or dishonest. For example, as mentioned earlier, many weight-loss centers have their clients write down and share their goals with as many people as possible, thereby decreasing the likelihood of failure.

The key to using FITD is to get the person to initially grant a small request. For example, if you were to ask someone, "Can I have just thirty seconds of your time?" most individuals would respond affirmatively. According to self-perception theory, the person would observe his own behavior and, in regard to this interaction, consider himself to be a helpful person. The second step in the FITD principle is making another, more involved request. "Can I try this on the stain on your carpet?" The person feels he should consent to the second request because he is "that kind of person." He has already seen himself do other behaviors in support of the product or service, so he willingly complies with the second request.

A 1966 study by psychologists Jonathan Freedman and Scott Fraser highlights just how effective FITD is. In their study, a researcher posing as a volunteer canvassed a California neighborhood, asking residents if they would allow a large billboard reading "Drive Carefully" to be displayed on their front lawns. So they'd have an idea of what it would look like, the volunteer showed his recruits a picture of the large sign obstructing the view of a beautiful house.

Naturally, most people refused, but in one particular group, an incredible 76 percent actually consented. The reason for their compliance was this: Two weeks prior, these residents had been asked by another volunteer to make a small commitment to display a three-inch-square sign that read "Be a Safe Driver" in their windows. Since it was such a small and simple request, nearly all of them agreed. The astounding result was that the initial small commitment profoundly influenced their willingness to comply with the much larger request two weeks later.

With another group of homeowners, Freedman and Fraser sent petitions requesting their signatures in support of helping to keep California beautiful. Of course, nearly everyone signed. Two weeks later, another volunteer went around and asked them if they'd allow the big "Drive Carefully" sign to be placed in their yards. Amazingly, about half of the homeowners consented, even though their previous small commitment was to state beautification and not safety.[11]

Freedman and Fraser were also interested in discovering whether or not they could persuade homemakers to carry out a very large request. They asked the women of the house if they would permit a group of five or six strangers to freely look through their cupboards and storage spaces for two hours, for the purpose of classifying the women's household products. Prior to this request, however, researchers had asked some of the women to take a survey about household products. Of those surveyed, approximately 50 percent consented to allowing the men to go through their household products. Of the women who had *not* been surveyed, only 25 percent agreed to let the men examine their storage spaces.

Another study involved testing to see whether introductory psychology students would rise early to take part in a 7:00 A.M. study session on thinking processes. In one group, the students were told at the beginning of the call that the session would begin promptly at 7:00 A.M. Of these students, only 24 percent agreed to participate. In the second group, the students were first told what the study was and that their participation was desired. The 7:00 A.M. time was not mentioned until after they had consented to take part, which 56 percent of them did. When the opportunity to change their minds was presented to them, however, none of them took advantage of it. Ninety-five percent of students actually followed through and showed up for the 7:00 A.M. session.[12]

In another case, social psychologist Steven J. Sherman wanted to see if he could increase the number of people who would be willing to collect door-to-door donations for the American Cancer Society. He called a sample of residents and simply asked them what their response would be if they were asked to volunteer three hours of their time to collect charitable donations for the American Cancer Society. Not wanting to seem uncharitable, many responded that they would indeed volunteer. The final outcome? When a representative of the American Cancer Society actually called and asked for volunteers, there was a 700 percent increase of individuals agreeing to participate.[13]

Using FITD Effectively

When utilizing this technique, you must first determine exactly what end result you are seeking. This will be the big commitment you ask for. You should then create several small and simple requests that are related to your ultimate request, making sure they can be easily satisfied. As the examples above demonstrate, taking these measures will greatly increase the likelihood that your ultimate request will be granted.

Here are some more key points to remember in using FITD:

1. *The First Request:* The first request needs to be "of sufficient size for the foot-in-the-door technique to work,"[14] but, on the other hand, it cannot be so big that it seems inappropriate and/or is not easily and readily accomplished. Basically, you want to present the largest possible request that will still realistically be accepted.

2. *Your Prospect's Viewpoint:* The FITD tactic is not effective if your prospect senses that you are acting in your own self-interests instead of in hers or society's. What is in it for you? Why are you requesting this from her?

3. *External Incentives:* The FITD technique loses impact if your prospect is offered external incentives for agreeing to your first request. Researchers typically use self-perception theory to explain this phenomenon.[15] For example, if you are given a gift for listening to a salesperson, you will not consciously or subconsciously perceive yourself to be one who is willing to readily listen and agree to the salesperson's offer. Instead, you agree to listen only for the incentive being offered to you.

4. *The Source of the Request:* Having different people employ the initial and subsequent requests when using the FITD technique can be an effective

strategy. This way, the same person isn't required to make both the initial and the follow-up requests and your prospects won't feel like they are being taken advantage of.

Three Steps to Using the Law of Dissonance

Step One: Get a Commitment

You can create or reveal commitments in your prospects by ensuring that the commitments are public, affirmative, voluntary, and effortful (PAVE).

Public

Make your prospect's stand as public as possible. Get a written commitment and make that written commitment public. Involve family and friends in the proposed action. Engage your customer in a public handshake to seal the deal in front of other employees and customers.

Affirmative

You want to get as many "yes" answers as possible because yeses develop consistency within the person that will carry over into your major request. This technique reduces dissonance and makes it easier for prospects to say yes to your final proposal. Even if it is a watered-down, easy request, getting a yes to any request makes it easier to evoke the same response down the road.

Close with a series of questions—ideally six—that all end with a yes. Desire increases with each yes, and decreases with each no. Every time we say yes to a benefit, our desire goes up.

Voluntary

When getting commitments, start small and build up to larger commitments later. You cannot force commitments. Long-term approval has to feel like it comes from your prospects' own will, something they want to do or say. They have to volunteer to test drive the car, write on the contract, or request more information. When they make a commitment, you can make the action more voluntary and solidify the commitment by saying things like, "Are you serious? Do you really mean that? You're not just pulling my leg, are you?"

Effortful

The more effortful and public the commitment is, the more commitment it will create down the line. The more effort your prospects exert in making the commitment, the more it seals the deal. You don't want to ask a prospect to do something extreme but you do want them to exert extra effort.

Remember the car dealer example? Car dealers often offer a great deal on a car just to get people in the lot. The prospect then makes a commitment to come in and look at the car only to find that it's already been sold. Already committed to being there, they browse the lot and find another car they like. They then start to fill out the paperwork, talking terms and completing forms. These are all small effortful commitments that later lead to full commitment. Many times, the car dealer will continue obtaining these small commitments only to come back and say he can only give $2,000 for the trade in instead of $2,500 like he promised. At this point, the buyer has exerted so much effort and has created so many small commitments that the extra $500 won't break the deal.

Step Two: Create Dissonance

Once you have the commitment, you can create the dissonance. You create that dissonance or imbalance by showing your prospects they have not kept or are not keeping their commitment. For example, "You said you needed this right away. Why do you have to think it over and come back tomorrow?" The person's self-image is squeezed from both sides by consistency pressures. The prospect feels great internal pressure to bring self-image in line with action. At the same time, there is pressure from the outside to adjust this image according to the way others perceive us.

Step Three: Offer a Solution

As a Master Persuader, whenever you create dissonance, you always need to offer a way out. You need to show, prove, or explain how your product or service can reduce the dissonance your prospect feels. For example, "If you donate right now, we can continue to feed the homeless children in Africa."

Keep in mind that the final solution or major request is what you ultimately want to accomplish. You prepare your whole persuasive presentation around the moment when you will ask for that major request. Once your prospects accept the solution, they have convinced themselves that they made the right and only choice. As a result, they feel great about their decision. This makes the cognitive dissonance disappear. The decision was their personal choice and they have solved the dilemma in their own minds. They know exactly what to do.

The solution is your call to action.

4

The Law of Obligation
How to Get Anyone to
Do a Favor for You

Nothing is more costly than something given free of charge.
—JAPANESE SAYING

OBLIGATION HAS BEEN USED as a persuasive technique since the beginning of time. Door-to-door salespeople offer free brushes, free encyclopedias, and free estimates in the hope of securing a sale. People throw parties in their homes, serving refreshments and giving away free Tupperware or other products. We all know how hard it is to attend a friend's party, eat their food, take their free gift, and then go home without buying a thing. So, what do we do? We order the cheapest item in the catalog to get rid of the obligation or indebtedness we feel to the host.

During World War I, some soldiers were given a special assignment to make sorties into enemy territory in order to capture and question enemy soldiers. A particularly skilled German soldier was instructed to fulfill one such mission. As he had on numerous other occasions, he negotiated the area between fronts and caught an enemy soldier off guard, eating his lunch alone in a trench. Unaware of what was happening, the startled soldier was easily captured. Not knowing what else to do, the soldier tore off a piece of bread and gave it to his captor. The German was so surprised by the friendly gesture that he couldn't follow through with his assignment. Turning away from the soldier, he headed back into neutral territory and on to face the wrath of his superiors.[1]

Maybe this has happened to you. You are attempting to buy a car and are playing hardball with the sales rep. You've negotiated back and forth and are getting nowhere. You are ready to walk away when he says that he will talk to his manager one last time. As he gets up, he says, "You know, I'm thirsty, so I'm going to get myself a soda. Would you like one?" "Sure!" you say, oblivious to his tactic. He comes back with the soda and a better deal from his manager. It's not the deal you wanted, but you feel it's the best you're going to get. So, you accept it. As you think about it later, it dawns on you that you bought the car because of a subconscious trigger. The moral of the story is to never take a drink from the car sales rep before you've settled on a price. That drink serves as an obligation trigger. You feel indebted to the car dealer because of this small courtesy, and he knows it. He created the obligation with a fifty-cent can of soda. You return the favor and get out of his debt by buying a $20,000 car.

Definition of the Law of Obligation

The Law of Obligation, also known as "reciprocity," states that when others do something for us, we feel a strong need, even a push, to return the favor. Returning the favor rids us of the obligation created by the first good deed. The adage "one good turn deserves another" seems to be a part of social conditioning in every culture. And, even beyond that, the maxim serves as an ethical code that does not necessarily need to be taught but nevertheless is *understood*. For example, when someone smiles or gives a compliment, we feel a great need to return the smile or compliment. Even when these gestures are unsolicited, we feel a sense of urgency to repay the person who has created the mental or psychological debt. In some cases, our need to repay this debt is so overwhelming that we end up dramatically exceeding the original favor. The obligation trigger created by the car salesman's soda offer is a classic example of this principle.

People often conscientiously trigger feelings of indebtedness and obligation in others by carrying out an uninvited favor. Even if we don't want or ask for the gift, invitation, or compliment, we still feel the need to return the favor when we receive it. Merely being indebted, even in the slightest sense of the word, can create enough psychological discomfort (and sometimes even public embarrassment) that we go to extraordinary lengths to remove the burdensome obligation we feel. This is when we often disproportionately reward the original giver.

When my family moved to a new area, we gave a small Christmas gift to all our neighbors. I don't think the gifts cost more than five dollars each. We were new on the block and wanted to get to know our neighbors. About thirty minutes after hand-delivering the gifts to our new neighbors, the doorbell rang. There stood one of the neighbors with a large box of truffles in one hand—this box had to have been holding at least fifty dollars worth of chocolates. She said, "Welcome to the neighborhood, and Happy Holidays," and with that she was off and on her way. She couldn't cope with the sudden debt she felt toward my family so, to rid herself of her feelings of obligation, she gave back ten times more than she'd originally received. This is why many people buy extra holiday presents to have on hand just in case someone delivers a gift they did not count on.

The Law of Obligation also applies when there are favors we wish we could ask, but we know we are not in a position to repay them or perhaps even ask for them in the first place.[2] The psychological and emotional burden created by such circumstances is often great enough that we would rather lose the benefits of the favor by not asking for it at all than experience the embarrassment and likely rejection that might come from asking. For example, a woman who receives expensive gifts from a man may complain that, although she is flattered by and likes getting the gifts, she feels an uncomfortable sense of obligation to repay her suitor. Furthermore, she may express frustration at the perception held by the suitor that, because of his gifts, the woman would or should be more sexually accessible. Studies have shown that the converse is also true: When individuals break the reciprocity rule by showering favors on someone without giving them a chance to repay, there is an equal amount of discomfort.[3]

The drive to alleviate feelings of obligation is so powerful that it can make us bend toward people we don't even know. One university professor chose names at random from a telephone directory, and then sent these complete strangers his Christmas cards. Holiday cards addressed to him came pouring back, all from people who did not know him and, for that matter, who had never even heard of him.[4]

The Law of Obligation can be used to eliminate animosity or suspicion. In one study, Cornell University researcher Dennis Regan had two individuals try to sell raffle tickets to unsuspecting workers. One individual made a conscientious effort to befriend the workers before attempting to sell any tickets. The other individual made a point of being rude and obnoxious around the workers. While on a break, the individual who had previously been rude to his prospects bought them drinks before trying to get them to buy tickets. The results of the study showed that the rude individual actually sold twice as many raffle tickets, even though the other had been so much nicer and more likable.[5]

On another occasion, a man was stranded on the side of the road because his car had run out of gas. A young man pulled over and identified himself as a friend of the man's daughter. He took the man to get gas and then brought him back to his car. Of course, feeling indebted, the man said, "If you ever need anything, just ask." Three weeks later, capitalizing on the offer, the young man asked if he could borrow the man's expensive car. The man's best judgment screamed, "Are you crazy? You don't know if you can trust this kid to get it back to you in one piece!" But the mental pressure to satisfy his obligation to the young man won out over his better judgment and he loaned the young man his car.

The pressure to reciprocate is strong enough that when people don't return the favor, they are viewed with contempt and disgust. Accepting gifts or favors without attempting to return them is universally viewed as selfish, greedy, and heartless. It is often strictly due to this internal and external pressure that people conform to the rule of reciprocity.

The Law of Obligation and Marketing

A film-developing company thrived on the Law of Obligation. They would send a roll of film in the mail along with a letter explaining that the film was a free gift. The letter then outlined how the recipient should return the film to their company to be processed. Even though a number of local stores could process the film at a far lower price, most people ended up sending it to the company that had sent them the film. The technique worked because the company's "pre-giving" incurred a sense of obligation to repay the favor. We often see this method at work when companies give out complimentary calendars, business pens, T-shirts, or mugs.

The same principle applies when you go to the grocery store and see those alluring sample tables. It is hard to take a free sample and then walk away without at least pretending to be interested in the product. Some individuals, as a means of assuaging their indebtedness, have learned to take the sample and walk off without making eye contact. Some have taken so many samples, they no longer feel an obligation to buy or even pretend they're interested in the products anymore. Still, the technique works, so much so that it has been expanded to furniture and audio/video stores, which offer free pizza, hot dogs, and soft drinks to get you into the store and create instant obligation.

Pre-giving is effective because it makes us feel like we have to return the favor. Greenburg said this feeling of discomfort is created because the favor threatens our independence.[6] The more indebted we feel, the more motivated we are to eliminate the debt. An interesting report from the Disabled American Veterans Organization revealed that their usual 18 percent donation response rate nearly *doubled* when the mailing included a small, free gift.[7]

A local clothing store offers free pressing as well as free dry cleaning for suits bought in their store. This creates a sense of obligation among their customers, who when they next decide to buy another suit are more likely to buy it from the store that offered the freebie.

Another study found that survey takers could increase physician response to a long questionnaire if they paid the physicians first.[8] When a $20 check was sent along with the questionnaire, 78 percent of the physicians filled it out and sent it back. When the $20 check was promised to arrive after the questionnaire was completed and sent in, only 66 percent followed through. The pre-giving incentive increased the sense of obligation. Another interesting result of the study was this: Of the physicians who received the $20 check in the initial mailing but did *not* fill out the questionnaire, only 26 percent cashed the check. Of the physicians receiving the $20 check who did fill out the questionnaire, 95 percent cashed the check![9]

This demonstrates that the Law of Obligation works conversely, as well. The fact that many of the physicians who did not fill out the questionnaire also did not cash their checks may be interpreted as a sign of their psychological and emotional discomfort at accepting a favor that they were not going to return. If they cashed the checks, they would have to cope with their indebtedness by complying and filling out the questionnaire. Rather than take on that uncomfortable sense of obligation or indebtedness, it was easier to sacrifice the benefit of gaining $20 altogether.

The Law of Obligation also presents itself in the following situations:

- Taking a potential client out to dinner or to play golf
- Offering free tire rotation or fluid fill-up between services
- Someone washing your car windows at a stoplight whether you want them to or not
- Generating money at "free" car washes by asking for a donation after the service is rendered
- A carpet cleaner offering to clean your couch for free

Fundraising and the Law of Obligation

In the early 1980s, the Hare Krishna movement encountered difficulty in raising funds through their traditional means. The rebellion of the 1960s had given way to the more conservative 1980s, and the Hare Krishna members were now considered almost an affliction to society. To counteract negative public opinion, they developed a new approach that utilized the Law of Obligation. Their new fundraising strategy worked because it prompted a sense of obligation that outweighed the dislike or negativity felt toward the Hare Krishna movement.

The new strategy still involved solicitation in crowded, public places, but now, instead of being asked directly for a donation, the potential donor was first given a free gift—a flower. If someone tried to turn it down, the Krishna follower would, under no circumstances, take it back. The Krishna gift-giver might say, "Sir, this is a free gift for you to keep, and we welcome donations." Often the gifts just ended up in the trash cans, but overall, the strategy worked. In most cases, even individuals who ended up throwing the gifts away donated something. Although lots of people were extremely annoyed by the high-pressure gift giving, their sense of obligation to reciprocate was too strong to ignore.

Some of the movement's followers, looking like your normal, energetic college students, would hand out books. People graciously accepted the offer before realizing they were deep into obligation. Playing on their sense of indebtedness, the requesters would then ask for a donation. The process worked like a charm. When someone tried to give the book back, the Krishnas would not take it back, it being a gift. Others would leave upset but the pair would follow them in hot pursuit. I observed that most of the people felt an obligation to donate money in exchange for the free gift presented to them, whether or not they wanted it.

Applying the Law of Obligation

This is a very simple law to implement. All you need to do is create a need or obligation in the mind of the other person. Think to yourself of what you can do, give, or say that would create that indebtedness in the mind of your prospect.

As you think of the perfect persuasive situation, include one or more of the following items to help you create a greater sense of obligation: a service of some sort, information or concessions, secrets, favors, gestures, compliments, smiles, gifts, invitations, attention, or your time. Any one, or a combination of several, of these will create a need to reciprocate in your prospect—as long as your act is perceived as altruistic. If, however, your pre-giving is read as manipulating, bribing, or "tricking," it will understandably *not* be met with much compliance.

Take caution with this strategy. The use of obligation will backfire if your prospect sees your actions as a bribe to comply. Feeling tricked, your prospect will not be pressured to comply or reciprocate. "When pre-giving is perceived as a bribe or a pressure tactic, it actually decreases compliance."[10] The obligation you create must be perceived as an unselfish act.

Reciprocal Concessions

Researchers have found that when someone persuades you to change your mind, they will be inclined to do the same if approached by you. Conversely, if you resist that person's attempts and do not change your mind, then he will likely reciprocate in a similar fashion, resisting *your* attempts to change *his* mind. Consider how you can use this to your advantage if you approach a person with whom you wish to deal in the future and say something like, "You know, I got to thinking about what you said, and you're really right . . ."

Give a Favor, Expect a Favor in Return

Before a negotiation, it is wise to offer some sort of gift. Note, however, that offering the gift *before* and not during the negotiation is of prime importance, or your token will come across as bribery. Your gift will almost always be accepted, even if only out of social custom and courtesy. Whether your recipient likes or wants your gift or not, the psychological need to reciprocate will take root, increasing the likelihood that your request will be met affirmatively. Of course, even when giving the gift *before* you make your request, be sure your motives come across as a sincere effort to help the recipient rather than yourself.

Secrets Create Obligation: The Secret of Secrets

Everybody loves secrets. We all love to be in the know. When you share something personal or private with another person, you create an instant bond and sense of obligation and trust with them. For example, imagine saying in the middle of a negotiation, "Off the record, I think you should know. . . ." or, "I shouldn't be telling you this, but. . . ." These statements show that you are confiding in your listener. By offering him inside knowledge, you've created a sense of intimacy and made your listener feel important. Your listener will feel a need, and often even the desire, to reciprocate the information or to share something personal about himself in return. He will begin to open up and share useful information with you.

Judges especially have to deal with their jurors being influenced by "secret information." Attorneys often strategically introduce information that the jury really isn't supposed to evaluate. When this happens, the judge can either declare a mistrial or tell the jury to ignore the information. In most cases, the jury is told to ignore the information, but the perpetual dilemma is that doing so heightens the information's validity in the minds of the jury members. In an exhaustive study on this issue by the University of Chicago Law School, a jury was to decide the amount of damages in an injury lawsuit. When the professor made it known that the defendant had been insured against the loss, the damages went up 13 percent. When the judge told the jury they had to ignore the new information, the amount went up 40 percent.[11]

Be extra careful not to plead and beg for your prospects to open up. Let them know you truly care and have a desire to know out of genuine concern, not curiosity. Pleading quickly becomes a red flag that shows your prospects you just want to know the juicy details rather than having any real desire to help them. As with the other laws of persuasion, be sincere by showing you really care and truly have their best interest at heart.

Caution

The Law of Obligation can backfire on you or become a matter of ethics if it's used for the wrong reasons. Manipulation is the flip side of obligation. If you use obligation to manipulate, I guarantee that you will lose your ability to persuade. People will catch on to your tactics, quickly declining any gifts you might offer or even refusing to be around you. Your gifts will be perceived as set-ups. People will instinctively know that it's only a matter of time before you come back around asking for that favor to be reciprocated.

Understand that there is a great difference between obligation and coercion. To become a Master Persuader you must first master yourself. It is essential that you have a foundation on which to build.

5

The Law of Connectivity
Contagious Cooperation

The most important single ingredient in the formula of success is knowing how to get along with people.
—THEODORE ROOSEVELT

WE HAVE ALL HAD THE EXPERIENCE of feeling an instant connection or bond with someone after just a few seconds of being in their presence. This is the Law of Connectivity. We have probably all met someone whom we instantly did not like and did not want to be around. This is caused by a lack of connectivity and usually takes only a few seconds to manifest itself. The Law of Connectivity states that the more we feel connected to, part of, liked by, or attracted to someone, the more persuasive they become. When you create an instant bond or connection, people feel comfortable around you. They will feel like they have known you for a long time and that they can easily relate to you. When we feel connected with someone, we feel comfortable and understood; they can relate to us and a sense of trust ensues.

There are four main factors in connectivity: attraction, similarity, people skills, and rapport. Each of these points will be discussed in detail in the following pages. However, before proceeding, it is important to note that really connecting with others requires an attitude of sincerity, a lot of practice, and a true interest in the other person. Whatever you do, don't take your relationships with people for granted.

Attraction: The Halo Effect

Attraction operates by making one positive characteristic of a person affect other people's overall perception of him. Sociologists describe this as the *halo effect*. Because of this halo effect, people automatically associate traits of kindness, trust, and intelligence with people who are attractive. We naturally try to please people we like and find attractive. If your audience likes you, they will forgive you for your "wrongs" and remember your "rights." In fact, studies show that people who are physically attractive are better able to persuade others. They are also perceived as friendlier and more talented, and they usually have higher incomes.[1] "Attractive" means more than just looking beautiful or handsome. It also encompasses having the ability to attract and draw people to you.

The effect of attractiveness transcends all situations. For example, the judicial system, which is supposed to be based upon evidence, has documented cases where attractiveness made a dramatic difference. In one Pennsylvania study, researchers rated the attractiveness of seventy-four male defendants at the start of their criminal trials. Later, the researchers reviewed the court records for the decisions in these cases and found that the handsome men had received significantly lighter sentences. In fact, those researchers found that the attractive defendants were twice as likely to avoid jail time as unattractive defendants. In the same study, a defendant who was better looking than his victim was assessed an average fine of $5,623; but when the victim was the more attractive of the two, the average compensation was twice that much.[2] What's more, both female and male jurors showed the same bias.

The halo effect also affects political elections. In 1974, a Canadian Federal election board found attractive candidates received more than two and a half times as many votes as unattractive candidates. When voters were surveyed about their bias, 73 percent denied, in the strongest possible terms, that they were influenced by attractiveness. Another 14 percent would only allow for the possibility.[3]

Consider these everyday examples of one's appearance influencing their circumstances: Have you ever noticed that height often seems to have some relationship to one's position? It often seems that the taller people get better jobs and have higher salaries.

Did you ever notice that there are some children who seem to be able to get away with anything? There has been some research showing that attractive children who misbehave are considered "less naughty" by adults than less attractive children. In elementary school, teachers often presume the more attractive children are even more intelligent than the less attractive children.[4]

When we come in contact with someone of the opposite sex, the attractiveness concept is magnified. Attractive females can persuade men more easily than unattractive ones, and attractive males can persuade females more easily than unattractive males can. We see obvious examples of this all around us. At conventions and trade shows, large corporations fill their space with sexy and attractive females. In one study, men who saw a new car ad that included a seductive female model rated the car as faster, more appealing, more expensive looking, and better designed than did men who viewed the same ad without the model.[5] Additionally, female students who are perceived to be more attractive by their professors often receive substantially higher grades than unattractive females. It is not uncommon for a store manager to assign an attractive female sales associate to the young man who walks in the door. Most store managers (although they won't admit it) hire attractive salespeople to attract more customers.

Research has shown that looks matter outside of advertising as well. In various studies, attractive men and women, when compared to those who were considered to be less attractive, were judged to be happier, smarter, friendlier, and more likable. They were also considered likely to have better jobs, be better marital partners, or to get more dates. The halo effect causes us to see such people only in a positive way, which gives them persuasive power. Because of the way we view them, we want to be like them and we hope for them to like us in return.[6]

The attractiveness of our clothes can also evoke the Law of Connectivity. Researchers Freed, Chandler, Mouton, and Blake conducted a now-famous experiment on how easy it would be to encourage people to ignore a "Don't Walk" sign at a city intersection. When a well-dressed individual ignored the sign and walked into the street, 14 percent of the people who had been waiting for the light to change followed him across. When the same person repeated the experiment the next day, now dressed in sloppy clothes, only 4 percent of the people followed him across. A similar effect has been found in hiring situations. In one study, the good grooming of applicants in a simulated employment interview accounted for more favorable hiring decisions than did their job qualifications. This happened even though the interviewers claimed that appearance only played a minor role in their choices.[7]

I know that when I travel, how I am treated and how often I am upgraded is directly related to how I am dressed. I can persuade the airline attendant to give me better seats, a better flight, or the help I need much better and faster when I am in a suit than when I am wearing casual attire.

When I have on jeans and a T-shirt, I am viewed as less attractive and, as a result, get less cooperation.

Not only can we focus on our other abilities to make us appear more attractive, but we can also increase our physical attractiveness in many different ways. Attractiveness lies in the simple things that many people overlook, like being in shape and watching your weight, picking nice clothes to wear, paying attention to your accessories (i.e., jewelry, glasses, earrings, etc.), and having well-groomed hair. Keep track of hair and clothing styles. Styles can change dramatically, and if we ignore fashion, our persuasive ability may be put in jeopardy. When in doubt, look to national newscasters as conservative role models in style.

Similarity: Similar Is Familiar

Similarity theory states that familiar objects are more liked than less familiar ones. The same holds true with people: We like people who are similar to us. This theory seems to hold true whether the commonality is in the area of opinions, personality traits, background, or lifestyle. Consequently, those who want us to comply with their wishes can accomplish that purpose by appearing similar to us in a variety of ways.

Studies show that we tend to like and are more attracted to those who are like us and with whom we can relate. If you watch people a party, you will see them instantly gravitate towards people who seem to be similar to themselves. I can remember walking in a foreign country, taking in the unfamiliar sights and sounds, and then running into someone from my own country. We could have been from opposites sides of the nation, but there was an instantaneous bond between us, all because we had something in common in a mutually unfamiliar place.

Have you ever heard the saying, "People buy from people they like"? This is true even in the judicial system. If jurors feel that they share some common ground with you and, better yet, *like* you—even subconsciously— for that similarity, then you will have a markedly better chance of winning your case. Anytime we establish something about ourselves that others will identify with, we increase our persuasive powers. In one particular study, antiwar demonstrators were more inclined to sign petitions of those similarly dressed, and often didn't even bother to read the petition before signing![8]

Similarly, we gravitate toward people who dress like us. In the 1970s, when young people tended to dress in either "hippie" or "straight" fashion, researchers studied the effects of clothing styles. Experimenters donned hippie or straight attire and asked college students on campus for a dime to make a phone call. When the experimenter was dressed in the same way as the student, the request was granted in more than two thirds of all instances; when the student and requester were dissimilarly dressed, the dime was provided less than half the time.[9] Numerous studies conclude that your audience is most responsive to individuals who dress and act similarly to them.

An especially apt illustration can be found in a study done by psychologists at Columbia University. Researchers placed wallets on the ground containing $2.00 in cash, a check for $26.30, the "owner's" ID, and a letter giving evidence that the wallet had already been lost before. The letter was written to the owner from the original finder, expressing his intentions to return the wallet as soon as possible. The letter was sometimes written in perfect English, while other times it was written in poor English, as though created by a foreigner. Researchers wanted to see whether the wallet would be returned more frequently when finders felt some commonality with the writer of the letter. The study found that only 33 percent of the respondents returned the wallet when the person who wrote the letter was seen as dissimilar, while 70 percent returned the wallet when they thought they were similar to the letter writer.[10]

Do you remember all the "cliques" in junior high, high school, or even college? People associate and interact with those they view as similar to themselves. Cliques are often based on such commonalities as gender, age, educational background, professional interests, hobbies, and ethnic background. In one study, researchers examined the social networks of prison inmates.[11] Their "cliques" were typically centered on commonalities of race, geographical origin, and the types of crime committed. One group of three men stood out to the researchers because they shared a tight companionship yet seemed to have no common backgrounds. Just as the study was coming to a close, the three men escaped together, demonstrating that we also build alliances based on common goals.

Researchers McCroskey, Richmond, and Daly say there are four critical steps to similarity: attitude, morality, background, and appearance.[12] When receiving a persuasive message, we ask the following questions subconsciously:

1. Does the speaker think like me?
2. Does the speaker share my morals?
3. Does the speaker share my background?
4. Does the speaker look like me?

Of the four similarity factors, attitudes and morals are the most important.[13] Master Persuaders are always looking for similarities or common beliefs to form the basis of common foundations with their prospects. We want to be persuaded by those who are like us and with whom we can relate. We see real-world examples of this in advertisements. We want to see people we can identify with, and the advertising execs accommodate us. When we see a particular commercial, we think, "Hey, he is just like me! He doesn't have time to pick up his socks, either. That couple has a messy, cluttered house, too." We see ads showing the average Joe or Jill because they create that similarity.

Your audience will connect with you when they perceive the similarity. O'Keefe found two important points regarding similarity and persuasion. First, the similarity must be relevant to the subject or issue being persuaded. Second, to persuade someone, the similarities must involve positive rather than negative qualities.[14]

People Skills: Winning Instant Acceptance from Others

The ability to work well with people tops the list for common skills and habits of highly successful people. Studies show that as much as 85 percent of your success in life depends on your people skills and the ability to get others to like you. In fact, the Carnegie Institute of Technology found that only 15 percent of employment and management success is due to technical training or intelligence, while the other 85 percent is due to personality factors, or the ability to deal with people successfully. A Harvard University study also found that for every person who lost his job for failure to do work, two people lost their jobs for failure to deal successfully with people.

In this era where technology is taking over our lives, it is tempting to think that personality and the ability to deal with people are not important qualities. On the contrary, we crave personal interaction now more than ever. People still want to get to know you and like you before the doors of persuasion and influence are unlocked. We most often prefer to say yes to the requests of people we know and like.

Network marketing companies rely on the effects of people skills. Marketing techniques are arranged in such a way so as to capitalize on the fact that people are drawn to buy products from people they know and with whom they are friends. In this way, the attraction, warmth, security, and obligation of friendship are brought to bear on the sales setting. For example, at Tupperware home parties, the strength of the social bond is twice as likely to dictate whether or not someone will buy a product as is the preference for the product itself.

People skills are crucial because they have a huge impact on our success. First impressions are made within only four minutes of initial interaction with a stranger,[15] so we don't have time to *not* have good people skills. Whole books have been written on people skills, but let's address some of the most important and basic communication and interaction techniques.

Goodwill

Goodwill in persuasive practice comes courtesy of Dale Carnegie, one of the "greats" in terms of understanding human nature. He told us that by becoming interested in other people, you will get them to like you faster than if you spent all day trying to get them interested in you.[16] Having goodwill entails appearing friendly or concerned with the other person's best interest. Aristotle said, "We consider as friends those who wish good things for us and who are pained when bad things happen to us."

This caring and kindness means being sensitive and thoughtful. It means acting with consideration, politeness, civility, and genuine concern for those around us. It is the foundation for all interactions and creates a mood of reciprocity. You will win hearts and loyalty through compassion.

You invoke goodwill by focusing on positives. Don't be harsh or forceful when dealing in areas where the other person is sensitive or vulnerable. Additionally, make statements and perform actions that show that you have the audience's best interest in mind.

Bonding: Name Calling Works

One of the quickest ways to form an immediate bond with people is by using and remembering their names. How can you effectively remember a name? When someone tells you her name, clarify the pronunciation, clarify the spelling, relate the name to something, and use it again quickly—before you forget. Research shows that if you use a person's first name at the beginning and end of a sentence, your chance of persuasion increases. It's a simple technique that is easy to implement and which creates an instant bond. Don't use the age-old excuse, "I can't remember names." Remembering someone's name is a function of listening, not a function of memory.

Humor

Humor can be a powerful tool of persuasion. Humor makes the persuader seem more friendly and accepting. Humor can gain you attention, help you create rapport, and make your message more memorable. It can relieve tension, enhance relationships, and motivate people. The actor John Cleese once said, "If I can get you to laugh with me, you like me better, which makes you more open to my ideas. And if I can persuade you to laugh at the particular point I make, by laughing at it you acknowledge its truth." Professional persuaders, such as advertisers, know that humor can be a powerful tool; humor is used in 36 percent of all television ads in the United Kingdom and 24 percent of television ads in the United States.[17]

Humor can also distract your audience from negative arguments or grab their attention if they are not listening. Herbert Gardner said, "Once you've got people laughing, they're listening and you can tell them almost anything." Humor may divert attention away from the negative context of a message, thereby interfering with the ability of listeners to carefully scrutinize it or engage in counterarguments. If listeners are laughing at the jokes, they may pay less attention to the content of a message. Humor can "soften up" or disarm listeners.

Humor must be used cautiously, however. If used inappropriately, it can be offensive and may cause your audience to turn against you. Humor should only be used as a pleasant but moderate distraction. As a rule of thumb, if you are generally not good at telling jokes, don't attempt it when you are in a persuasion situation. Be sure that you have good material. Nonfunny humor is not only ineffective but irritating. Modify your humor so that it is appropriate for your audience.

Smile

The safest way to increase people skills is to give away smiles. A smile is free, generates a great first impression, and shows happiness, acceptance, and confidence. Your smile shows that you are pleased to be where you are, meeting this person. As a result, he in turn becomes more interested in meeting you. Smiling also conveys a feeling of acceptance, which makes your listener more trusting of you. It has been shown that sales representatives who smiled during the sales process increased their success rate by 20 percent. However, as with traditional humor, use a smile appropriately.

Respect

In order for your audience to take your message seriously, they have to have some level of respect for you. The more they respect you, the more successful you will be. Building respect often takes time, but there are things you can do to facilitate it. You need to show gratitude—be thankful for what others do for you. Never criticize others or talk about your problems. People want to talk about two things: themselves and their problems. If you listen when people tell you their problems, they will think you are wise and understanding. Remember, how others feel about you is often influenced by how you make them feel about themselves. Being a person who makes other people feel good will go a long way toward increasing your likeability in their eyes.

Rapport: The Instant Connection

Rapport is the secret ingredient that makes us feel a tangible and harmonious link with someone else. It is equivalent to being on the same wavelength with the other person. Rapport is the key that makes mutual trust materialize.

Have you ever met a perfect stranger and just hit it off? Finding plenty to talk about, you almost felt as if you had met before. It just felt right. So comfortable were you in talking about practically anything that you lost track of time. You developed such a strong bond with that person that you knew what he was going to say. Everything just clicked between the two of you and you felt very close to this person. It might have been a physical attraction, or it might have just entailed being on the same wavelength. You felt your ideas were in sync and you enjoyed your time with each other. This is rapport. When there is rapport, we can differ in our opinions with someone else but still feel a connection or bond with that person. Rapport can even exist between two people who share very few similarities.

In our discussion of rapport, we are going to elaborate on two concepts: body language and mirroring. Both of these ideas will help you to develop rapport faster.

Body Language: Attracts or Distracts

Whether we realize it or not, we are constantly reading and being read by others. Even without the utterance of words, the language of the body speaks volumes. Often, interpreting body language is a subconscious thing. We may not make a conscientious effort to think through all the details of *why* someone has just folded their arms across their chest and narrowed their eyes at us, yet somehow this body language registers subliminally and makes us feel uneasy. The subconscious instantaneously interprets these actions to indicate resistance, suspicion, or spite, even if we have not made a conscious study of the opposing person or their background.

Using body language to its fullest not only involves mastering your own use of outward gestures to create and maintain rapport, but also entails acquiring the ability to read the body language of another person. When you can effectively read body language, you can identify the emotions and discomfort of others. You can see tension and disagreement. You can feel rejection and suspicion. You have to understand that your body language adds to or detracts from your message. In other words, your subconscious gestures and expressions can either help or hurt your ability to persuade others. You can create rapport by understanding and adopting the right body postures and countenances for your prospect.

Everything about you, be it outward or subtle, communicates something to somebody else. The words you use, your facial expressions, what you do with your hands, your tone of voice, and your level of eye contact will determine whether people accept or reject you and your message. To be persuasive, you have to present not only openness, but also authority.

Albert Mehrabian says we are perceived in three ways:

1. 55 percent   Visually (body language)

2. 38 percent   Vocally (tone of voice)

3. 7 percent   Verbally (spoken words)[18]

Other research estimates that as much as 93 percent of your message's impact depends on nonverbal elements.[19] This includes facial expressions, body movement, vocal cues, and proxemics (the study of spatial separation between individuals).

Body language and gestures are an innate part of our psyche. There have been many interesting studies conducted on body language and the use of gestures. In one particular experiment, twelve children with perfect vision and twelve children who were blind since birth were observed to see whether either group gestured more than the other. The results showed that the blind children actually gestured just as much as their full-sighted counterparts, even when they knowingly spoke with other blind children. The researchers concluded that gesturing is an innate part of our expressive and communicative patterns, and that speech and body language are highly interconnected.[20]

Furthermore, the researchers asserted that speech and body language also bear strong ties to our thought processes. One article discusses how gesturing can serve as a memory aide. Subjects had a more difficult time remembering words when they had to keep their hands holding on to a bar than when their hands were free.[21]

There is a direct correlation between our ability to read body language and our relationships. In another study, college students were tested to see whether they could accurately identify the meanings behind certain facial expressions and tones of voice. Significantly, the research consistently showed that the students who made the most errors in interpreting the meanings were those who had troubled relationships and/or greater feelings of depression.

Eyes

Ralph Waldo Emerson said, "The eyes of men converse as much as their tongues." The more common phrase we hear is "the eyes are the windows to the soul." Through our eyes, we can gauge the truthfulness, intelligence, attitude, and feelings of a speaker. *Not* making eye contact when we ought to can have devastating results. Note the following true example:

Pennzoil Oil took the Texaco Oil Company to court over Texaco's allegedly interfering with a contract Pennzoil already had with Getty Oil. Throughout the trial, Pennzoil's counsel was accused of trying to sway the jury by encouraging their witnesses to make eye contact and joke with the jurors. To show that they were serious and did not consider the circumstances a joking matter, Texaco's counsel told witnesses not to joke at all and to avoid eye contact with the jurors. Unfortunately, the advice proved to be unwise and cost Texaco dearly in the end. Pennzoil was granted more than $2.5 billion in damages— the largest damage award in U.S. history. Why? Afterwards, jurors expressed distrust toward the witnesses who had avoided eye contact, even going so far as to call them "arrogant" and "indifferent."

Our eyes' pupils are one of the most sensitive and complicated parts of our body. They react to light but they also respond to our emotions, betraying a variety of feelings. When a person is aroused, interested, and receptive, the pupils dilate. This is an attempt by the eye to allow the entry of more light and more information. Being able to see each other's pupils is so important to our communication that we often distrust a person wearing sunglasses. Consciously or subconsciously, we assume that use of the glasses is a direct attempt to hide the eyes in fear that they will reveal the truth.

Making eye contact can also convey love or passion. In a number of studies on eye contact and attraction, researchers found that simply looking into one another's eyes can create passionate feelings. In one particular case, two members of the opposite sex who were complete strangers were found to have amorous feelings toward each other after merely gazing into one another's eyes.[22] In another study, beggars were interviewed about their "tactics" for getting donations from passersby. Several of the beggars stated that one of the very first things they tried to do was establish eye contact. They claimed that making eye contact made it harder for people to pretend they hadn't seen them, to ignore them, or to just keep walking.[23] Other studies have shown that public speakers who make more eye contact, use pleasant facial expressions, and incorporate appropriate gestures into their speeches have more persuasive power than speakers who do not.[24]

Hands

The way we use our hands tells others a lot about what we are thinking or feeling. For example, if your hands are tucked away in your pockets or behind your back, you may be perceived as holding something back. Clenched fists may portray anger or tension. Holding your hands up around your face—over your mouth, by your ear, etc.—may portray dishonesty. Stroking your chin shows you are thinking about what has been said. If you place your hands flat on the table in front of you, you may be sending a signal that you agree. On the other hand, placing your hands on your hips may express defiance or dominance.

The way we shake hands also tells people a lot about us. It is customary in business situations to shake hands with someone when we first meet them or when we are sealing a deal. Even if we don't realize it, a firm handshake conveys cooperation and alliance. Weak or limp handshakes, on the other hand, portray just that: weakness, incompetence, or maybe even disinterest. Be sure your handshakes are always firm and appropriately energetic.

Head

If you notice your prospect tilting her head toward you, it is very likely that she is interested in the deal. If her head is tilted away, however, she may not be totally sold, and, in fact, she may feel some distrust or dissatisfaction toward you or the offer. If she rests her head on her hand, she is bored or not really interested. If she keeps looking around, you can bet she is most likely thinking: "Get me out of here." Obviously, nodding her head would express agreement and interest.

Legs

If your prospect is pointing his feet in your direction, he is most likely facing you and is therefore likely to be very interested in your offer. If his legs or feet are pointed away from you, however, he may just be enduring your pitch and may be feeling ready to leave as soon as he has the opportunity. If his legs are crossed when he stands, he may still be feeling some awkwardness about the deal. On the other hand, if his legs are crossed when he is seated, he may be feeling some resistance to you or your offer. If he keeps tapping his foot, he's either wishing you would shut up and let him talk or he's feeling bored.

Other Types of Nonverbal Communication

As mentioned above, putting your hands or fingers to your nose or mouth can send a message that you are lying. As a general rule, keep your hands away from your face and head when engaging in the persuasion process. Here are a few more nonverbal indicators:

- Leaning closer = interest and comfort
- Learning away = discomfort with the facts or with the person
- Nodding = interest, agreement, and understanding
- Relaxed posture = openness to communicate
- Hand to cheek = evaluating or considering
- Sitting with hands clasped behind head = arrogance or superiority
- Tapping or drumming fingers = impatience or annoyance
- Steepling fingers = closing off or creating barrier

- Fidgeting = boredom, nervousness, or impatience

- Clutching objects tightly = anxiety or nervous anticipation

- Chin stroke = deep thinking or intently listening

From what we have discussed, you can see that resistance can be easily detected in your prospect. Check to see if your prospect's body is leaning away from you. Observe whether she faces you at an angle. Look to see whether her arms, legs, or both are crossed. She may glance from the corner of the eye and make minimal eye contact. She may tap her finger or foot—or her feet may point away from you. Generally, if she is resisting your persuasive efforts, her posture is closed. When you persuade, avoid adopting this body language. By opening yourself up, you may prompt her to follow suit.

Touch

Touch is another powerful part of body language—important enough to devote a whole section to it alone. Touch can be a very effective psychological technique. Subconsciously, we like to be touched; it makes us feel appreciated and liked. It is true, though, that we do need to be aware and careful of a small percentage of the population who dislikes being touched in any way. In most instances, however, touch can help put people at ease and make them more receptive to you and your ideas.

Touch can create a positive perception in the person being touched. Touch carries with it favorable interpretations of immediacy, affection, similarity, relaxation, and informality.[25] In one research study, librarians did one of two things when handing back library cards to university students checking out books: either they did not touch the person at all during the exchange or they made light, physical contact by placing a hand over the student's palm. Invariably, those students who were touched during the transaction rated the library service more favorably than those who were not touched at all.[26] Waiters/waitresses who touched customers on the arm when asking if everything was okay received larger tips and were evaluated more favorably than those waiters who didn't touch their customers. Attractive waitresses who touched their customers received the highest tips of all. Touch also induces customers to spend more time shopping in a particular store. In one study, physical contact on the part of salespeople induced customers to buy more and to evaluate the store more favorably.[27]

In another example, touch was found to increase the number of people who volunteered to score papers, sign petitions, and return money that had been left in a telephone booth. Syracuse professor Jacob Hornik discovered that touching bookstore customers on the arm caused them to shop longer (to be exact, 22.11 minutes versus 13.56 minutes), to purchase more ($15.03 versus $12.23), and to evaluate the store more positively than customers who had not been touched. Hornik also found that supermarket customers who had been touched were more likely to taste and purchase food samples than nontouched customers.[28]

We know that certain areas of the body can be freely touched while other areas are off limits. Women don't mind being touched by other women and they are fairly tolerant of being touched (appropriately) by men. Men usually don't mind being touched by an unfamiliar female—but things get harder to predict in cases where men are touching other men. In general, men don't like being touched by unfamiliar men. Safe areas of contact include the shoulders, forearms and hands, and sometimes the upper back. This all depends on the situation and relationship between the two parties prior to the touch.

Mirroring and Matching

John Grinder and Richard Bandler, founders of neurolinguistic programming (NLP), developed the concept of "mirror and matching." The idea is to align your movements and body image with your prospect's demeanor. The goal is to mirror or reflect their actions, not to imitate them. If people think you are imitating them, they may feel like you're mocking them and they may become offended. They will see you as phony and no longer trust you. Instead of directly imitating, just mirror or match the overall tone and demeanor of your prospect. You can safely mirror their language, posture, gestures, and mood.

When you mirror your prospects, you build rapport with them. Because of your similar demeanors, your prospects will feel a connection with you. Remember, people are inclined to follow and obey those they perceive as similar to themselves. If they shift in their posture, you should eventually do so, too. If they cross their legs, you should cross your legs as well. If they smile, you smile too. When you do this, your prospects will subconsciously feel that you have much more in common with them than is actually the case.

We often unconsciously mirror others, without even realizing it. It is just a natural thing that we do. Have you ever noticed at social gatherings how people tend to match each other in their body language and their attitudes? For example, when two people greet each other, they typically tend to use the same posture and behave with the same demeanor. When you are a Master Persuader, you will make skillful and conscientious use of mirroring.

Mirroring Language

You will be amazed at the effectiveness of using vocabulary or "lingo" similar to that of your prospect. Pick up on and use some of the words or phrases that your prospect uses. You may also find it helpful to mirror his rate of speech. If he speaks in a slower and more relaxed tone, you can do the same. Nevertheless, be sure to keep the enthusiasm high. If he speaks quickly, feel free to do the same.

Matching Breathing

See if you can adopt the same breathing pattern as your prospect. In doing so, it is helpful to observe the rise and fall of your prospect's chest or shoulders for cues. Of course, use your peripheral vision to do this so you are always maintaining eye contact. Synchronized breathing between you and your prospect is such a subtle thing, yet it creates connectivity.

Matching Voice

This is different from matching language. It refers to the actual tone or inflection of your prospect's voice. Be very careful, however, that you do not come across as mimicking. The "mirrored" voice you use should never be so different or foreign from your own that you arouse suspicion. Just minor and subtle adjustments in tone are all that are necessary to get the desired results.

Mirroring Moods

When you reflect your prospect's mood, you give validation to what he is saying and feeling. We often verbally mirror another's mood by restating what he or she just said: "So, what I hear you saying is . . ." or "I think I would feel that way too, if I also experienced. . . ." Be sure when you mirror your prospect's mood that your tone is very sincere. When you sincerely acknowledge your prospect's comments, concerns, and feelings, your persuasive power increases.

Matching Energy Level

Some people always seem to be relaxed and mellow. Others seem to be constantly active or vivacious. Seek to mirror your prospect's energy level. This will be another subtle way you are in sync with your prospect. This technique is also effective when giving a group presentation: Match the overall energy level present in the room, or adopt the level of energy emanating from the group.

Breaking the Mirror

Certainly, there are occasions when you may not want to mirror someone else. For example, a lawyer will often seek to create anxiety or uneasiness in a witness. To accomplish this, the lawyer needs to *avoid* mirroring. While the witness is slumped back in the seat looking at the ground, the lawyer may hover or stand rigidly and look intensely at the witness's face. Have you ever noticed or felt the uneasiness when someone stood in the middle of a conversation where everyone was seated? Have you ever experienced the awkwardness of glancing at your watch when you're in the middle of a conversation with someone and they notice? "Breaking the mirror" breaks the synchronization that makes everyone feel calm and comfortable. If you need to break the mirror, simply stop mirroring and sit, speak, or gesture differently from the person you're dealing with. You can create even further distance by altering your demeanor abruptly or suddenly.

As you study persuasion, you must realize that connecting with your audience is critical. Many persuaders don't know how to maintain that rapport throughout the entire persuasive situation. You see people in sales break the ice, find similarities, build rapport for the first five minutes, and then launch into their presentation. All of a sudden, they get serious and change their demeanor. What is the prospect going to think? The person he has been talking to for the past five minutes has now changed. Which one is the real person? The two were getting along, having fun, and all of a sudden, without warning, the salesperson becomes serious and dives into a sales pitch. This breaks rapport and seems incongruent to the prospect. You both know why you are there and what the ultimate goal will be, so continue to build on that rapport.

Connectivity takes time, research, and practice to master. You need to learn how to read your prospect and your customer. Learn how to determine whether your prospect is relaxed, nervous, confident, or indifferent.

6

The Law of Social Validation
The Art of Social Pressure

The greatest difficulty is that men do not think enough of themselves, do not consider what it is that they are sacrificing when they follow a herd.
—RALPH WALDO EMERSON

WE ARE SOCIAL ANIMALS. We all have an innate desire to belong to a social group. It is precisely because we value this sense of belonging so highly that the more other people find an idea, trend, or position appealing or correct, the more correct that idea becomes in our own minds. The Law of Social Validation recognizes and builds on our innate desire to be part of the main group. It also recognizes that we tend to change our perceptions, opinions, and behaviors in ways that are consistent with group norms.[1] Even if we don't admit it, or maybe even realize it, we care about what others think. As such, we use others' behavior as a guide in establishing the standard for the choices and decisions we make.

We seek to find out what others are doing as a way of validating our own actions. This method is how we decide what constitutes "correct" behavior. We see the behavior as more correct when we see others doing it. The more people do it, the more correct it becomes. Professor Kirk Hansen of the Stanford Business School demonstrated this when he boosted downloads for best-selling files on the Web by personally downloading those files over and over so the counter was artificially high. He and his team then observed that these boosted downloaded files were downloaded even more frequently. The high number on the counter indicated popularity, and people were most interested in downloading the files that were already ranked the highest. Whether the question is what to do with an empty can of soda at the park, how fast to drive in the city, or how to eat the soup at a restaurant, the validation of others gives us our answers and therefore guides our actions.

We feel validation when we see others do what we want to do. We learned early in life that we make fewer mistakes when we follow the social norm. There are two types of norms: explicit and implicit. *Explicit norms* are openly spoken or written. For example, road signs, employee manuals, or game rules are all examples of explicit norms. *Implicit norms* are not usually stated openly. For example, most people don't have to be directed to say hello or to smile when they see someone, but they do it anyway. Or, somehow you know better than to put your feet up on the dinner table when you're a guest in someone's home, even though your host most likely will not request that you refrain from doing so.

If we don't know the norm, we look around and find it. The Law of Social Validation becomes a way to save time and energy in figuring out what is correct. We use others' behavior to guide our own actions, to validate what we should or should not do. We don't always have to look at the positive and the negative in every situation. This automatic trigger saves us from thinking. We compare what we do against the standard of what everyone else is doing. If we find a discrepancy between what we observe and what we do, we tend to make changes in the direction of the social norm.

Going with the Crowd

Social validation compels us to change our behaviors, our attitudes, and our actions, even when what we observe doesn't really match our true feelings, style, and thoughts. We go against our better judgment because we want to be liked, accepted, and found in agreement with everyone else. When we are part of a crowd, we "no longer feel individually responsible for our emotions or actions. We can allow ourselves to shout, sing, cry, or strike without temperament imposed by personal accountability."[2]

We seek out social norms to help us know what we should be feeling or doing. For the most part, this is not a conscious process. We subconsciously accept many ways of behaving that are determined by our surroundings and the actions of others, such as raising our hands to speak in class, how we behave at a concert, or how we act at work because of the corporate culture. When we become part of a group, our once divergent emotions and feelings tend to converge.[3]

Usually, as long as most people agree with what we are doing or about to do, we feel social validation. For the most part, we are all conformists.

We will do what the crowd does. We might not like to admit that, but it is true. Only 5 to 10 percent of the population engages in behavior contrary to the social norm.

We see this law operating in groups, in organizations, in meetings, and in day-to-day public life. In all of these circumstances, there is a certain standard or norm. In churches, the moral code determines the standard behavior acceptable for the group. In organizations, the bylaws and years of tradition establish a standard operating procedure. Because we want to fit into these groups and maintain our membership with them, we conform our actions to the norm.

When we find ourselves in a foreign situation where we feel awkward or unsure of how to act, we look for those social cues that will dictate our behavior.[4] This could be at a party, during freshman orientation, while attending a family gathering, or on one's first day on the job in a new company. When the social information we are seeking is at all ambiguous, we don't know how to respond and thus continue seeking out social clues. Imagine if you were sitting in the movie theater enjoying your show when somebody shouted, "FIRE!" Do you think you would jump up and run for it? Well, if everyone else did, you would, too. If everyone remained seated, you would remain seated also.

The Law of Social Validation at Work

The Law of Social Validation is in action all the time, everywhere: publicly passing the donation plate to help with a community project; doing the wave at sporting events; going to popular dance clubs when you don't enjoy the surroundings; being afraid to raise your hand in class to ask a question; franchise owners having their athletes sign their contracts in public; stacking the top ten most popular books right in the entryway of a bookstore; choosing restaurants according to which have the longest lines or the most cars; choosing movies according to which ones everyone is talking about; washing our hands in public restrooms only when somebody else is watching; and restaurants seating their first patrons near the window for everyone else to see.

Sometimes theaters even employ "professional audience members," or claques, to start laughter, clapping, and even standing ovations! When audience members see others stand and cheer or applaud, they are more inclined to do so. Performers commonly "salt the tip jar" by placing some money in the jar themselves. When people see that others have already made contributions, they assume this is the appropriate and acceptable thing to do. Salting the tip jar is a common practice among pianists, bartenders, bus drivers, and even the homeless on the street. Even in churches, the practice of "salting the collection plate" is often employed. People are more inclined to donate if they are passed a plate that already holds some bills.

Researchers from Arizona State University reported that before one of Billy Graham's televised crusades, his organization had coached thousands of volunteers on when to come up front, when to sing, and when to clap, all to give the appearance of great, religious intensity.[5] In televised fundraisers people manning the phones are instructed to pretend they are talking to someone when the camera turns their way, to make it appear that there is a huge volume of calls. This gives social validation to the at-home audience that this charity is popular and an acceptable organization to which to donate money.

Your video rental stores use social validity as a means of increasing rentals on high-profit movies. Older movies return the highest profit for video rental stores. When storeowners noticed that many customers check the return stacks to see what videos other people were watching, they had workers put older movies into the return bin. Social validation increased the rentals of the older movies significantly.

Do you recall MCI's "Friends and Family" campaign? The result was a gain of ten million customers in less than ten years! If we believe friends and family—people we know so well—are participating in the program, then we feel social proof and family pressure that it must be a good company or product. That's why referrals are some of your best prospects! Referrals are your greatest source of social validation.

Etiquette is also a form of social validation. When we eat, what we order, what we drink, where we put our napkins, and how we cross our silverware when finished, all are forms of social validation. Have you ever noticed that no one wants to be the first to order dessert? If the majority does not want dessert, it's likely that no one will.

I recently attended a business opportunity seminar that was promoting a home business for $4,000. Throughout the course of the event, I saw many elements of social validation. The organizers used testimonials from people who were successful. The testifier stood up and claimed that this business opportunity was the answer to his economic woes. Then, as a form of social validation, all those who were ready to sign up had to walk to the back of the room to do so. The first few people ran to the back sign-up table. This was proof enough of the soundness of the business idea, and a storm of people followed suit to sign up. Of course, once at the back, there was a gentleman with a credit card machine running everybody's card through, tempting everyone's ears with that familiar sound of the credit card machine being swiped.

Gangs exhibit a powerful manifestation of social validation. New initiates allow older members to beat them up just so they will be able to belong. Fraternity hazings also reduce the initiate to a subhuman level—all because of an overwhelming desire to belong to a group. During one fraternity hazing, new members were forced to drink so much alcohol that one guy passed out. Members, oblivious to the seriousness of the situation, thought he was asleep and left him there to sleep it off. Unfortunately, it turned out he was found dead the next day, in the same spot where they had left him the night before.

CNN reported on the vicious way in which some Marines are initiated into the military. In the initiation ritual called "blood pinning" the recruits' badges are literally pinned into their chests. Psychologists have identified people belonging to these organizations with what is now called "gang syndrome." Gang syndrome manifests itself when participants feel shame for the crimes they committed (acts they've committed or pain they've endured) but went through with them anyway so they could finally have a sense of belonging, or a sense of family—typically a feeling they never experienced in their own home lives.[6]

I once attended a college football game between two fierce cross-town rivals. Emotions were high, and we all wanted our home team to win. One of the fans near me was using a megaphone to taunt the other team and its fans. He only meant it in good fun, but it was not too long before a rent-a-cop came up to the man and told him he could not use the megaphone during the game. The rent-a-cop stood in the middle of the aisle of the sold-out game. The fan said he was just having fun but the rent-a-cop stressed that it was strictly against the rules. Then the social pressure and validation kicked in. Other fans nearby told the rent-a-cop that the fan's overzealous actions were okay and that there was no problem. The rent-a-cop tried to persist, but the crowd only grew louder in their protests. Finally, the rent-a-cop decided it wasn't worth the hassle and left.

Even watching someone else "do what's right" will give your cause social validation. For example, one study asked 10,000 high school students to give blood. The study found that students who had been exposed to thirty-eight photos of high school blood-drive scenes were 17 percent more likely to donate blood than the students who had not seen the photos. Seeing others do the right thing prompts us to socially validate the cause and to jump on board.[7]

Social Validation: The Power of the Group

In another study, researchers had very young children who were terrified of dogs watch a little boy play with his dog for twenty minutes a day. After only four days, 67 percent of the children were willing to sit in a playpen with a dog and even remain with it when everyone else left the room. The results were lasting, too: One month later, the same children were just as eager to play with dogs.[8] In a similar study, children who were afraid of dogs were influenced just as readily by *films* of a child playing with a dog as they were when watching a *live* child play with a dog.[9]

In another study, participants were asked to identify the longer of two lines displayed on a screen. One line was clearly longer than the other, but some participants had been privately instructed prior to the study to state that the *shorter* line was longer. The surprising result was that several of the unsuspecting participants actually gave in to social pressure and changed their answers! Over the course of the entire study, 75 percent of the participants gave the incorrect answer at least one time. In a related study, it was determined that even when the correct answer is obvious, individuals will knowingly give the incorrect answer 37 percent of the time, just to go along with the consensus.[10]

You know how you often you have heard canned laughter on television sitcoms even when there isn't anything really funny happening? Studies prove that using canned laughter actually influences audience members to laugh longer and more frequently, and to give the material higher ratings for its "funniness."[11] Even for the portions of the show that seem to have no humor at all, producers use laugh tracks to get us to laugh along. The sad part is that it actually works! There is evidence that canned laughter is most effective when the joke is really bad.[12] When two audiences watch the same show, and one hears a laugh track while the other doesn't, it's always the audience that hears the laugh track that laughs the most!

Another study was set up to test whether passersby would stare up into the air if there was another group of people already doing so. The researchers arranged groups of one to fifteen people to congregate in New York City at 33 West 42nd Street. A video camera was set up on the 6th floor to catch the results on tape. Sure enough, the more people in the group who were already gawking and looking into the air, the more passersby who stopped, came over and stared, and looked up themselves![13]

When participants were asked to view a political debate among George H. W. Bush, Bill Clinton, and Ross Perot, it was found that the mere presence of a confederate who cheered for one of the candidates influenced the participant's overall evaluation of that candidate in a positive manner.[14] Obviously, when receiving information in a social setting, the audience can be skewed to perceive the information the way the group tends to hear it.

In yet another study, researchers wanted to see whether mothers who had just given birth to their first child would be more likely to adhere to guidelines for their new babies' nutrition when instructed individually or in a group.[15] The mothers were told that it could be important to give their new babies cod-liver oil and orange juice. The mother's were taught either one-on-one by a nutritionist associated with the hospital or in groups of six. The study found that when taught in a group setting, the mothers were far more inclined to give their babies cod-liver oil and orange juice than those who had been taught individually.

The Dark Side of Social Validation

Bystander Apathy

Numerous studies demonstrate that when someone is in trouble or in need of help, as the number of bystanders increases, the number of people who actually help decreases. Termed "bystander apathy," this effect occurs because, in almost any situation, the more people that are present, the more we feel a diffusion of responsibility. Our sense of social pressure is lessened when we feel that there might be any number of people more capable of helping than we are.

Have you ever been in a situation where, because of the numbers in your group, you didn't really give it your all? For example, maybe on an academic group project you weren't as diligent as you would have been had you been solely responsible for the assignment. Or, maybe you've helped push a stalled car to safety with some other people but didn't really push your hardest. When we find ourselves in groups, there is a diffusion of responsibility. Sometimes we don't know whether we should even involve ourselves in the first place, since there are so many other people who could take action. Have you ever seen someone pulled over on the side of the road, but you just kept driving along with all the other cars speeding by? When there are large numbers of people involved, we tend to assume someone else will respond and take action first, or we might conclude that our help is not really needed.

One particular case in history stands out as a classic example of bystander apathy. Catherine Genovese, a young woman living in New York City, was murdered one night when returning home from work. The unfortunate truth of the matter was that, in a city like New York, her death was just another of countless murders. Consequently, the incident didn't receive any more coverage than a few short lines in the *New York Times*. Genovese's story would have remained an obscure and incidental case had it not been for the publicity given one additional fact of her killing.

A week later, A.M. Rosenthal, editor of the *New York Times*, went out to lunch with the city police commissioner. Rosenthal asked the commissioner about another homicide in the area, but the commissioner, mistakenly thinking he was being asked about the Genovese case, revealed a shocking piece of information that had been uncovered by the police. Genovese's death had not been a silent, hidden, or secretive occurrence. Rather, it had been a loud, drawn-out, public event. As her attacker chased her down and stabbed her three separate times in a 35-minute period, thirty-eight neighbors watched from their apartment windows and didn't even call the police!

Rosenthal promptly assigned a team to investigate this incidence of "bystander apathy." Soon after, the *New York Times* came out with a lengthy, front-page article detailing the incident and the alleged reactions of the neighbors:

For more than half an hour, 38 respectable, law-abiding citizens in Queens watched a killer stalk and stab a woman in three separate attacks in Kew Gardens. Twice the sound of their voices and the sudden glow of their bedroom lights interrupted him and frightened him off. Each time he returned, sought her out, and stabbed her again. Not one person telephoned the police during the assault; one witness called after the woman was dead."[16]

Everyone was completely stunned and baffled. How could people just witness such a scene and do absolutely nothing? Even the very neighbors alluded to in the article didn't know how to explain their inaction. Responses included, "I don't know," "I was afraid," and "I didn't want to get involved." These "explanations" didn't really answer anything. Why couldn't one of them have just made a quick, anonymous call to the police? Different branches of the media—newspapers, TV stations, magazines, radio stations—pursued their own studies and investigations to explain the incredible scenario, all of them finally arriving at the same conclusion: The witnesses simply didn't care. They concluded that there was just no other explanation, or so they thought.

Do you really think thirty-eight people did not care enough to make an anonymous phone call? Did the researchers not understand the diffusion of responsibility? The neighbors did not react, thinking someone else would help or someone else would call the police. Most of us are good people. If each individual neighbor knew it was up to them to phone the police and get help, I guarantee they would have made the call.

Another experiment conducted in New York highlighted this tendency for "bystander apathy." It determined that when a lone individual observed smoke leaking from under a door, 75 percent of those studied reported the smoke. In groups of three, however, reporting incidences dropped to 38 percent. If in that group two people encouraged the third person to do nothing, reporting of the smoke dropped to 10 percent.[17]

Often we don't know whether we are really witnessing an emergency or not. For example, if we see a man collapsed on the floor, we might waver between two conclusions: Did he just have a heart attack or did he pass out because he'd been drinking too much? So, bystanders may be "apathetic" more because of uncertainty than insensitivity. And if they are uncertain, then they often don't help because they don't know if they're responsible for doing so.

Everybody else observing the event is also likely to be looking for social evidence. Because most people prefer to appear poised and levelheaded when in the presence of others, they are likely to search for that evidence with brief glances at those around them. Therefore, everyone sees everyone else looking unflustered and failing to act. When people clearly know their responsibilities in a recognized and obvious emergency, however, they are remarkably quick to respond.

De-Individuation

Social psychologists Festinger, Pepitone, and Newcomb coined the term "de-individuation" in 1952.[18] De-individuation refers to how, when we find ourselves in a group, we become less self-aware and also less concerned with how others will evaluate us.[19] Think of all the people you've heard yell obscenities at sporting events. Do you think they would do that if they were in a small, intimate group watching that same event? Basically, de-individuation means that when in a group, we feel more anonymous and therefore less individually responsible for our actions, often causing us to say or do things that we would not normally feel comfortable with.

Diener, Fraser, Beaman, and Kelem conducted a study that showed how de-individuation can lead to antisocial behavior.[20] On Halloween, researchers evaluated 1,352 trick-or-treaters—either alone or in groups—who had the chance to steal candy from twenty-seven Seattle homes. The researchers figured that Halloween would be the perfect occasion to conduct such a study because the children would be in costume, making them more anonymous. When the children came to doors where they were greeted by experimenters, they were told they could choose only one piece of candy. In some cases, the experimenter asked the children their names, while in other cases the children were allowed to remain anonymous. The experimenter would then leave the room, as though they had to go get something. Unseen observers took careful note of how the children responded: When alone, 7.5 percent took more than one piece of candy; when in groups, 20.8 percent took more than one piece! It was also interesting to observe that the children who remained anonymous stole more candy than did the children who gave out their names. De-individuation prompted many of the trick-or-treaters to go against what was socially acceptable and steal more candy.

Social Validation and Conformity or Groupthink

Anytime we find ourselves part of a group, we feel some susceptibility to peer pressure and/or the opinions of others in the group. The more respect we feel for the group, the more their opinions matter to us, and therefore the more we feel pressured to align our own opinions with those of the group. Even when we don't really agree with the group, we will often go along with the group in order to be rewarded instead of punished, or liked instead of scorned.

In a way, this is an obvious observation. Anyone who has ever been to the movies knows that the size of the crowd in the theater has a big effect on how good the movie seems: The larger the crowd, the funnier the comedies are. The larger the crowd, the scarier the horror flick is. Consider the following other examples:

- Conforming because you believe everyone else is correct
- Conforming because you fear the social rejection of not going along
- Conforming simply because it's the norm
- Conforming because of cultural influences

Social Validation and Marketing

Certainly a huge part of advertising is to make a product seem very popular. As marketing psychologist and business consultant Max Sutherland explains:

> The more a brand is advertised, the more popular and familiar it is perceived to be. We as consumers somehow infer that something is popular simply because it is advertised. When people are buying gifts for others, social proof is one of the most effective tactics that a sales-clerk can use."[21]

Many salespeople find great success in telling clients that a particular product is their "best-selling" or "most popular" on hand because such a tactic increases the social validation of the product in the mind of the buyer. When customers feel that something is more popular, they spend more money to acquire it, even if there is no proof other than the salesperson's word. So it is with advertising: Simply asserting that a product is in super-high demand or that it is the most popular or fastest selling, etc., seems to provide proof enough! When consumers *think* a product is popular, that's often all they need to go out and buy it.

The creation and use of social validation is rampant: Clubs make their spots look like "the place to be" by allowing huge waiting lines to congregate outside their facilities, even when the place is practically empty inside. Sales-people often recount the many other people who have purchased the item in question. Sales and motivation consultant Cavett Robert said it best: "Since 95 percent of the people are imitators and only 5 percent initiators, people are persuaded more by the actions of others than by any proof we can offer."[22]

Making Social Validation Work

The power of social validation can be used to your benefit in any persuasive situation. If your product or service is socially validated, people are most likely to use it or to switch to it. People are always looking around and comparing themselves to see if they line up with everyone else. If they feel a discrepancy between where they are and where everyone else is, they will most likely conform to the group standard. Consider the following ways you can enhance the effects of social validation to your benefit:

1. *The larger the group, the better.* The larger the group, the more people will conform. Social theory shows us that when a group grows, so does conformity to that group.

2. *The greater the familiarity, the better.* The more a person can identify with the group, the more that person will be influenced to change their behavior and/or opinions. Social validation is more powerful when we observe people we consider to be just like us.[23]

3. *The clearer the principle of social validation, the better.* Find the best use of social validation in your product or service. Is it the best selling, the most popular, used by the elite, the fastest growing? Is it part of a trend or is it the industry standard? Who uses it? Do you have testimonials from other clients or users?

7

The Law of Scarcity
Get Anyone to Take Immediate Action

Without a sense of urgency, desire loses its value.
—JIM ROHN

ONLINE AUCTIONS DRIVE ME NUTS. In most auctions, I find an item I like and I put in what I think is a reasonable, winning bid. I promise myself that I won't bid higher. But I always get caught. When I get the outbid notice, I can't believe somebody outbid me. What if I can't find this item again? They obviously think this item is worth more than I do. Then I find myself wanting it even more—whatever it is—and I bid far more than I originally intended. The thrill of winning usually outweighs the pain of the price I paid.

In 1996, Jackie Kennedy's personal belongings were put up for auction. Everyone knew such items would reel in top dollar. More than 100,000 catalogs were sold prior to the auction. Hardcover catalogs sold at ninety dollars a copy, while paperback catalogs cost forty-five dollars a copy. The week the belongings were on public display, more than 40,000 people took part. The hype and anticipation surrounding the event catapulted prices far beyond the originally anticipated prices. For example, a brooch estimated at $6,000 to $8,000 sold for $415,000; John F. Kennedy's golf clubs were estimated at $700 to $900 but sold for $772,500; a wooden cigar box estimated at $2,000 sold for $547,500; even a cigarette lighter inscribed with the letter "J"—estimated at $300—sold for $85,000.[1]

Think about potatoes. Nothing special, right? There was a time in history (late 1700s) when potatoes were not a popular food. The French thought potatoes were connected with leprosy, the Germans thought they were nothing better than feed for livestock, and Russian peasants actually thought they were poisonous! Then Catherine the Great came along and turned potatoes into gold. She had high fences installed to enclose her potato fields. Signs dotted the land warning the Russian citizens not to steal her potatoes. With the potatoes suddenly off limits, they became the talk of the town! Imagine what those peasants were thinking as they watched those big, tall fences go up: "Why are they fencing in the potato fields? Why are the rich keeping the potatoes all to themselves? Why are we restricted to the same old beef stew every single day? We deserve potatoes, too! We *need* potatoes! Give us potatoes!"[2]

Why Scarcity Drives Us Wild

The Law of Scarcity plays a large role in the persuasion process. Opportunities are always more valuable and exciting when they are scarce and less available. We want to be the ones to own the rare items or to get the last widget on the shelf. The more the scarcity of an item increases, the more the item increases in value, and the greater the urge to own it.

Whenever choice is limited or threatened, the human need to maintain a share of the limited commodity makes us crave it even more. Scarcity increases the value of any product or service. Scarcity drives people to action, making us act quickly for fear of missing out on an opportunity. Potentially losing something before we've even had an opportunity to possess it drives people to action. We don't want to miss out on anything we could have had. We want to get around any restriction placed upon us. We feel uptight and want back our freedom. This causes tension and unrest. The Law of Scarcity not only pertains to physical products, but also to time, information, price, and knowledge.

The Threat of Potential Loss

Anytime someone feels their freedom—to choose, think, or act—is being restricted, they "experience psychological reactance and attempt to restore their freedom."[3] With this restriction on freedom we are driven to latch on to that thing which we fear will be restricted even more. Instead of standing by and saying, "Okay, I'll give that up," we take the opposite approach. Suddenly, that restricted item is even more important to us. Researchers call this tendency "reactance."[4] An intensely motivational state, reactance causes us to be emotional, single-minded, or even irrational. We hate feeling restricted, so we are highly motivated to resolve anything that creates that feeling. It is due to reactance that we act, and that we want it now.

A study involving a group of male toddlers illustrates just how powerful the Law of Scarcity is, even in very small children. In the study, the toddlers were brought into a room that held two equally exciting and appealing toys. A Plexiglas barrier was set up so that one of the toys sat *next* to it, while the other sat behind. The barrier wasn't very tall, so some of the toddlers could simply reach over the top and grab for the toy. For others, though, the barrier was still too high to reach over, so they could only reach that particular toy if they went around and behind the Plexiglas. The researchers wanted to see if the obstructed toy, being more "scarce," would draw more attention and be more desirable. The boys who could easily reach over the top showed no preference toward the obstructed or the unobstructed toy; the unobstructed toy was approached just as frequently and just as quickly. For the boys who could *not* reach over the top, however, the obstructed toy was clearly the more desirable of the two—in fact, the boys made contact with it three times faster than with the unobstructed toy![5] Even in toddlers, there was an urge to defy restriction of choice!

You Can't Have It

In another study involving children, researchers told the children they could select from a wide array of candy bars. They then pointed out a particular candy bar and told them they should not choose that one, but any of the others would be fine. The children reacted to the threat to their freedom of choice by choosing the bar they'd been told not to select. In doing so, they felt they had preserved their freedom to select whatever bar they wanted.[6] It makes you wonder if that is also why Adam and Eve, who had the entire Garden of Eden to play in, couldn't stay away from the forbidden fruit.

The Law of Scarcity works because it makes people feel like they will lose their opportunity to act and choose if they don't do so immediately. The threat of such loss creates urgency in our decision making. Have you ever noticed how people tend to be more motivated when faced with potentially losing something than when they might take steps of their own accord and gain something of equal value? Studies have verified that this is a common and consistent phenomenon.[7] For example, do you think homeowners would feel more urgency to act if they were told how much money they were going to lose if they didn't improve their insulation, or if they were told how much money they would save? They are more likely to act if they are told about their potential loss.[8]

The mental trigger of potential loss causes such great anxiety in people that they act to prevent the loss—even though they likely are not really interested in the product itself. Imagine making a decision where you have all day to make up your mind and you have the reassurance that when you return tomorrow, the item will still be available at the same good price. You could take days to make that decision.

However, when scarcity enters the picture and you feel that the availability of the product, the timing, or even the price is bound to change without notice, the mental trigger of scarcity begins to operate. You are driven to acquire something to alleviate the threat of potential loss. That's why shoe salespeople always bring you back the last pair of shoes available in your size at the sale price—which ends today. What we can't have is always more desirable and exciting than what we already possess. As the adage says, "The grass is always greener on the other side of the fence." Any parent knows the result of telling a child she can't have or do something. The child will immediately drop everything and want the one thing she can't have. Look at Romeo and Juliet. The forbidden nature of their relationship made it even stronger and more appealing to them. Parents need to be cautioned about forbidding their child's friends and lovers because the Law of Scarcity will come back to haunt them.

The manner in which an object *becomes* scarce also contributes to making it more desirable. In a particular study, researchers gave subjects a cookie jar containing ten cookies. Then, taking the jar back, the subjects were given a new jar containing only two cookies. One group of subjects was told their cookies had been given away to other participants because of the demand for their study. Another group was told their cookies were taken away because the proctor had made a mistake and had given them the wrong cookie jar. The results indicated that the cookies that had become scarce through social demand were rated considerably higher than the cookies that had become scarce through the proctor's oversight. Not only this, but they were also the most highly rated of all the cookies used in the study![9]

The Law of Scarcity works even when the desired object or thing isn't going to really benefit the recipient. A county in Florida enacted legislation forbidding the sale and use of laundry detergents containing phosphates, as phosphates negatively impact the environment and don't help clean the clothes. Before the ban went into effect, stores experienced an increase in sales of the phosphate-containing detergents. After the ban was underway, stores within the city saw a drop in laundry detergent sales overall, while stores in surrounding counties not affected by the ban saw an increase in sales of the phosphate-containing detergents.

Later, when consumers were polled as to which detergents were better, the residents where the ban had taken place rated the restricted detergents higher than any others in all categories. The Law of Scarcity had made the limited product dramatically more appealing.[10]

The Law of Scarcity in Marketing

Psychologist Anthony Pratkanis of the University of California, Santa Cruz, is recorded as saying, "As consumers we have a rule of thumb: If it is rare or scarce, it must be valuable and good."

Department stores use the Law of Scarcity to bait consumers into an uncontrollable shopping frenzy. Fights break out at department stores when people are going after those scarce items, which are being offered at bargain prices for a limited time only. The lower prices are bait—a loss leader for the store, but certain to generate a buying frenzy that is contagious. Blinded by scarcity, consumers will buy anything and everything even if they don't need it. For example, you see patrons buying three DVD players. You ask them why "three," and they don't know. All they know is that the store said supplies were limited, the sale was only for today, and each shopper was limited to three. So they bought three DVD players.

Some stores have this "limited number" thing down to perfection. Often when we go shopping, we are only casually interested, telling the salesperson, "Just looking, thanks." We glance over the packaging, examine the sale sign, etc. Then the salesperson plays the number's game. Approaching us, she says, "It's a great model, isn't it? Especially at this price! Unfortunately, I just sold our last model." We suddenly feel disappointed. Now that it's no longer available, we feel that we really want it, even though we were only mildly interested before. We ask whether there might be another one in the back or at another location. "Well, let me see what I can do. If I can get another one for you at this price, will you take it?" she baits. Trapped!

Funny thing is, we don't even realize the trap is being set, so the technique works like a charm. We are asked to commit to a product when it seems like it will soon be totally unavailable, and therefore seems incredibly desirable. Threatened with potentially losing a great deal, we agree. Then, of course, the salesperson comes back with the great news. The product will be shipped to the store in three days. In the meantime, all you have to do is sign the sales contract.

We also see the Law of Scarcity being frequently employed by home-shopping television networks. They know that rare things are highly valued in our society, so they always have a little clock running in the upper corner of the screen. You only have ten minutes to purchase this precious item, and the clock lets you know how little time you have left to make this buy of a lifetime. Home-shopping channels make time the scarce resource.

They often have a counter on the screen too. Sometimes the counter runs down with every sale. So the host says, "We only have a limited number of these imported widgets, and when they're all gone, we will never sell them again." And the counter showing the number of items remaining continues to tick down. The counter creates the impression of scarcity.

Creating a Demand: Can You Say "Limited Supply"?

Have you ever wondered why some "in" restaurants continue to have waiting lines outside? Long lines seem to make the restaurants even more fashionable, increasing the length of the line by an even greater degree. Why don't restaurants eliminate the waiting line by increasing their prices? They don't because removing the lines would eliminate the scarcity factor, and demand would collapse.

Consider how the Law of Scarcity created the Beanie Baby phenomenon. When Ty Warner, the creator/mastermind behind Beanie Babies, took certain Beanie Babies off the shelf and limited their availability, prices skyrocketed for the discontinued and suddenly rare and valuable Beanies. Spurred on by the threat of losing out, collectors began hoarding the stuffed animals and speculating as to which ones would be retired next.[11]

The Law of Scarcity was also used to create demand for diamonds. In spite of a dramatic leap in production from 15 million carats to a whopping 100 million carats, DeBeers, the company maintaining a monopoly over diamond supply, still managed to render the diamonds scarce. Running only ten diamond sales per year and inviting only a select number of dealers, DeBeers easily controlled the supply and pricing. Not only this, but each invited dealer got only a limited amount of diamonds. DeBeers selected for them, and if they complained, they were not invited back![12]

An owner of a successful beef-importing company decided to conduct a study among his staff. The staff members were assigned to call the company's customers and ask them to purchase beef in one of three ways. One group of customers just heard the usual presentation before giving their orders. Another group was given the usual presentation, but they were also presented with evidence that imported beef was expected to be in short supply in the coming months. A third group was given the usual presentation as well as the information about the beef's upcoming scarcity, but they were *also* told that this news was not available to the general public, and that the information provided was exclusive to the company. Not surprisingly, the sudden demand for beef created by these phone calls exceeded the supply on hand, and the company had to scramble to fill the orders. Customers alerted to the coming scarcity of the beef bought double the amount of those receiving only the standard sales pitch, and those learning both of the coming scarcity and that this was "secret information" bought *six times* the amount as those hearing only the standard sales pitch![13]

How about when you take your child to be photographed? They take ten different shots and then send you a proof for each. You're told to select the shots you like best and how many copies of each you'd like. *Then,* you're told the negatives will be destroyed within a certain number of months. Of course, you feel like you'd better get all the copies of all the shots you want *now,* or you won't be able to later!

Creating Allure

Think about when a woman wants to come across as more attractive to a certain man. If she can set things up so she will just happen to meet him while on a date with some other successful, attractive man, then she will appear to be more desirable than if she were merely to meet him alone at some club or bar. Or what if you were selling real estate? You'd be smart to have several interested people along for the tour of the property, since the interest of one client will heighten the interest of another. Instead of your potential buyer thinking, "Okay, I'm going to try to wheel-and-deal here," he will think, "I'd better jump or this other guy's going to get it before I do!"

In one experiment, students were given a written description of a particular novel. Half of the students' copies included the description, "a book for adults only, restricted to those twenty-one years and over," while the other half contained no such restriction. When polled about their feelings about the novel, students reading about the restriction indicated that they thought they would like to read the book, while students who had not read the restriction expressed significantly less interest.[14]

Restricting access to information or material often makes it that much more appealing. Although this topic typically brings to mind material of a sexually explicit nature, scarcity can apply to anything. Consider a form of censorship at the University of North Carolina. When students learned that a speech in favor of coed dorms was banned, they became more smitten with the idea of coed dorms. It is of great significance to realize that, without ever having heard the actual speech, the *censorship* alone heightened the students' interest. The students didn't even need to hear the speech to be persuaded to support or become more committed to the notion of coed dorms.[15]

Think again about the study conducted by the University of Chicago Law School that was discussed in Chapter 4, The Law of Obligation. The Law of Scarcity was also at work in this scenario. When the judge ruled that evidence on the defendant's insurance was inadmissible, and therefore had to be disregarded, the jurors actually increased the award amount. The censored information was actually embraced even more, jumping the damage payment by $13,000![16]

Additional Forms of Scarcity in Marketing

Consider the following "scarcity" tactics we see day-to-day:

- Clubs and restaurants that create exclusive membership requirements

- Disney videos and DVDs that are offered for sale once every five years

- Airlines that only hold your seat for twenty-four hours, informing you that "These seats might sell out"

- Collectors who specialize in hard to find antiques and rare baseball cards

- Special "by invitation only" sales

- Going-out-of-business sales

- Offers "not available" in stores

- Exclusive, one-time offers

- Memberships in an exclusive club

How to Use the Law of Scarcity

Sometimes scarcity is necessary to help us make a decision. Most of us fear the point of making a decision, so we naturally want to put it off and allow ourselves time to think about it. As a persuader, however, be aware that when your prospects put off the decision, chances are they won't make one.

You could have the perfect product for them—something they really need right now—but if you let them go, they will probably not come back later and tell you, "Okay, I finally decided. Let's do it." Creating scarcity helps your prospects make their decision. It also eliminates the amount of time you waste tracking down prospects who are still undecided about your product or service. You can create legitimate scarcity with your product or service without violating your morals.

To create scarcity, be sure you have the following elements firmly in place:

1. *Deadlines.* Give your prospects a deadline or a point of no return. We all operate on deadlines at home and in our businesses. They are what cause us to take action. If there is no immediate reason to take action now, we won't. Many people don't pay their bills until they have to. Judging by the lines outside the post office at midnight on April 15th, most of us don't pay our taxes until the last possible second. No deadline means no action.

2. *Limited Space, Numbers, or Access.* If your prospect feels like they are competing for a limited resource, they will be much more motivated to take action. When people fear they're going to miss out on a great deal, they feel an urgency to act. Think of shoppers at closeout sales. They've got to speed over there and check things out before all the stuff is "picked over." Otherwise, with the store's limited supplies, they'll miss the deal forever! This limit can also include access to information. Our response to banned information is a greater desire to receive that information and a more favorable outlook toward it than we had before the ban was set in place.[17]

3. *Potential Loss.* Prospects must recognize that they might be limited in their actions if they don't take advantage of your offer. People will always overvalue the thing you are restricting. Create a state of emotion in which your prospect fears the loss. This is an overwhelming feeling they won't be able to ignore. Motivated by restriction, this prospect becomes an emotionally motivated buyer. They will not be denied. The more you deny them, the more energy you give to your cause. You have denied their right to something, so they'll do anything to have it. I can recall occasions when I tried to talk people out of purchasing a certain product because I honestly felt it was not appropriate. The more I took the product away, the more they wanted it.

Think about all those sweepstakes messages that say, "You may already be a winner!" They used to say, "You can be a winner!" but the notion that you may *already* be a winner spoke even more loudly! Do you think people can throw away such an envelope without even opening it just to check and make sure? With the change in slogan, the sweepstakes company experienced a marked increase in their response rates. Suddenly, people were afraid they might lose something they potentially already had!

4. *Restrict Freedom.* We want what we can't have. If we are told a product is or will soon be unavailable, we want it even more. Our desire goes up and so does the urgency to act. Create a scenario where you tell your prospect that the offer is only good for so long. Tell them they have to act now to take advantage of the opportunity or they will lose out. This technique works so well because we have all walked away from offers like this before, and they really haven't been there when we returned. Walk through clearance stores and you will see "Sold" signs on the furniture. These signs create urgency because somebody else has found a deal, and so should we.

In sales, this urgency is called the "take away" close. If you take away your prospects' opportunity to get involved with your product or service, they naturally want it more. This strategy also works well when you want to see if your prospect really is interested in what you are providing. If you are stuck and not sure how much time you want to spend with a prospect, or if they are just looking and not willing to make a decision, do a take away. If they are truly interested in your product, they will perk up and become more interested. If not, they will walk away. Either way, you have saved yourself time and energy.

8

The Law of Verbal Packaging
The Leverage of Language

Real persuasion comes from putting more of you into everything you say.
Words have an effect. Words loaded with emotion have a powerful effect.
—JIM ROHN

OVER 60 PERCENT OF YOUR DAY is spent in oral communication, in which you could be persuading, explaining, influencing, motivating, counseling, or instructing. You can create movement, excitement, and vision with the words you use. The right words are captivating; the wrong words are devastating. The right words make things come to life, create energy, and are more persuasive than the wrong words. As Mark Twain said, "The difference between the right word and the wrong word is the difference between lightning and a lightning bug." The bottom line is that the words you use attract or repel your prospects.

The Law of Verbal Packaging states that the more skillful a person is in the use of language, the more persuasive they will be. People are persuaded by us based on the words we use. Words affect our perceptions, our attitudes, our beliefs, and our emotions. The words we use in the persuasion process make all the difference in the world. Language used incorrectly will lose the deal you might otherwise have closed. Word skills are also directly related to earning power. Successful people all share a common ability to use language in ways that evoke vivid thoughts, feelings, and actions in their audiences.

Typically, news broadcasters are trained to inflect their voices downward at the ends of sentences because doing so suggests confidence and authority. Upward inflections tend to suggest lack of confidence and doubt. Numerous studies have shown that a common trait of successful men and women is their skillful use of language. This correlation has also been manifested in their incredible ability to persuade.

The Inherent Power of Words

Words communicate abstract or vague things. We can use them to explain events, to share feelings, and to help visualize the future. Words shape our thoughts, feelings, and attitudes towards a subject. They help decide if we stay neutral or take action. Just reading words can affect your thoughts, attitudes, and feelings. For example, read these six words slowly and vocally, taking notice of how they make you feel.

> Murder   Hate   Depressed   Cancer   Sad   Despair

Now read the following six words slowly and vocally, noticing how the words affect you as you do so.

> Wealth   Success   Happiness   Health   Inspiration   Joy

How did these words make you feel? Successful persuaders know how to use the right words to create the desired response in their audiences. Speakers with greater verbal skills come across as more credible, more competent, and more convincing. Speakers who hesitate, use the wrong words, or lack fluency have less credibility and come across as weak and ineffective.

The Fundamentals of Language Usage

The use and packaging of language is a powerful instrument that can be fine-tuned to your advantage. We all know the basics of language, but mastery of both the aspects of language usage and the verbal situation can control human behavior. The proper use of verbal packaging causes you to be adaptable and easy to understand. This type of language is never offensive, and is always concise.

To create an effective verbal package, you need to understand the following critical aspects of language:

Word Choice	Vocal Techniques
Double-speak	Emphasis
Packaging Your Numbers	Pace

Positive Word Choice	Vocal Fillers
Emotion-packed Words	Pitch
Word Choice in Marketing	Volume
Use of Silence	Articulation
Vivid Language	Pauses
Simple but Powerful Words	
Simple Statements	
Attention-grabbing Words	

Word Choice

Understand that proper language varies from setting to setting, and from event to event. One word choice does not work in every circumstance. Word choice can also be critical to defusing situations and in getting people to accept your point of view. Even one word can make the difference in perception and acceptance. In a study by social psychologist Harold Kelley,[1] students were given a list of qualities describing a guest speaker they were about to hear. Each student read from either one of the following two lists:

1. Cold, industrious, critical, practical, and determined

2. Warm, industrious, critical, practical, and determined

Of course, the students who read #1 had less than positive feelings about the speaker. The interesting thing, though, is that the lists are exactly the same except for one word! It seemed that the differing word's placement at the head of the list conditioned how the reader felt in reading through the rest of the list. It didn't matter that none of the following words were negative. Just reading the word "cold" tainted how the students read the rest of the list.

The airline industry has mastered the power of words. They know word choice is critical to getting their point across and to reducing panic. In one situation, a flight attendant had run out of steak as an option for dinner entrée. Instead of telling the customers their only option was chicken, the flight attendant said, "You can have a piece of marinated chicken breast, sautéed in mushrooms in a light cream sauce, or a piece of beef." Consequently, people chose the chicken because it sounded better. Once, as a plane I was on was about to take off, one of the engines caught on fire. Smoke billowed and the runway was suddenly filled with fire trucks. The pilot came on and called it "slight engine difficulties." I don't know about you, but the situation seemed like a little more than "slight" to me.

When you listen to the flight attendants' instructions before take-off, you also hear careful word choice. They tell you that in the event of a water landing, your seat cushion can be used as a "flotation device." Hello! What they're really saying is, "If we crash into water, grab your seat cushion so you don't drown." Notice they don't say "life preserver," but rather they call it a "flotation device." Also note that there is no "barf bag" on board—it's a motion discomfort bag. Or "we are experiencing a mechanical difficulty" instead of "the plane is broken." They don't clean the plane; they refresh it. Planes aren't late; they're merely delayed. And, my personal favorite, they never lose my luggage; they misplace it. Yes, airlines know the power of word choice in affecting their customers' point of view.

Sales professionals also use words carefully. They know that one wrong word can send their prospect's mind somewhere else and lose them the sale. Some examples of language that salespeople use to help diffuse a potentially tense situation include the following:

Words That Repel	Superior Words
Contract	Agreement/paperwork
Sign here	OK the paperwork /autograph
Sell	Get involved
Cancellation	Right of rescission
Salesperson	Business consultant
Commission	Fee for my services
Cost	Investment
Credit card	Form of payment
Problem	Challenge
Objections	Areas of concern

Expensive	Top of the line
Cheaper	More economical
Service charge	Processing fee

Words also have a strong bearing on how we remember certain details. For example, in a 1979 study conducted by Elizabeth Loftus and colleagues, when defendants were asked how fast they were driving when they "smashed" into the other car—as opposed to "hit" the other car—much higher speeds were reported. In another study, subjects were asked if they had headaches "frequently" or "occasionally" and how many per week. Those who were interviewed with the word "frequently" reported 2.2 headaches per week, while those interviewed with the word "occasionally" reported only 0.7 per week.[2]

In another study, one group of individuals was asked if they thought the United States should *allow* public speeches against democracy, while another group was asked if they thought the United States should *forbid* public speeches against democracy. Although they bear similar implications, notice the word choice makes them contrary to each other. Still, one might think the answers would be similar, since they drive at the same point. Because of the word *forbid*, which caused them to want to hear the speeches, there was a much higher response to the second question.

Have you ever noticed those pharmaceutical commercials currently on the air? They portray all these wonderful benefits and use a soothing, sophisticated voice to highlight these benefits. Then, at the end of the commercial, when they have to run through all the negative side effects: vomiting, headache, diarrhea, etc., they read through these negatives quickly using the same pleasant voice! The effect is that negatives are de-emphasized, and we, as viewers, are still left with an overall positive impression.

Double-Speak: Tame the Sting

The term double-speak means replacing an offensive word with a less offensive word to create less sting. Here are some examples of how double-speak has made its way into our society.

Offensive	**Repackaged**
Fired	Let go
Downsizing	Right-sizing

Used car	Pre-owned vehicle
Sex change surgery	Gender reassignment
Kentucky Fried Chicken	KFC (the word "fried" is taken out)
Garbage man	Sanitation engineer
Housewife	Domestic engineer
Interrogate	Interview
Cancer	Growth
Fail	Not passing
Buried	Interred
Fatty (beef)	Marbled (beef)
Final exam	Celebration of knowledge

Package Your Numbers

Often salespeople, or people in any sort of persuasive situation for that matter, need to either play up or play down the greatness or smallness of certain numbers. When playing up a number, persuaders use this type of language:

- More than three quarters . . .
- Almost eight out of every ten . . .
- Better than two out of three . . .

When playing down a number, they use this type of language:

- Less than half . . .
- Fewer than two out of three . . .
- Under three quarters . . .

Positive Word Choice

You can use positive words to help prospects feel more confident, safe, or happy. You can also use negative words to trigger depression, anxiety, or sadness. When you use positive words, you capture and keep the attention of your listeners on the points you want them to concentrate on. The words you choose to use can mentally keep them on track. For instance, if you want to plant seeds of doubt, you would use negative forms of speech. When we are in a positive mindset, we don't ask as many questions. Positivity puts our mind in a comfortable, more persuadable area. When the negative is triggered, it requires more mental effort and our mind begins to search for incongruities or weaknesses in the argument.

Former Speaker of the House Newt Gingrich published a guidebook called *Language: A Key Mechanism of Control*.[3] In it, he advised Republicans to use positive governing words for themselves and negative words for their opponents. This pamphlet encouraged them to use the words "common sense, courage, dream, duty, empowerment, fair, family, and freedom" when talking about Republican ideals. He then advised them to use the following words to talk about their Democratic opponents and their position: "betray, bizarre, cheat, collapse, corruption, crisis, destroy, devour, and disgrace."

Remember how in 1980 Chrysler almost closed its doors and declared bankruptcy? Their only hope was $2.7 billion in loan guarantees from the federal government. This seemed hardly possible. Why would Congress approve such a sum for a private corporation? Chrysler and its lobbyists knew the right language would tip the balance. They positioned their argument so it was about the government providing a "safety net" for its companies, the same way it does for individuals. They further argued that this was an "American problem" belonging to everybody and not a unique situation only to themselves. Their strategy worked! The argument won Congress over, and Chrysler got the financial guarantees it needed.

Master persuaders use very assumptive and assertive language. For example, instead of saying, "If you get the report done by Friday, we'll leave early and go out to dinner," they would say, "When you get the report done by Friday, we'll leave early and go out to dinner." Effective persuaders also speak positively when accepting responsibility. Instead of saying, "That's not my problem. You'll have to talk to someone else," they would say, "I'll have the person responsible give you a call."

Emotion-Packed Words

The words we use can hurt others and cause tension and resentment. Words can even cause wars. Humans tend to create and use words that hurt or label. Hitler used labeling and name-calling during his rule in Germany. He called the Jews many negative things, including "vermin", "sludge", "garbage", "lice", "sewage", and "insects." Labels also extend far beyond the names people are given, into the way we describe things in a negative light, such as "broken home," "single-parent family," or "blended family." Whereas we think of theses terms as essentially neutral, the words can carry significant negative weight to those people to whom the terms apply.

As you design your persuasive message, you must consider the emotional impact of each word and phrase. When you want to create emotion, choose words that will trigger feelings. If you want to downplay the event or situation, use an unemotional word. Notice the following words generally have the same definition but carry different emotional weight, for example, calling someone "thrifty" versus "cheap," "traditional" versus "old-fashioned," "extroverted" versus "loud," "careful" versus "cowardly," and "eccentric" versus "strange."

There are many words that are emotionally loaded and represent different values to different people. These words can get people to pay attention and alert them to know what significance the message has for them. It is hard to find a neutral word. Your word choice will paint different pictures for different people because the way we define words is based on our belief systems, our past experiences, and our social roles. The beliefs we hold about a word will dictate our actions and how we respond. For example, some cultures view death as a celebration of life; others view death as a tragedy.

Sometimes, if used improperly, positive words can still lead to a negative response. For this reason, persuaders will often avoid certain words, although generally positive, and instead use words that may still bear positive associations, but are more ambiguous. For example, in the world of politics we hear phrases like "freedom of choice," "fiscal responsibility," or "responsible taxation." When politicians use such generalities, people of differing viewpoints can actually both be appeased. They will fill in the blanks and provide their own definitions.

Words can convey emotional color by how long or short they are. Generally, shorter words are more blunt, direct, harsh, or sharp. Consider words like "kick," "hit," "force," "stop," or "no." Longer words, like "lonely," "depressed," or "painful" are drawn out to evoke colors of melancholy or suffering.

Word Choice in Marketing
Word choice in marketing and advertising is absolutely critical. When advertisers spend millions of dollars each year, you can bet they have tested every

word they are going to use. They want their word choices to psychologically lead you to believe their product is the best, that it will change your life. Skilled advertisers can get us to absorb their message unconsciously. They might even package an identical product with different words and phrases to reach a wider segment of the public.

Psychologist Daryl Benn conducted a study on how advertisers use word choice and catch phrases to sell different, but identical in effectiveness, brands of aspirin. Consider the following:

Brand A: proclaims 100 percent pure, claims nothing is stronger. Benn notes that governmental tests also showed no brand was weaker or less effective than any of the others.

Brand B: advertises "unsurpassed in speed—no other brand works faster." The same governmental tests showed "B" works no faster than any of the others.

Brand C: declares it used an ingredient "that doctors recommend." Governmental tests revealed that "special ingredient" is nothing more than regular aspirin.[4]

The word choices in these advertisements work because the positive connotations make us assume that each advertised brand is the best. Advertisers know that changing just one word in their ad can dramatically increase the response rate. One advertiser changed the word "repair" to "fix" and saw a 20 percent increase in response.

There are other words advertisers employ, which are known as "weasel words." These words confuse their audience and don't allow you to put an exact number on the advertiser's claim. They let you justify and believe what you want. They are called "weasel words" because weasels are notorious for breaking into the chicken coop and sucking out the inside of the eggs without breaking the shell. The eggs look fine but in reality are hollow and empty, just like these words. Watch out for these words:

- Helps
- May
- Possibly
- Improved

- Up to
- Almost
- About
- Approximately

Probably the biggest challenge with word choice in marketing comes when billion-dollar corporations want to translate just the right English word into the perfect equivalent in another language. The most famous marketing fiasco based on translation was the Chevy Nova. Translated into Spanish, Nova meant "Doesn't Go."

"Come Alive, You're the Pepsi Generation" translated into Chinese means, "Pepsi, Bring Your Ancestors Back from the Grave." When American Airlines wanted to advertise its new, leather, first-class seats in the Mexican market, it translated its "Fly In Leather" campaign literally, which meant "Fly Naked" (*vuela en cuero*) in Spanish! Coors put its slogan, "Turn It Loose," into Spanish, where it was read as "Suffer from Diarrhea." The Dairy Association's huge success with the "Got Milk?" campaign prompted them to expand advertising into Mexico. It was soon brought to their attention that the Spanish translation read, "Are you lactating?"

Frank Perdue's chicken slogan, "It takes a strong man to make a tender chicken" was translated into Spanish as "It takes an aroused man to make a chicken affectionate." The Coca-Cola name in China was first read as "Kekoukela," meaning "bite the wax tadpole" or "female horse stuffed with wax," depending on the dialect. Scandinavian vacuum manufacturer, Electrolux, used the following in an American campaign: "Nothing sucks like an Electrolux."

The Use of Silence

Sometimes the right word is no word. On occasion we need to remain silent and let the other person talk. We have heard in sales that the first one to talk after the close loses. After the persuasion process and the final decision is ready to be made, make your proposal and shut up. The silence is nerve-wracking, but it's a critical time to let the prospect make the decision without you rambling on and on about the product or service.

How often have you noticed a sales rep overselling a product? You were ready to make the purchase by handing over your credit card. The sales rep felt you needed to know everything about the product and he started to fill you in. This caused doubt to creep into your mind and you ended up leaving, telling the salesman you would think about it. When someone has been persuaded and convinced, there is no reason to say any more. Strike when the iron is hot!

More communication is not necessarily better persuasion. In fact, the less you talk, the smarter people think you are. The more you say, the more common and less in control you appear. Many individuals try to impress people with what they know by flaunting all their wisdom, but usually this strategy is just a turn-off.

Using Vivid Language to Paint Pictures

Complete this imagination exercise with me: Pretend you are standing in a beautiful, sunny kitchen. You reach across the counter and grab a bright, juicy orange. You can feel it is heavy with sweet, ripe juice. You can smell the delicious orange scent as you rub the oil of the skin on your hand. Reaching for a knife, you slice the orange and begin to peel back the skin. The aroma only becomes stronger as you tear the sections apart. One of the sections drips bright, sticky orange juice over your finger. You raise this juicy section to your lips and take a bite. As your teeth sink into the orange, you feel the juice burst out and swish around your teeth and tongue. The juice is incredibly sweet! You savor it a moment, cradling a puddle on your tongue before swallowing.

Did your mouth water? Almost everyone's does. The extraordinary thing is that if I had simply instructed you to produce saliva, you couldn't have done it. The vivid picturing technique works far better than the command because your mind cannot distinguish between what is imagined and what is real.

A Master Persuader has the ability to paint a picture with his words. The prospects will be able to see, hear, feel, and experience exactly what he is talking about. The prospects become part of the message and can more fully understand how the product or service will change their life. As a Master Persuader you stimulate your prospects' senses by using words that activate their mind. You present your message through positive emotions because the positive thoughts of the audience will color their perception of what you want them to do.

We can all say, "I walked on the beach," but that's not half as effective as saying, "The sun was up and shining brightly on the warm sand. I took off my shoes and felt the soft sand between my toes. The seagulls floated lazily across the ocean sky. The waves soothed my soul as they rhythmically crashed against the shore. I could taste the salt of the breeze on my tongue." I think you can feel the difference between the two. Words activate all that we do. The words we use can make you physically ill, emotionally drained, hungry, and even salivate. They can especially make you buy!

A utilities company, trying to sell customers on the advantages of home insulation, sent auditors to visit homeowners and point out the ways they were wasting energy. The auditors provided the homeowners with suggestions on how they could save money if they were willing to improve the energy inefficiencies. In spite of the clear financial benefits over the long term, only 15 percent of the audited homeowners actually went ahead and paid for the corrections. After seeking advice from two psychologists on how they could better sell the advantages of home insulation, the utilities company decided to change its technique by describing the inefficiencies more vividly. With the next audits, homeowners were told that the seemingly minute cracks here and there were collectively equivalent to a gaping hole the size of a basketball. This time, 61 percent of the homeowners agreed to the improvements![5]

When you find yourself in a situation where you really need people on your side, use words that are going to create strong mental images. Attorney Gerry Spence once said, "Don't say he suffered pain. Tell me what it felt like to have a broken leg with the bone sticking out through the flesh. Tell me how it was! Make me see it! Make me feel it!"[6] Words are more powerful when they have strong emotional connotations. You want your words to be clear and credible, but they will have greater impact if they also strike an emotional chord within your audience. You can avoid being melodramatic or sensational by being sure that your words truly reflect the circumstances and that they can always be backed up.

You can even package simple derogatory comments. Sure, you can call someone dumb or stupid, but when you can verbally package something, this is what you get:

- Dumber than a box of hair

- Got into the gene pool while the lifeguard wasn't watching

- If brains were taxed, he'd get a rebate

- All foam, no beer

- Sharp as a marble

- Too much yardage between the goal posts

- Her antenna doesn't pick up all the channels

- No grain in the silo

- Forgot to pay his brain bill

- Studied for a blood test and failed

- Gates are down, the lights are flashing, but the train isn't coming

- The wheel is spinning, but the hamster's dead

Simple but Powerful Words

We know certain words have more pull than others, but who would have thought that simple words like "because" and "you" would have the power to move mountains? In a study by Langer, Blank, and Chanowitz, researchers found certain word choices could influence people to act against their own self-interests. The researcher would approach a copier where a long line of students stood. She would try three different word choices at different times to see how the other students would respond to each request. She didn't change what she was asking, only the word choice. When she said, "Excuse me, I only have five pages. May I use the copy machine *because* I am in a rush?" 94 percent complied. When she said, "Excuse me, I have five pages. May I use the copy machine?" 60 percent complied. But when she said, "Excuse me, I have five pages. May I use the copy machine *because* I have to make some copies?" 93 percent complied.[7]

The magic was in the word "because." Even when she used an obvious reason, for example, just to make copies, she had a higher compliance. The word "because" is very powerful. "Because" prepares the mind for a reason. Even if the reason is not legitimate, it is still a reason.

Perhaps one of the most valuable words to learn how to use is "you." When you use the word "you" instead of a more general word like, for example, "people," there is a stronger sense of identity. Your listener will be more tuned in to what you are saying.

On the other hand, the one word that will impede your ability to persuade is "but." "But" negates everything you said before it. We all know the drill, "I love you, but . . ." or "I want to help, but. . . ." The word "but" puts the brake on persuasion. Practice your vocabulary and use the word "and" in your persuasive communication instead of "but." Another simple change is to use the word "can" instead of "could." For example, say "Can you carry this for me?" instead of "Could you carry this for me?" Similarly, it is better to use "will" than "would" and better to use "try" than "do."

The "Let's" Technique

Often in day-to-day living we find ourselves in circumstances where we need to direct, delegate, or even order. Usually our assignments are just short sentences, such as "Can you please do this or that?" You can create unity and alliance and lessen defensiveness when you use "let's" in place of "you," even when it's the other person, not you, who is carrying out the assignment. For example, "Let's be sure and get this out in the mail today, okay?" It's such a simple thing, yet you will find it works wonders. Make a habit of using the word "let's," and you will find more cooperation.

The Value of the Simple Statement

It is best to assume that with spoken language, simple is better than complex. Since we are unable to recapture or replay our spoken words, we hope that they will be correctly interpreted the first time they are heard. Unfortunately, spoken words can be the most misread and misinterpreted form of communication, and therefore, can be a great hindrance to effective persuasion. When you're in a persuasive situation, use simple, direct, and concise language, rather than fretting about how eloquent you're sounding. If you are preoccupied, you'll miss a lot of important cues. Moreover, complex language may not effectively deliver your point.

Persuaders normally try to speak to the lowest common denominator. The more advanced and complex your ideas and sentence structure are, the harder it is to follow your line of reasoning. You don't want your audience struggling to understand what you mean. Comprehension should be easy because then your audience is more open to persuasion. If your prospects are struggling to find your logical thread, their emotions will never get involved, except in a negative, accusatory way.

Clarity is of prime importance when persuading. Your persuasive attempts are useless if you are not clearly understood. Here follows a list of complex words we use when we are trying to sound educated but which actually only confuse and tire our audiences. Notice the much simpler choice on the right that would help your audience to both comprehend your message and be persuaded by your presentation.

Complex	Simple
Annually	Every year
Comprehend	Understand
Assistance	Help
Cultivate	Grow
Accomplished	Did
Essential	Necessary
Utilize	Use
Persists	Continues
Primary	First
Respond	Answer
Disseminate	Spread

Following are some simple guidelines to keep your speech and verbal packaging on the right track.

■ *Don't use jargon or technical language* unless you are sure every member of your audience understands the meaning.

■ *Don't use profanity or slang.* In general, using profanity damages your credibility.[8] Be sensitive to whatever language your audience might find offensive, profanity or politically incorrect. Avoid name-calling and other forms of abusive language.

■ *Speak in everyday language.* You want your audience to relate to you and to feel as comfortable with you as possible. Use language that will make you seem familiar and easy to follow.

■ *Keep your language simple and clear.*

■ *Keep your sentences short.* Use as few words as possible unless you are painting the picture—just one idea at a time.

■ *Use words that will engage the audience.* Use "you," "we," "us," and even "I" if you are relating a personal experience.

■ *Don't use vague and abstract words.* They muddle your meaning and confuse your listener.

■ *Don't talk down to your listener by using pompous and pretentious words.* Be direct; don't bluff or beat around the bush.

■ *Use verb-driven language.* By using verb-driven language, you will arouse a greater sense of action and motivation. Using action verbs will make your statement more convincing because your audience will engage their emotions, consciously and subconsciously. Verbs that are abstract or overused do not communicate excitement.

Sixteen Attention-Grabbing Words

With so many words in the English language to pick from, you must be very particular about which ones to use. Some will grab attention more than others. The following sixteen words are commonly used to effectively sell a product:[9]

Benefit	Money	Easy	New*
Free*	Now	Fun	Proven
Guarantee	Results	Health	Safe
How to	Save	Love	You/Your

*Always pulls best

Among all those on the list, the word "free" always gets attention anytime it is used. Suppose you were in charge of designing and wording the fliers your company is planning to send out in three weeks. Which phrase would you use?

1. Half price!

2. Buy one—Get one free!

3. 50 percent off!

Each of the three denotes the exact same offer, but the second phrase is the most effective. In fact, studies have shown that phrases using the word "free" outsell other phrases stating the exact same thing, only in different terms, by 40 percent![10]

"New" is another big word. Think about its use in politics. For Franklin Roosevelt, it was "The New Deal"; for John Kennedy, it was the "New Frontier." Then there were Ronald Reagan's "New Beginning" and Bill Clinton's "New Covenant." Politicians aren't the only ones selling with the word "new." Think of all the times you've seen advertisements proclaiming "introducing," "all new," or "first time ever."

Vocal Techniques: Keep People Attentive and Listening

How we say the words we choose is just about as important as the words themselves. Our voice is a powerful instrument that can motivate the troops or lull them to sleep. There is a huge difference between presenting and persuading. Your voice is a complete arsenal of persuasive techniques in and of itself. For example, you can say the same thing but mean five different things, depending on the tone of your voice. You can say "Thank you" laden with sarcasm, love, hate, anger, humor, or surprise—just by changing the tone and inflection of your voice.

Peter Blanck, in his research, found that judges communicated their bias and attitudes by the tone of their voice. The juries in California were twice as likely to convict trial defendants when the judges already knew the defendants had a record and prior convictions. The law simply states that a judge cannot share this private information with the jurors, but, as researchers found, judges can convey their attitude toward defendants when the words and tone of voice in their instructions to the jury lack warmth, patience, and tolerance.[11]

You can change your rate of speech, your vocal fillers (um, uh, ah), the volume, pitch, inflection, emphasis, and even the pauses that you use. You can keep an audience listening with both ears and with full energy, rendering them absolutely spellbound because of the power of your voice.

Your voice is who you are. It is your trademark and your calling card. Your voice must exude energy, confidence, and conviction. We tend to judge others by their voice: Is it confident, nervous, relaxed, energized, tired, weak, or strong? If you sound unsure and timid, your ability to persuade will falter. Persuasive voices have great volume, varied emphases, good articulation, and a pleasing pitch. Master Persuaders use vocal variety and frequently vary their pace.

The good news is you can change many characteristics of your voice. Tape your voice. What does it project? Your voice must be interesting and easy to listen to in order to help, rather than hinder, your ability to persuade. Does your voice work for you or against you?

Emphasis

Watch what happens when you place emphasis on different words in this sentence.

I didn't know he stole the car.

I **didn't** know he stole the car.

I didn't **know** he stole the car.

I didn't know **he** stole the car.

I didn't know he **stole** the car.

I didn't know he stole the **car.**

The exact same words form sentences of completely different meaning every time you change the emphasis to a different word. Emphasis brings your main point to the audience's attention. You are able to highlight and stress the more important issues throughout your presentation with proper use of emphasis.

Pace

Pace refers to how quickly you speak. Mehrabian and Williams found that people who spoke faster, louder, and more fluently as well as those who varied their vocal frequency and intensity were perceived as more persuasive than those who did not.[12]

Speeches delivered at fast speeds are more persuasive than those of slow or moderate speeds, because persuaders who speak faster appear more competent and knowledgeable. At these faster rates, receivers are not able to mentally engage in counter-arguing.

Pace and speed are also important to keep and capture attention. We can think three times faster than we can speak. We have all had conversations and were able to listen while thinking of other things. When we speak faster, we can keep attention longer. There is less time for our audience's mind to wander. Studies show that we generally like faster speakers and find them more interesting. Most speakers average 120 to 180 words per minute. But

102 | Maximum Influence

there is no ideal speed. Franklin Roosevelt spoke 110 words per minute while John Kennedy raced along at 180 words per minute. Persuasive speakers will speak fast enough to excite and energize the mood of the audience but will be able to slow their pace down to create a mood of anticipation.

To counteract boredom, use your basic pace most of the time, and vary it in one of two ways from time to time. *Slow your pace down* when you wish to appear thoughtful; when you want to give people the impression that you are working through a process of induction or deduction, even as you are speaking; when you have something particularly important or serious to say; or when you wish to show great respect. *Increase your pace* when you want to create excitement and energy.

Vocal Fillers

Fillers can destroy your presentation, hurt your credibility, and annoy your audience. Most people feel they don't have a problem with this, and most of them are wrong. You would be amazed when you tape yourself what words you use to fill in space during a speech. Fillers are not acceptable and need to be eliminated from all speech. Vocal fillers include the common "um," "er," and "uh." Some people have their own idiosyncratic way of filling in the silence between ideas that makes them uncomfortable. Some repeat the first two or three words of a sentence until their brain catches up and they decide what they're going to say. Others might say, "Okay" at the end of every sentence, as if they're checking audience comprehension.

Pitch

Pitch is the highness or lowness of the speaker's voice. Low is best. In our culture, deeper voices are generally interpreted as reflecting authority and strength, for both men and women. In addition, a deeper voice is stereotypically considered to be more believable, indicative of an individual's sincerity and trustworthiness. Many speakers practice lowering their voices because of the benefits of a lower pitch. Some speakers even drink hot tea before they speak, a technique that creates a lower sounding voice.

Remembering to employ variety in your speaking is a constant challenge, but it is of paramount importance. You can help people remain alert and pay attention while you speak if the pitch of your voice rises and falls. There are two main reasons why this strategy works. First, the varying pitches will prevent your voice from sounding monotonous. Second, the varying inflections can help emphasize a particular word.

Remember, if you are not an engaging speaker, you will not be persuasive.

Volume

Obviously you're not going to be very persuasive if no one can hear you. You've probably experienced the aggravation of straining and struggling to hear a speaker. Before your presentation, test the room to ensure you can be heard from all parts of the room. Also, test to see whether you're going to need amplification. If yes, be sure this equipment is available and properly set up prior to beginning.

Certainly, the converse is also true: Be sure you are not yelling or shouting at your audience. This understandably is just as aggravating for the audience, or even more so, as struggling to be able to hear.

Raising your voice for impact or dramatic effect is not as effective as *lowering* your voice. The technique can work, but you must be very careful about how you use it. Additionally, people who keep a calm and steady voice in emotional moments are often considered more credible and competent.

Articulation

Clearly articulate every sentence, phrase, and word. When your speech is clear and coherent, it conveys competence. When your articulation gets sloppy, it suggests lack of education and laziness. Consider how lawyers, doctors, supervisors, lobbyists, and the like *must* be articulate if they are to survive professionally. Good articulation conveys competence, experience, and credibility. Another practical reason to have good articulation is simply because it is so much easier to follow. As previously discussed, people will comply with you more if you are easy to understand.

Pauses

Treat your pauses like gold. Well-timed pauses attract attention to a particular part of your presentation, give others time to tune in and process your message, and help you gain poise and confidence if you're rattled. Use intentional pauses for the points you intend to drive home. Not only does a pause increase comprehension, but it also helps to highlight important points. Use pauses to create attention, emphasis, and mood.

A carefully planned pause usually comes *before* the point you want to highlight. It is a common mistake to not hold the pause long enough. Be sure you allow enough of a pause that the full effect will be felt. When you do this, the audience anticipates and listens closely to what you will say next. They can tell something important is about to happen. This strategy is made even more effective when you combine it with pitch strategies: Be sure that as you come to the pause, your pitch is high, thereby building suspense and giving momentum to what will follow. Inflecting your pitch downward will defeat the purpose, providing a feeling of resolution instead of suspension.

Dental Verbal Packaging

As a final example of the power of verbal packaging, think about what you hear during your appointments with your dentist—not a particularly pleasant situation in general and sometimes downright frightening. Dentists have mastered the art of verbal packaging to put patients more at ease.

What you won't hear	What you will hear
Painful	Uncomfortable
Does that hurt?	Does that bother you?
Blade	#12
Hatchet	Big H
Yank, Pull	Remove
Cut	Smooth
Drill	Prepare
Blood, Hemorrhage	Debris
Needle	Tip
Spit	Empty mouth
Grind	Prepare teeth
Shot	Injection
Pain	A little pressure

9

The Law of Contrast
How to Create Extra Value

In the long run, men hit only what they aim at. Therefore . . .
they had better aim at something high.
—HENRY DAVID THOREAU

HAVE YOU EVER TAKEN YOUR CAR to your mechanic and he tells you that you might need new brakes, a new transmission, a new fan belt, and that the timing sounds off? You go away thinking, "Oh man, I'm sunk. I might as well just buy a new car." Then when you come back, he tells you, "You just need new brakes." You feel as free as a lark, only having to pay $300 for what could have been a $3,000 repair job. Imagine if he had told you he thought he could fix it for $50 and the bill ended up being $500. That is the Law of Contrast in action.

The Law of Contrast explains how we are affected when we are introduced to two vastly different alternatives in succession. We know that contrasting two alternatives can distort or amplify our perceptions of things. Generally, if the second item is quite different from the first, we will tend to see them even more differently than they actually are. As a Master Persuader, you can use this contrast to steer your audience toward the object of your persuasion.

The use of contrast is based on our perception of items or events that happen one right after the other. If you've had a rotten day because you found out you're losing your job and you come home to a new scratch on your car, you will have a vastly different reaction than if you were having a great day because you're getting a promotion and then came home to the scratch on your car. It's the same scratch, but there are very different perceptions and reactions to it, depending on your personal circumstances.

Time can erode your ability to use the Law of Contrast. The key to this law is that the two contrasting items must be presented one right after the other. This has an effect on group meetings and decision making: If in a meeting you put forth your great idea right after another great idea, it won't have the impact it would have had if it had followed someone else's poor idea. Likewise, if we are talking to a beautiful woman or man at a party and we are then joined by an unattractive woman or man, the beautiful person will seem even more beautiful, and the less attractive person will seem even less attractive.

This is all about human perception. The human mind has to find a benchmark of comparison to make judgments, especially when we are talking about unfamiliar situations. People need to make comparisons with their past experience and knowledge. By presenting your prospects with contrast, you are creating those comparisons for them. The mind can't process everything at once and so it develops shortcuts to help make decisions. Instead of making a completely internal judgment, we look for boundaries, patterns, and polar opposites. We want to know the difference between our options, so we naturally contrast the two items. We mentally place things in our mind from best to worst, first to last, or highest to lowest. Do you want your prospects to compare your product or service to a second-hand used car or to a Rolls Royce? You get to decide where you want them to start their benchmark.

When using the Law of Contrast, keep in mind the powerful differences between positive and negative information. Psychologists have asserted for years that people automatically and subconsciously have extremely high expectations for the good over the bad. Because of this consistent tendency, negative information, when it comes, always seems to be given considerable weight because it is such a jarring contrast to what was expected.[1] For example, have you ever had a salesperson get you all excited about some incredible product you were about to purchase? You're totally *thrilled* with all the things this product is going to do for you, and then BAM! The salesperson hits you with the ghastly price. Suddenly the hefty price tag, just one negative detail, outweighs the product's twenty terrific features. Negative information has taken precedence over all the positive information. In fact, now it's consuming your thoughts. You drive home able only to think about how the precious item is going to cost you an arm and a leg.

Contrast works in many arenas. You can contrast just about anything and immediately see its effects. Try this experiment: Fill three buckets with water, one with hot water, another with cold water, and the third with tepid water. Simultaneously soak one foot in the hot bucket and the other one in the cold bucket for thirty seconds. Now place both feet in the tepid bucket and you will be shocked with the results. The water in the third bucket is considered warm, but to the hot foot it feels cold and to the cold foot it feels hot. It is the same water but two completely different reactions. This is the Law of Contrast. Any product or service can be contrasted to appear very different from what it actually is.

Types of Contrast

Some examples of the Law of Contrast fit into different categories. Let's examine the relationship among these categories and look at some examples of each.

Sweetening the Pot: Triple the Value

"Sweetening the Pot" is a technique often used by salespeople to make the deal seem "sweeter" than it really is, that is, making the prospect believe they are getting an exceptionally good deal. What can you add on as an incentive? What can you give as a bonus? What do you have that will add value to your product or service? It could be an added feature, a larger discount, free delivery, gift-wrapping, batteries, an extended warranty, or free consulting. Whatever it is, use it to create and contrast a higher value.

Think about the last infomercial you saw on late-night TV. You watch the salespeople display and demonstrate the product and you start to get interested. You begin to think about how this product will really make your life easier. They have not told you the price, but when they finally do, it is much higher than you thought. You were hoping to spend around $99, but the announcer said it was $499. Your heart drops but you keep watching because you are really getting into this product and how it will change your life forever.

Oh, now wait a minute—they are giving a special deal today. There is a temporary price reduction. This is your lucky day! Now they are offering it for $297! It's a good deal, but still a little expensive. Wait, they are adding three additional items to the package, an added value of $350. You can hardly believe it—you'll get over $800 worth of products for only $297. You are really interested now and you're just about ready to buy, when wait—it gets even better! If you order now, you can even make three easy payments of $99 for the next three months. You can't believe your luck so you order right away.

You were thinking of spending only about $99 and you ended up spending triple that amount—$297 to be exact. Why? Because of the Law of Contrast, you were going to get over $800 worth of product and the deal kept getting better. This law is critical for you to understand when showing others the value of your product. No one buys unless they feel like they are getting value for their money.

When you "sweeten the pot," you add bonus items to make the deal more and more valuable. We can all learn from the example of a high school bake sale: When the cashier told one group of customers they could purchase one cupcake and two cookies for a total cost of 75 cents, 40 percent of customers bought. The cashier then told another group of customers that they could purchase one cupcake for 75 cents. However, a few seconds later she added that because of a special they had going for that night, two more cookies would be thrown in as a bonus. By the end of the night, 70 percent of the customers purchased cupcakes and cookies when the "three for the price of one" technique was used, even though it was really the exact same deal.[2] It's all in the presentation—you have to "sweeten the pot"!

You see this technique used in supermarkets and in other advertisements when a company plans their packaging strategy to show the contrast between before and after prices. You may see diapers that have the "save 20 percent" slashed out and replaced with "save 30 percent." Or maybe their method is "buy five, and we'll give you another one free." It might also be that they have the 16 oz. slashed out and the new 20 oz. written in for the same price. Whatever the form it takes, this is an example of "sweetening the pot," the Law of Contrast in action. It isn't the actual price that is paid, but the add-ons that seem to make it such a better deal.

The same thing happens when an insurance sales rep presents you with the initial offer and *then* begins to give you special deductions based on your circumstances. Look, you are getting a better deal! If the opposite were to happen, you would feel cheated.

Put yourself in the mall candy store buying one pound of chocolate candy for your sweetheart. The young lady at the counter scoops up the chocolates and places it on the scale. She notices she does not have enough and starts to add more. The other alternative is that she dumps all the chocolates on the scale and begins to take them away. Which one will leave you the most satisfied? In the first scenario, you would feel as if you were getting more and that the deal was being sweetened, whereas under the second set of circumstances you would feel like you were being robbed.

Reducing It to the Ridiculous: Create Perspective

This technique involves paring down your request to something that seems manageable to your prospect. Let's say you are trying to convince someone to purchase a life insurance policy. The client wants a $250,000 policy and you feel that is not high enough for his needs. To adequately take care of his family, you suggest a $500,000 policy. He feels that the monthly payment for a $500,000 policy is too high. So you break it down for him, telling him that for an extra 50 cents a day, or the cost of a can of soda, he can insure himself and adequately take care of his family if something were to happen to him. With this contrast, your client can see that the extra 50 cents is worth it to have the extra $250,000 in coverage. You have reframed your request into simple terms to help your prospect see it fitting into his way of life.

Shifting Focus

Sometimes it is a good idea to simply give your prospects a different frame of reference, or to merely shift their focus slightly. This is kind of the "glass is half full" idea. University of Iowa researchers Levin and Gaeth conducted a study where they gave samples of ground-beef burgers to two groups of tasters. The burgers were exactly the same, but one slight difference in advertising strategy was employed: One group was told the burgers were 75 percent lean, and the other group was told the burgers were 25 percent fat. The group that was told the burgers were 75 percent lean rated them significantly leaner, of higher quality, and better tasting than the 25 percent fat group who rated the burgers as fatty, greasy, and of low quality.[3]

In the following example, notice the two different ways the doctors present the patient with the diagnosis:

Doctor One: I hate to tell you this, but the tests confirmed that you have extremely high blood pressure. You are most likely going to face some serious complications, and it could turn into a life-threatening situation. You've got to make some dramatic changes in your lifestyle immediately. You need to change your work situation, your sleep patterns, how you eat, and your exercise program.

Doctor Two: Well, overall, you're in pretty good shape except your blood pressure is a little higher than we want it. I'm really glad you came in so we can work together on some preventative measures. Actually, there are millions of Americans who have high blood pressure too, so we know of some steps you can take to bring it back under control. If you follow the steps I'll outline, you will quickly see and feel an improvement in your health overall.

Both doctors were talking about the same thing, but their presentations were very different. Doctor Two made sure her delivery was positive and did not overload the patient with all the negative details all at once. The patient will need to understand the reality of the situation and all its implications, but an initial positive and general discussion will better prepare the patient emotionally and psychologically to properly deal with the issue.

A university in Colorado was having trouble getting their grass to grow on campus because the students kept walking on it. They tried placing signs on it that read, "Don't walk on the grass," but the students ignored the requests and walked on the grass anyway. The university subsequently took a different approach. They put up another sign that said, "Give Earth a Chance." Like magic, the students stopped walking on the grass. The university simply changed the perspective of its students by making the issue an environmental one.

One last example of shifting the frame of reference comes from an experimental questionnaire administered to physicians:

A group of physicians were posed with the following scenario: "Imagine the United States is preparing for the outbreak of an unusual Asian disease, which is expected to kill 600 people. Two alternative programs to combat the disease have been proposed. Assume that the exact scientific estimates of the programs' consequences are as follows: If program A is adopted, 200 people will be saved. If program B is adopted, there is a one-third probability that 600 people will be saved and a two-thirds probability that no people will be saved. Which of the two programs would you favor?" Notice that in the wording, the focus was on the "lives saved." Seventy-two percent of the physicians chose program A over program B.

The same experiment was conducted again with a different group of physicians. This time, the focus was on how many people would die: "Imagine that the United States is preparing for the outbreak of an unusual Asian disease, which is expected to kill 600 people. Two alternative programs to combat the disease have been proposed. Assume that the exact scientific estimates of the programs' consequences are as follows: If program A is adopted, 400 people will die. If program B is adopted, there is a one-third probability that nobody will die and a two-thirds probability that 600 people will die. Which of the two programs would you favor?" You can see that this scenario is exactly the same as the first, but there was a dramatic difference in the results. This time, with the shift in focus, 22 percent of the physicians voted for the more conservative plan, plan A, while 72 percent voted for the risky plan, plan B![4]

Door-in-the-Face

"Door-in-the-face" is one of the most common techniques for implementing the Law of Contrast. Basically, an initially large and almost unreasonable request is made, likely to be declined—hence the "door-in-the-face" as the prospect rejects the proposal. Then a second smaller and more reasonable request is made. People accept the second request more readily than if they'd just been asked outright because the relativity between the two requests makes the second one seems so much better. The technique is effective because social standards state each concession must be exchanged with another concession. When you allow a rejection, it is considered a concession. The person you are persuading will then feel obligated to agree with your smaller request.

Demonstrating this point, researchers first asked college students to donate blood every two months for three consecutive years. Requiring a long-term commitment of not only time, but also of physical and emotional responsibility, the request was overwhelmingly turned down. When a day later the same students were asked to donate blood just one time—on the following day—49 percent agreed. The control group, wherein students were only approached with the second request, only demonstrated a 31 percent compliance rate.

The study continued the next day. As students showed up to donate blood, they were asked if they would provide their phone numbers so they could be called to see if they'd donate again later on. Of the first group (those who'd been given both requests), 84 percent consented to giving their phone numbers. Of the students in the control group, only 43 percent agreed to give their phone numbers.[5]

The main reason the door-in-the-face technique is so effective is because the contrast between the two requests makes your prospects feel like they are getting more/or less than they would have if they'd gone with the original offering. They feel like they've made a fair compromise, while you get exactly what you wanted in the first place. Alan Schoonmaker, author of *Negotiate to Win: Gaining the Psychological Edge,* makes an especially interesting point:

A conservative first offer also creates the bargaining room needed for the mutual concession ritual (you give a little; they give a little; you give a little; and so on). You may regard this ritual as silly, but many people insist on it. If you do not perform it, they may feel you are not negotiating in good faith. . . . It is far better for them to feel that they have defeated you, that they have driven you right to the wall. Lay the foundation for their victory with an initial offer that creates lots of bargaining room."[6]

By way of example, pretend your local scout troop is canvassing door to door to ask for donations to the scouting program. They ask you to donate $200, saying that all the other neighbors have donated this amount. After some discussion, the scouts ask for a $50 donation. You feel relief and give them $50—and you feel lucky that you got away with giving less than your neighbors.

In these examples, the second request seems much more logical and reasonable in comparison to the outrageous first request. We are creating a perceptual contrast whereby we are defining what we think the standard of comparison should be. When the second request comes along, it seems much smaller than the first request, and in our case, much smaller than the request would seem if presented alone.

In my university class, students learning about the Law of Contrast were asked to write letters to their parents requesting money. They were instructed to create a scenario so the request seemed inconsequential.

Dear Mom and Dad,

I hope this letter finds you both well and happy. I wish I could say that is how I feel. I know you love me, but it is hard to come to you in such an embarrassing situation. Now, I don't want you to worry too much. I can see Mom now, already skimming through this letter to find out exactly what is wrong, so I guess I'll cut right to the chase. I'm really worn out, but I'm getting better. At least I have a place to stay, especially during this cold winter weather.

The last couple of weeks I have been sleeping on the streets, looking for food and shelter. I finally met this nice man who is letting me stay in his room for free. It sure is nice to have a roof over my head. Sometimes I still get wet at night though, because there's a crack in the wall on my side of the bed. But with five of us sharing the room, we've got some body heat going and that helps out. We hope that between the five of us, we can make rent this month. They sure have been nice letting me stay here, and letting me keep out of sight. It seems there is some type of warrant out for me and I am unfortunately "on the run," as they say.

I'm afraid I can't tell you exactly where I am; I don't want to endanger you with too much information in case the authorities come to question you. As you may guess, I am in desperate need of a large sum of funding so that I can settle my accounts before another, more ruthless party begins to hunt me down. I was hoping for, but not counting on, your assistance. I know I have done wrong, but I plead for your forgiveness and prayers.

Just kidding! I wanted you to see my problems in the proper perspective. I crashed my car last weekend. No one was hurt. I did have $300 in damage to my car though. I was wondering if you could send me the money so I could get back on my feet.

I love you forever,

Jill

_____

In the negotiation process, the door-in-the-face technique can be a powerful tool. Watch a skilled property developer. He may look for quality properties that have been on the market for some months, often because of the seller's high asking price of $500,000. To drive down the seller's expectation, the property developer employs an agent who, acting anonymously, displays great enthusiasm for the property and then makes a very low aggressive offer—say $350,000—which the seller angrily rejects. The developer then moves in and offers a much more reasonable price—say $430,000—which, after some negotiating, is accepted. Labor negotiators frequently deploy this tool as well. They begin with extreme demands that they expect to be turned down. Abruptly, they repeat a series of smaller demands, or concessions, which will then be more easily accepted. These smaller demands are the real target of the labor group.

The door-in-the-face technique can also save you from lots of headache and hassle. You can get people to go from hating you to thanking you for the same exact thing. For example, when I assign my college students a ten-page final paper, it makes the students tense and vocal. They complain about time, length, font size, etc. You name it; they'll bring it up. I was getting tired of the complaining, so I changed the way I approach the subject of the paper. I use this principle: I bring up the paper and wait for the moans, but then I tell them this twenty-page paper will have to include the following. . . . The uproar starts: "Twenty pages! I won't have time for that!" I then graciously acquiesce and tell them if they promise to do a great, concise paper with the proper research, I will make it only ten pages. The cheers erupt and everyone is happy. The students see the ten-page paper as a great deal compared to the twenty-page paper. Now the students thank me rather than hate me.

Many times, we can fly under the radar with the contrast principle. There is a theory called the "Just Noticeable Difference" (JND),[7] which means the minimum amount of difference in the intensity of the stimulus that can be detected. What does this mean? How much can you raise the price of a product without anyone noticing? How many ounces can you take out of a can of soup before people start to catch on? Can we really tell the difference between 21 ounces and 20.25 ounces? Many marketers would rather change the packaging and offer less of their product than resort to charging more. When we don't notice the difference, we think we are getting the same deal.

Just the opposite is true if we want to promote a new, larger-size product or a significant price reduction. In this case, we want to pass that threshold and make the change extremely noticeable. This is also true for taste. Companies want the best taste for the lowest cost. The quality of the ingredients causes people to notice or not notice the quality of the product.

Comparison Effect: Taking Their Temperature

The last form of contrast is the more general Comparison Effect. This is closely related to the door-in-the-face technique except that instead of presenting an outrageous request upfront, the persuader presents his prospects with an undesirable form of what they are looking for. Then, when the good (or even mediocre) item is presented, the prospect grabs hold of the offer a lot faster. The Comparison Effect focuses on how the prospect is able to compare two options simultaneously and come to the conclusion that the second option really is desirable.

Some real estate companies maintain what they call "set-up" properties. These are run-down properties listed at inflated prices, which are used to benefit the genuine properties in the company's inventory by comparison. Agents show customers the set-up properties first, then they show them the homes they really want to sell, both of them listed at the same price. The latter home looks much better in comparison to the dump they first saw. This strategy works just as well when showing a $120,000 home after viewing a $90,000 home.

The comparison principle comes into play in our everyday lives. It can even influence how we perceive the physical attractiveness of our partner. A study at Arizona State and Montana State Universities tested to see whether we might think our own spouses or partners were less attractive because of the media bombardment with ads showing very attractive models. In the study, students were first shown pictures of models before rating the attractiveness of members of the opposite sex who were not models. These students rated the nonmodels as significantly less attractive than did students who had not first looked at pictures of models.[8]

In another study, sales for billiard tables were monitored to see whether "up-selling" or "down-selling" was more effective. For a number of weeks, customers were first shown the less expensive tables, and then shown the more expensive models. The average sale worked out to be approximately $550 per table. For the second half of the experiment, customers were first shown top of the line tables, priced as high as $3,000. After seeing the most expensive tables first, the customers were shown gradually less and less expensive tables. This time, the average sale turned out to be over $1,000 per table. After seeing the really nice, high-quality tables, the low-end tables were less appealing, so customers tended to buy higher priced items.[9]

A similar example uses the same concept with a different product: funeral caskets. Funeral directors exploit the contrast principle to get families of the deceased to spend more money. Directors show the deceased's family the expensive model first, and then they show them a very plain, cheap one. They know that the family members are grieving and will do anything for their loved one. The grieving loved ones are often shocked by the contrast in the two caskets and rebound back to the more expensive casket.

These principles also apply when you're in a position where you have to compare people. The Law of Contrast is constantly at work, even influencing judgments in job interviews. If you first interview an outstanding candidate, and then immediately following you interview someone who is less favorable, you will be inclined to underrate the second person even more than if you had not interviewed the outstanding candidate first. Certainly the reverse is also true: If an average candidate follows someone who has interviewed very poorly, you may view that individual as better than average.

We see diet ads that use contrast to convince us to use their products. The "Before" and "After" pictures are intentionally made to look like stark opposites. The "Before" picture is in black and white, with the person slouching, frowning, and pale. The "After" picture is of the same person in full color with a smile, erect posture, and tan skin. We look at the two pictures, see the comparison, and decide we want to be more like the "After" picture.

How to Use the Law of Contrast

By reviewing the examples that were just outlined, you can guess the steps you need to take when employing this law. But let's try to simplify the process a little bit by looking at a few different elements of the Law of Contrast.

Starting High

As the name "Starting High" suggests, make sure your initial request is really big—not so big that it is totally unrealistic, but big enough that you know you will get a "no." Then, follow this initial request with smaller offers that will bring about the result you really desired all along.

For example, fundraising organizations often send letters asking for donations in amounts that are usually pretty high for most people's pocket books. Soon after the letter is sent out, the organization places a follow-up telephone call. The person making the call asks whether the letter was received and then makes a request for a smaller donation.

Timing

For contrast to be effective, it is important that the two scenarios, options, or offers are presented one right after another. Researchers Dillard[10] and

Fern[11] argue that the timing between the initial and follow-up requests in-fluences the successfulness of using this technique. Specifically, in order to increase compliance, the delay between the two requests must be short. If there is too much of a delay between the first and the second request, your prospect may not remember that you are comparing the two items or re-quests, and your ability to persuade will falter.

The effects of timing play a key role in people's reactions and the actions they take. Let's say that you just found out your twelve-year-old son took the family car for a joyride and was brought back by the police. You might be understandably upset. However, what if you just found out instead that your nineteen-year-old son had taken your car out for a joyride seven years ago? In both scenarios you discovered the same news, but your reaction would be entirely different. You can see how the passage of time dulls the impact an event or situation can have. The same holds true with your re-quests—the passage of time will dull their impact.

Situation

"Situation" applies to most of the persuasion laws, and certainly to the Law of Contrast. You have to think about the situation that you are in before you can choose which method to use and to what degree to implement the law. It is easy to see that the feelings of a funeral attendee will be different from those of a wedding guest. Each event puts the attendee in a different frame of mind. So, if you approach the funeral attendee with a happy, fun presentation, obviously their sentiments will not compare to yours, making the approach totally inappropriate.

You can also determine the best time to bring up your topic by assessing each individual situation. Should you ask close to the time you want some-one to take action, or as far in advance as possible? The answer is, "the sooner the better." Make your request as far in advance of an event as possi-ble. As the event approaches, and as the "realness" of what the prospects have to do sets in, the greater will be their anxiety and the less likely it will be for you to gain cooperation. If you need help with something right away, studies suggest that you should find someone who is not rushed or preoccu-pied with something else. The ability to gain cooperation from someone who is not under a time constraint goes up dramatically when compared with someone who is preoccupied or rushed.

Automobile dealers use the contrast principle. They wait until the final price for a new car has been negotiated before suggesting one option after another that might be added on. After committing to $15,000, what is an extra $200 for undercoating, an extended warranty, or a CD player? The trick is to bring up the extras independently of one another. After you've already decided to buy a $1,000 couch, what is $70 for fabric protection? Your prospects will always pay more for accessories or add-ons they buy after the purchase has been made.

Airlines also contrast news to you one piece at a time. They will say there is a slight delay, but they add that they should be ready to go in a few minutes. Then a later announcement comes stating that while everything is fine, they don't want to take any chances, so they are going to replace the part. They come back on loudspeaker and say they are close to being finished and will announce when they are ready to go. The next announcement you hear is that they are waiting for final clearance and will be taking off shortly. These small announcements, in relation to each other, keep the passengers calmer and more peaceful than if the airline had just come right out and announced a two-hour delay.

We also see the contrast technique used at large amusement parks. If we hear ahead of time how long the lines are going to be, we won't stand in them. You look to see how long the lines are, then, finding them reasonable enough, you get in. After you think you are almost there, you see another section of ropes and people. This happens three more times until finally, two hours later, you are at the front of the line.

Here is another charity example: Often when solicitors call for a donation, they begin by asking you how you are. Usually you reply, "Fine," or "Doing well," or something like that. After you have announced that your circumstances are favorable, the solicitor then proceeds to say, "I'm glad you're doing so well. I'm calling to see if you would make a donation to help the unfortunate victims of . . ." Now what? You don't want to seem stingy or unfeeling, especially now that the solicitor has reminded you of your easy life compared to those that his company is soliciting for. In one study, 18 percent of the people donated when they were approached *without* the initial "How are you doing this evening?" while 32 percent donated when the initial greeting was employed.[12]

10

The Law of Expectations
The Impact of Suggestion

If I accept you as you are, I will make you worse; however if I treat you as though you are what you are capable of becoming, I help you become that.
—JOHANN WOLFGANG VON GOETHE

THE LAW OF EXPECTATIONS uses expectations to influence reality and create results. Individuals tend to make decisions based on how others expect them to perform. As a result, people fulfill those expectations whether positive or negative. Expectations have a powerful impact on those we trust and respect, but, interestingly, an even greater impact on perfect strangers. When we know someone expects something from us, we will try to satisfy him or her in order to gain respect and likability.

You have probably heard the saying, "What gets measured, gets done." The same is true for expectations. That which is expected is what actually happens. People rise to meet your expectations of them. This is a powerful force that can lead to the improvement or destruction of a person. You can express an expectation of doubt, lack of confidence, and skepticism, and you will see the results. If you believe in someone, show confidence in them, and expect them to succeed, you will see different results. Author John H. Spalding expressed the thought this way: "Those who believe in our ability do more than stimulate us. They create for us an atmosphere in which it becomes easier to succeed."[1] When you create expectations, you change people's behavior. Whenever you label specific behaviors or characteristics, the action is expected. When those expectations are not met, you can see anger, disgust, surprise, or dissatisfaction.

We communicate our expectations in a variety of ways. It may be through our language, our voice inflections, or our body language. Think of a time when you've been introduced to someone. Usually, if they introduce

119

themselves by their first name, then you do the same. If they give their first and last name, you do likewise. Whether you realize it or not, you accept cues from others regarding their expectations and you act accordingly. Similarly, we all unknowingly send out our own cues and expectations. The power is in using the Law of Expectations *consciously*!

Numerous studies have shown how the Law of Expectations dramatically influences people's performance. For example, in one study, girls who were told they would perform poorly on a math test did perform poorly. In another, assembly line workers who were told their job was complex performed less efficiently at the same task than those who were told it was simple. Another case study demonstrated that adults who were given complex mazes solved them faster when told they were based on a grade-school level of difficulty.

By adding the Law of Expectations to your persuasive repertoire, you can change your audience's expectations of you—and their expectation to buy your product, service or idea—and you will be infinitely more persuasive.

Most of us have heard about the famous Pavlov dog experiments. Ivan Pavlov, a physiologist who won a Nobel Prize, trained dogs to salivate at the sound of a buzzer. The training was effective because the dogs had learned to *expect* food when they heard the buzzer—the Law of Expectations. The dogs behaved in a certain way because the Law of Expectations was at work. Shockingly reminiscent of Pavlov's experiments, the Law of Expectations has been used ever since in advertising to make humans salivate when viewing a commercial or thinking of a certain brand of food.

Expectations as Assumptions: Expect with Confidence

Often our expectations are based on the assumptions we have about people or groups of people. The same is true of us. Have you ever noticed how your expectations become reality in your personal life? Expectation is literally a self-fulfilling prophecy. We do this consciously and subconsciously. Remember the kid in grade school who was always really rowdy and disruptive? Sometimes if people already assume they are perceived a certain way, then that is indeed exactly how they will act, even if they don't mean to. The rowdy kid in grade school knew everyone perceived him as disruptive, and so he was. The teacher expected bad behavior, and the expectations were fulfilled.

Consider the profound impact this can have in your own life. Are the assumptions and expectations you have about yourself liberating or victimizing? There are countless examples of "self-fulfilling prophecies," or the Law of Expectations at work in everyday life. Ever notice how people who think they're going to be fired suddenly experience a drop in the quality and enthusiasm for their work? Then what happens? They get fired! Their belief causes them to act a certain way, and those expectations then work to bring about the very thing that at first was only a figment of their imagination.

In another study, second graders listened to statements from their teachers before taking a math test. There were three types of statements: expectation, persuasion, or reinforcement. The *expectation statements* went something like, "You know your math really well!" or "You work really hard at your math." *Persuasion statements* involved sentences like, "You should be good at math." or "You should be getting better math grades." Finally, for the *reinforcement statements*, teachers said things like, "I'm really happy about your progress" or "This is excellent work!" Now, what do you think the results were? The scores were the highest in the "expectation" category! Why were the expectation statements the most effective? They created personal assumptions within each student. Those assumptions conditioned the actual external results.[2]

Expectations of Others Affect Behavior

The expectations we create for others often become reality. This can have interesting effects when applied out in the real world. This section contains multiple examples of how expectations have changed the lives and persuaded the behavior of other individuals.

School Teachers

Under the umbrella of expectations, teachers can be the greatest asset or the greatest negative influence in a child's life. We know what happens when a teacher labels a student a "troublemaker" because it creates certain expectations for the student's actions. We have seen the labels "slow learner," "stupid," and "ADD" become projections for a student's future academic success. There is the story of the substitute teacher who came to class and found a note from the regular teacher labeling one of her students as a troublemaker and another as helpful. The substitute teacher began the class looking for these two students. When she found them, she treated them accordingly. However, when the teacher returned, she was amazed when she discovered the substitute felt the troublemaker was helpful and the helper was trouble. She had gotten them mixed up! The children's behavior was based on the substitute's expectations. This is often called social labeling. People tend to live up to the positive or negative label bestowed on them.[3]

We have all had teachers who had high expectations of us and brought us to the next level. Can you imagine how powerful this becomes? Imagine the first day of class as the teacher looks around the room at her students. What if there is a student who is the son of a distinguished Asian professor, another one who it the brother of a former student who was a class clown, and one who is heavily pierced and wearing all black? What do you think her assumptions and expectations would be? Her expectations would probably be fulfilled without ever even speaking to the students.

One interesting experiment revealed how teachers' expectations influenced students. Two Head Start teachers were selected who were as equal as possible in potential and in practice. Then, two classes were formed from pupils who had been carefully tested to ensure that they were as similar as possible in background and learning potential. Next, the principal spoke with each teacher alone. He told the first teacher how fortunate she was. "You have a class of high potential pupils this year! Just don't stand in their way. They're racers and ready to run." The second teacher was told, "I'm sorry about your pupils this year. But you can't expect top students every year. Just do the best you can. We'll be understanding, regardless of the results." At the end of the year, the two classes were tested again. The first class scored significantly ahead of the second.[4] The major differentiating factor appeared to be each teacher's expectations.

Grubby Day

Many schools have "dress-up days," where, for example, students can dress up for Halloween, Spirit Day, Pajama Day, or Fifties Day. In one high school, they had a "Grubby Day." As you can imagine, on this particular day, the student behavior was less than outstanding. The administration received more complaints about student behavior on this day than on any other. The dress code set up certain assumptions, which further set up certain expectations. Then, of course, the expectations were fulfilled by the bad behavior.

Littering

We know that children tend to put their trash directly on the floor. In one elementary school, students were given individually wrapped pieces of candy. Of course, most of the wrappers ended up on the floor and not in the garbage can. Over the next two weeks, the teacher frequently commented on how neat and tidy the children were. On a visit to the classroom, the principal remarked to the children that their classroom was one of the neatest and cleanest in the school. Even the custodian wrote a note on the blackboard telling the children how clean and tidy their classroom was. At the end of the two weeks, the children were given individually wrapped pieces of candy again. This time, most of the wrappers ended up in the trash can.[5]

Parental Expectation

One thing you notice with toddlers and small children is that they behave according to the expectations of their parents. When I was single, I noticed that when children fell down or bumped their heads while running and playing, they would look at their parents so they would know how to react. If the parents showed great concern and pain in their eyes, the children would start to cry in an effort to get the attention they wanted. This would happen regardless of whether the child really felt pain or not.

One of the techniques my wife and I tried as new parents was the exact opposite of this approach. We changed the expectation, and it has worked great! When our children hit their heads or get a small scrape, they look up to us and we all laugh. The amazing thing that happens is that they begin to laugh too. They realize it's not a big deal and go off to resume their activities, often laughing with us. Children act based on the expectations of their parents. You create the expectations in your voice, in your actions, and with the words you use.

Studies show that children will live up to the expectations of their parents whether those expectations are positive or negative. According to Bill Glass, over 90 percent of prison inmates were told by parents while growing up, "They're going to put you in jail."[6]

Blood Drive

When blood drive organizers make reminder calls, they may end their conversations with something like, "We'll see you tomorrow at 10:00 A.M. then, okay?" and then wait for the person's commitment. Why do they do this? Studies have shown that when you create an expectation, attendance rates dramatically increase.

Sales Applications

The power of suggestion can also be extremely effective when you engage the emotions in your tactics. For example, when your car salesman says,

"You're really going to love how this car handles in the mountains," he is shifting the focus away from the sale and creating an exciting image in your head. He is also speaking as though you had already agreed to the sale because you wouldn't be driving it in the mountains unless you were going to buy it. He's acting like it's a done deal—and the truth is, the more he does this, the more it is!

I love seeing door-to-door salespeople use this law to their advantage. They approach a door, ring the bell, and with a big smile tell the prospect they have a great presentation that person needs to see. Of course, they employ this strategy while they are wiping their feet on the person's doormat in expectation of being let in the house. You would be surprised how often this technique actually works. You see the salesperson handing the prospect his pen in expectation of signing the contract. Have you ever felt bad leaving a store or situation where you have not bought something? The store has created the expectation that you would make a purchase.

Presupposition: Assuming the Sale

Using expectations, we can create immediate reactions to stimuli so the subject doesn't even have to think—they just perform the action. Discounts, closeouts, going out of business sales, and coupons are used to draw traffic to stores. Consumers assume they will receive a reduced purchase price by presenting the coupon or by going to a "going out of business sale." One tire company made an error in printing their coupon and the misprinted coupon offered no savings to recipients. However, this coupon produced just as much customer response as did the error-free coupon.[7]

Presupposition is often utilized by using words and language that indicate your assumption that your offer has already been accepted. It is a technique that is used both consciously and subconsciously. Consider the following examples (the assumption is expressed in parentheses):

"When do you want your couch sent?" (You want the couch.)

"Should I call you Tuesday or Wednesday?" (You want to talk again.)

"Your first class will start next Monday." (You're signing up for the class.)

You'd be amazed how often people will just go along with your proposal! They don't even stop and think about their response because now they're already finishing the deal in their mind!

Another way to use presupposition is to put it in writing. People always think that if something's in writing, then it must be true. We often go along with something without questioning it, just because it's what the directions say to do. For example, a particular "candid camera" stunt involved a stop sign placed on a sidewalk, even though there was no reason to stop there. The sign was in an odd place and there was no danger of oncoming traffic, but everyone obediently stopped and waited at the sign, just because it said to do so! In another spoof, a sign reading "Delaware Closed" actually made people start asking for how long Delaware was going to be closed![8]

The Placebo Effect: Persuasive Suggestions

One form that expectations can take is in the shape of a placebo. A placebo is a nonmedicinal substance that is given to patients so they believe they are receiving medicine. Placebos were used during the Korean War when MASH units ran out of morphine. When medical workers gave wounded soldiers placebos, 25 percent of the soldiers reported a reduction in pain. The placebo works because the expectation that the "medicine" will help is so strong that our brains actually translate it into reality. In some studies, placebos worked 25 percent to 40 percent of the time![9]

Not only can our expectations make us well, but they can also make us sick. You may think, "I feel the flu coming on," and you will probably get it. Or if one of your coworkers says, "You look terrible. Are you coming down with something?" you probably will. Expectations have also been related to the occurrence and timing of death. Most elderly people view nursing homes as the end of the line, the last step in life. After admission to the nursing home, mortality rates, for both men and women, double compared to people of the same age and health still living in their own homes.

The Nazi concentration camps fed off of the psychological expectation of death. Prison guards instilled hopelessness in prisoners. They created a psychological environment whereby the prisoners came to expect no chance at survival. Prisoners exhibited powerlessness, an inability to cope, and a diminished will to live—in a sense, a self-imposed death sentence.

One amazing example of the placebo effect occurred in Israel in 1991. Israeli citizens were seen wearing gas masks during scud bombings. Shortly thereafter, hospitals reported dozens of people complaining of symptoms from weapons that were never used. The gas masks were just a form of protection in case of chemical or biological warfare, but just seeing others wearing one caused people to become ill!

I have even used the placebo effect on my daughter. At times, she has trouble sleeping at night and needs a little nudge. I tell her I have a special pill (vitamin) that will put her right to sleep in five minutes. Without fail, she is happily sleeping before the five minutes are up.

Time Expectations

In our modern world, we are bound by time. This being the case, we have certain expectations about how time works and how long it will take us to accomplish something. Often, time becomes distorted through our perceptions and expectations. Why do some afternoons speed by faster than others? And why do we finish projects one minute before our deadline?

Parkinson's Law states that work expands to fill the time available. So, if a project is given a three-month deadline, it will take the full three months to complete. If that very same project is given a six-month timeframe, it will still take the full six months. It may sound strange, but the law has bearing because the time allotted for completion sets our expectations. It is actually our expectations that influence how we will work on a project and therefore when it will be completed. Ever notice how there's a sudden burst of activity right before the deadline appears? We all have the tendency to procrastinate, waiting until the deadline to do most of the work. This is why it is often effective to set multiple deadlines for large projects. Projects without deadlines never seem to be accomplished, no matter how good the intentions are.

Reputation Expectations

The most effective psychological tool for getting someone to follow through is to let him know that you believe he is the type of person who will follow through. Using phrases such as "You're the kind of person who . . ." or "You've always impressed me with your ability to . . ." or "I've always liked the fact that you . . ." invoke the powerful psychological law of internal consistency. Winston Churchill, one of the greatest masters in dealing with people, said, "I have found that the best way to get another to acquire a virtue, is to impute it to him."

When people are aware of the good or bad opinions other people have about them, they usually live up to those opinions. This is why we act out the roles assigned to us. If we receive praise, we want to be worthy of that praise. There was a police officer who always seemed to be able to get even the toughest criminals to open up and tell him everything. His technique was to tell the criminal, "I know you have a reputation for being the tough guy who's been in a lot of trouble, but everyone tells me the one thing that stands out about you is that you never lie. They tell me that whatever you say, it's always the truth, no matter what."

Honestly assess how you think you make others feel when they're around you. Do you make them feel small and unimportant, or do you inspire them to achieve more? Your actions towards others will tell them how you feel or think about them. The German writer and poet Johann Wolfgang von Goethe once stated, "Treat a man as he appears to be and you make him worse. But treat a man as if he already were what he potentially could be, and you make him what he should be."

First Impression Expectations

Have you ever noticed how the people you assume are going to be jerks turn out to be just that? And if there is someone you're especially excited to meet, then you meet her and she seems great! Often our assumptions and expectations about someone we're about to meet for the first time play out exactly as we've already mentally conceived them. Once again, even when first meeting someone, you will send subconscious messages about how they are to respond and behave.

In a particular study, a group of high school students were brought together to hear a speech on how the minimum driving age should be raised. Half the students were told to focus on the speaker's speaking style, while the others were forewarned that the speaker considered teenagers to be horrible drivers. Two weeks after the presentation, the students were asked to fill out a questionnaire. Overall, the first group rated the speaker favorably and even leaned in favor of the position he asserted. The second group rated the speaker as hostile and seemed to have tuned out his message altogether. Because of the expectations set up for them, the second group of students were already defensive before the speech even started, leaving little room for persuasion.

Embedded Commands

An embedded command is a technique used to communicate to the conscious mind while also sending a message to the subconscious mind. The idea is to actually bypass the conscious mind and communicate directly to the subconscious mind. Embedded commands are commonly used in marketing and advertising. Embedded commands are hidden suggestions within written or spoken language. The conscious mind is unaware of their existence. Embedded commands create expectations without creating inner resistance. For example, Pepsi used to have the slogan "Have a Pepsi Day." The embedded command was "Have a Pepsi."

The most effective embedded commands are short and concise; they should be no longer than two to four words. It is much easier to use these commands in persuasive writing because you can visually highlight the command. When using this technique, first determine what exactly you are trying to say to your audience. Then, create the sentences where the embedded words and phrase will logically and contextually fit. Finally, set the embedded commands apart in some visual way: italicize, bold, underline, highlight, or use a different color.

Embedded commands are also a powerful tool in speaking. Certain phrases have specific command forms that follow the "two to four words" rule. Phrases can include word associations, cause and effect statements, presuppositions, questions, hidden suggestions, or analogies. Essentially, we are looking for phrases that jump out at us. Consider the following examples:

Become wealthy	Buy now	Use this material
How good it feels	Going to happen	Read each word
Feel good	Follow my lead	Act now
Change your life	Become really interested	You will understand
Use this process	Learn quickly	Enjoy life
Use this skill	Learn how	Improve your results

Studies show that embedded commands can actually change our attitudes or beliefs, even if we are totally unaware that this has happened.[10] It is in this way that the embedded commands are effective: The conscious mind has no opportunity to analyze or evaluate the material. We then can create expectations of behavioral changes with embedded commands as well as with and direct and indirect suggestions. The subconscious mind will create an internal reality to match the commands.[11]

Goal Setting: Creating Personal Expectations

Many people don't like the idea of goal setting; in fact, just the mere mention of the words makes them cringe. However, there is no doubt that goal setting works. The problem is that most people aren't doing it the right way. I am not going to spend time talking about the many aspects of goal setting—the bottom line is that goal setting works and is an important aspect of the Law of Expectations. If you can help others make goals, it increases their future expectations for themselves. Visualizing themselves reaching their goals also makes achievement of those goals more tangible.

Goals must have the power to stretch and inspire, and they must be realistic in the mind of the person being persuaded. Research shows that goals dictate future performance. Conscious goals influence our overall performance. In one study, there was a large difference in the performance between asking someone to do their best and helping them set their goals or standard for their performance.[12]

It is a general rule of thumb that greater or more difficult goals actually increase performance. The reason for this is that lofty goals set a higher expectation, and, as discussed already, expectations strongly influence behavior. In a production plant, workers with little experience were divided into two groups. One group was told to simply observe the experienced workers and try to be able to perform at a skilled level themselves within twelve weeks. The second group received specific weekly goals that were progressively more and more demanding. Needless to say, the second group fared much better.[13]

Environment

Your environment and the expectations of that environment should be persuasive. In a theory they call the Broken Window Theory, criminologists James Wilson and George Kelling suggest that a building full of broken windows will cause people to assume that no one cares for the building or its appearance. This in turn will spur more vandalism. In other words, the environment's condition gives suggestions that lead people to hold certain assumptions, and people then act on those assumptions. The broken window invites greater vandalism and crime.[14]

In his book, *The Tipping Point*, Malcolm Gladwell uses an example of the Broken Window Theory as he explains the New York City subway clean-up. The subway system was in dire need of rebuilding—a multibillion-dollar endeavor. With the system about to collapse, the focus was understandably on issues like reducing crime and improving subway reliability. As a consultant hired by the New York Transit Authority, George Kelling urged officials to utilize his Broken Window Theory. Hired to clean up the subways, David

Gunn immediately assigned people to start cleaning up all the graffiti. Removing the graffiti seemed to be of such little consequence compared to everything else there was to worry about, but Gunn was insistent. In his own words:

The graffiti was symbolic of the collapse of the system. When you looked at the process of rebuilding the organization and morale, you had to win the battle against graffiti. Without winning that battle, all the management reforms and physical changes just weren't going to happen. We were about to put out new trains that were worth about ten million bucks apiece, and unless we did something to protect them, we knew just what would happen. They would last one day and then they would be vandalized.[15]

Gunn set up specific goals, timetables, and even cleaning stations. If any train came back with graffiti, it had to be cleaned immediately before it could go out again. For the vandals who had spent their nights, toiling into the wee morning hours painting their murals, it sent a strong message. Seeing their masterpieces already painted over again by the cracking of the next morning's light told them they were wasting their time. The entire anti-graffiti campaign took years, but finally, the incidence of graffiti subsided.

The hope and expectations you can create in your persuasive environment will forecast your ability to persuade. One experiment was conducted on the influence of light. Lab rats were placed in jars of water to see how long they would keep trying to swim before giving up. Some of the jars were placed in complete darkness, while others had light shining into them. The results were dramatic! The rats in the dark swam for about three minutes before succumbing. The rats with the light swam up to thirty-six hours—more than 700 times longer than the rats in the dark![16]

In another study, volunteers were asked to participate in an experiment on prison environments. Half of the volunteers posed as prison workers, while the other half posed as prison inmates. The results were astounding. Previously tested to be psychologically sound people, the participants rapidly became more and more hostile, crude, rebellious, and abusive—both those acting as inmates *and* as guards! One "prisoner" became so hysterical and emotionally distressed that he had to be released. The study was supposed to last two weeks but was called off after only six days![17]

Pacing and Leading

Another application of the Law of Expectations is the concept of pacing and leading. This is part of NLP, or "neurolinguistic programming." *Pacing* involves establishing rapport and making persuasive communication easier; *leading* involves steering your prospect toward your point of view. Pacing and leading will enable you to direct a person's thoughts so they tend to move in your direction.

When you pace, you validate your prospects either verbally or nonverbally; that is, you are in agreement or rapport with your prospects. As a result, they feel comfortable and congruent with you. Pacing entails using statements everyone accepts as true. By doing so, you eliminate disagreement and get others to agree with what you are saying. The topic either can be proven true or is commonly accepted as true.

An example of a pacing question (obviously true):

> Most people would love to be financially free and
> end their money worries forever.

Once you have established rapport and harmony with your prospect, you can create expectation of agreement. You must have general agreement before you can lead your prospect to your point of view. You then begin to use statements that you want your prospect to agree with, even though they haven't consciously and/or publicly acknowledged that they do.

An example of a leading question (you want your prospect to accept):

> The answer to your financial problem is providing the
> right training at the right time by the right person.

So to put pacing and leading in a nutshell, pacing statements are obviously true, so the prospect has to accept their validity. Leading statements can't necessarily be proven true, but they represent what you want your prospect to believe.

11

The Law of Involvement
Create and Awaken Curiosity

Without involvement, there is no commitment. Mark it down, asterisk it, circle it, underline it. No involvement, no commitment.
—STEPHEN COVEY

THE LAW OF INVOLVEMENT suggests that the more you engage someone's five senses, involve them mentally and physically, and create the right atmosphere for persuasion, the more effective and persuasive you'll be. Listening can be a very passive act; you can listen to an entire speech and not feel or do a thing. As a persuader, you need to help your audience be one step closer to taking action. As a Master Persuader, your goal is to decrease the distance someone has to go to reach your objective.

When you get a prospect to start something, it is most likely they will follow through and complete your desired outcome. The more involved they become, the less psychological distance between the start and the finish. The desired outcome becomes more and more realistic instead of just an idea you are proposing. If you put on your shoes to go to the store, you are more likely to continue in that direction. If you sit down and turn on the TV, your goal of going to the store is less likely to be reached.

There are many ways to use involvement. We are going to focus on the following:

1. Increasing Participation

2. Creating Atmosphere

3. Maintaining Attention

4. Using the Art of Questioning

5. Telling Mesmerizing Stories

6. Repeating and Repackaging

7. Building Suspense and Distraction

8. Generating Competition

9. Engaging the Five Senses

Increasing Participation

You can create involvement through increased participation. The more we take an active role and get involved, the more open to persuasion we become. When we take an active part in something, we feel more connected to and have stronger feelings for the issue at hand. We have a personal stake in what we are doing.

One of the keys to successful participation is making your problem their problem. This technique creates ownership and a willingness to help on the part of your prospects. Obviously, asking for help is much milder than telling someone what to do or think. You will have more success involving your prospects in the solution if you give them the option of participating. Feeling that it was their choice and their solution, your prospects will take ownership—they have persuaded themselves. It becomes their own problem and their own solution. By nature, people will support what they help create.

Store and mall owners understand the concept of participation. They attempt to get you participating by making eye contact with you, by arranging their stores to force you to spend more time in them, and by saying hello as you pass. When you shop for goods in Mexico, for example, the storeowner knows that if he can get you in the store and get you involved, there is a greater chance of persuasion and a purchase. As such he will make eye contact and do everything in his power to get you in the store. If you don't go in the store, he might follow you for blocks, showing you his products and trying to get you to buy.

The amount of time one spends in a store is directly related to how much one will buy. The more time spent, the more money spent. For example, in an electronics store, non-buyers averaged about five minutes and six seconds shopping time while buyers averaged nine minutes and twenty-nine seconds in the store. In a toy store, the longest any non-buyer stayed was ten minutes, while shortest time spent for a buyer was just over seventeen minutes. In some cases, buyers stayed up to four times longer than non-buyers.[1]

Many other arrangements are made by stores to persuade people to get interested and get involved. For example, hallways and walking paths at malls are made of hard marble or tiles. But the floors of individual stores are soft and carpeted—encouraging you to stay longer. Have you ever noticed that it is easy to get disoriented in a mall you are unfamiliar with? Malls purposely design their structures with hexagonal floor plans, which are the most difficult to navigate: complicated hallways, confusing angles, and consistent temperature and lighting. The Mall of America in Minnesota, the largest mall in America, wants you to get lost—you can walk forever and still not know exactly where you are.

This is also the reason why malls place department stores at opposite ends of each other. Department stores are draws, so for people to get from one to another, they will have to walk past every other store in the mall before they reach the opposite one. Grocery stores place their milk at the back of the store so customers have to walk through the rest of the store to grab a carton. All of these techniques increase the time that customers spend in the store. And as we know, increased time in a store means increased sales.

Role-Playing

One way to get your audience more involved is to use role-playing. This technique has proven to be effective in getting people to actually convince themselves of something. Role-playing is the single most powerful way to induce attitude change through vicarious experience. In essence, you are getting people to make up arguments against their own beliefs. Do you want to know just how powerful role-playing is? One experiment used role-playing to convince people to stop smoking. The subjects role-played cigarette smokers having x-rays, receiving news of lung cancer, and coughing with emphysema. When compared with a control group of smokers, those who role-played this situation were more likely to have quit than those who passively learned about lung cancer.[2]

In another study, students were tested to see what types of persuasion techniques were most effective in delivering an anti-smoking message. One group was assigned to write, stage, and put on the presentation, while the other group was simply required to watch the presentation. As you might imagine, the group that was more involved in the presentation held more negative feelings about smoking than did the group that had just passively listened.

During World War II, the U.S. government had to ration traditional meats such as beef, chicken, and pork. However, Americans tend to be very picky about the meats they eat and often do not accept meat substitutes. The Committee on Food Habits was charged with overcoming the shortages of popular foods. How could they overcome the aversion to eating other meats?

Psychologist Kurt Lewin devised a program to persuade Americans to eat intestinal meats. Yes, your favorite—intestinal meats. He set up an experiment with two groups of housewives. In one group, the housewives were lectured on the benefits of eating intestinal meats. Members of the committee emphasized to them how making the switch would help the war effort. The housewives also heard fervent testimonials and received recipes. The second group of housewives was led in a group discussion about how they could persuade other housewives to eat intestinal meat. This group covered the same main topics as the other group. Of the group that was more involved in "role-playing" and discussing the question of "how they would persuade and convince others to eat intestinal meats," 32 percent of the housewives went on to serve their families intestinal meats. This was compared to 3 percent of the first group.[3]

Asking for Advice

Another way to get people to participate with you is to ask their opinions or advice. Simple phrases such as, "I need your help" "What is your opinion?" "What do you think about . . . ?" "How could I do this?" "How would you do this?" "Do you think I am doing it right?" and "Do you have any ideas?" can immediately spark the interest of your listener.

Watch how another person brightens up when you ask for his or her advice. For example, if you ask your neighbor, "Frank, how about helping me fix my fence?" he will probably tell you he is busy and has plans for the next twelve weekends. But suppose you said, "Frank, I have a challenge with this fence that I can't solve. I don't know what I am doing wrong and can't seem to get anywhere. I am not sure if I am doing it right or what to do next. Do you have ideas about how I could mend this fence? Could you come take a look?" You will see a marked difference in response between the first request and the second.

People have an innate desire to feel wanted and needed. When you fulfill this need, you open the door to persuasion and action, a fact that has been proved beyond a doubt by records kept on industrial workers. Workers who have no voice whatsoever in management, who cannot make suggestions, or who are not allowed to express their ideas simply do not do as much work as workers who are encouraged to contribute. The same is true in families. Family-relations expert Ruth Barbee said, "It is surprising how willingly a child will accept the final authority of the father, even if the decision goes against him, provided he has had a chance to voice his opinions, and make his suggestions, before the final decision is reached."[4]

Our opinions play an enormous role in changing our minds about issues. For action to occur, the change must be internalized. Consider this example: Suppose you surveyed people's opinions on some topic, let's say capital punishment, then divided them into two groups. Both groups are to write an essay on capital punishment that is against their true views. One group is "required" to write the essay, while the other group is asked to "volunteer" to write the essay. Both groups are then surveyed again for their opinions on capital punishment. What do you think the results would be? When this experiment was actually tried, the individuals who were required to write the essay showed almost no change at all in their opinions. Those volunteering to do so showed changes in opinion when tested later, even though their essays were written from a standpoint in conflict with their true views. From this, we learn two things: First, there was greater compliance from those who were given the choice and not forced to participate; second, as discussed in an earlier chapter, when people feel conflict or dissonance internally, they will often adapt or even change their position.

Visualization

Another participation technique is to use visualization. No one can follow through on an act or message without first thinking or seeing in his or her mind that it is possible to accomplish it. You can mentally achieve participation by helping your audience visualize and see in their mind how your product or service will help them. Real estate agents attempt to help their clients visualize living with their family in a certain home. When showing the home, the agents want the people to envision it as their own.

A group of researchers went door-to-door selling cable TV subscriptions. When they included the phrase "imagine how cable TV will provide you with broader entertainment," they immediately achieved more success. Forty-seven percent of those who were told to imagine cable TV bought a subscription while only 20 percent of the control group did. The mind is activated when you help your prospect visualize your product or service.[5]

In many persuasive situations, your audience may not be interested in your message, service, or product at all. How do you pull in passers-by? Many times when we see a persuasive situation, we like to remain anonymous. We don't want to feel any pressure so we watch from a distance. If someone at the clothing store asks if we want help we say "no." We avoid the involvement because deep down we know that becoming involved will decrease our resistance.

I remember spending some time on Key West in the Florida Keys. Every night before dusk, everyone would gather at Sunset Pier to watch the sunset and enjoy the view. It is a great time of the day to unwind and enjoy nature's beauty. It is also the perfect opportunity for vendors and street performers to hawk their wares. We saw jugglers, sword swallowers, magic tricks, the works. One night, as I watched people walk by, many of them wanted to watch but felt timid unless a crowd had already gathered around the performers. The performers knew if they did not get a crowd, they would not make any money. When someone remains anonymous, they feel little pressure to donate. I saw someone who was doing a magic act call over to someone who was trying to remain anonymous. Soon, the performer got the man involved in his act. This attracted more people to watch and also got a donation from the gentleman, who no longer was anonymous.

If you see someone around you or in your audience who is avoiding or rejecting your message, try to get him or her involved. You can get a volunteer from your audience and by getting him to willingly participate, you will completely change his perspective. Pet storeowners are famous for this. They see children come in just to look around. The parents don't want to have a dog in the house, but their son or daughter still wants to look. The owner waits patiently to see the child's eyes light up and instantly fall in love with a new puppy. The child holds and hugs the puppy and the dad knows he is in for a struggle. The owner is wise and does not want to fight the father. He just says, "It looks like she has fallen in love with this puppy. I understand your apprehension about having a new puppy—who will be in charge of it? Tell you what—just take the puppy home for the weekend and if it doesn't work out, bring him back." Of course, you know that the rest is history. Who can't fall in love with a puppy after a weekend? The owner has successfully pulled a reluctant customer to get involved.

One of the most influential salesmen for the U.S. Army was Major General Walter S. Sweeney. In one city where he and his troops were staying, there was a strong feeling of hostility toward the troops. The general wisely invited one of the civic clubs to lunch. There, club members were served by army members—while they listened to the army band play—and heard different speeches. The meeting was successful, and others followed. It was not long before the hostility was forgotten. General Sweeney knew that the only way he would gain support was if he could involve and get to know the civilians.[6]

Physical Movement

Making your audience physically move can also affect the way your message is received. Involvement can be something as simple as getting people to say "yes," to raise their hands, or even just to nod their heads "yes." The more movement and involvement you can create, the greater your ability to persuade. Great persuaders look for times when they can get affirmation from their audience. They engineer their persuasive message to get as many verbal, mental, or physical "yeses" as they can throughout their presentation. And there is good evidence to support this practice. One study brought in a large group of students to do "market research on high-tech headphones." The students were told that the researchers wanted to test how well the headphones worked while they were in motion (while wearers were dancing up and down and moving their heads to the beat of Linda Ronstadt and the Eagles). Following the songs, the researchers played an argument about how the university's tuition should be raised from $587 per semester to $750 per semester. One group of students had been told to move their heads up and down throughout the music and the speaking. Another group was told to move their heads from side to side. A last group was told to make no movements at all.

After "testing the headsets," the students were asked to fill out a questionnaire about not only the headsets, but also the university's tuition. Those nodding their heads up and down (yes motion) overall rated a jump in tuition as favorable. Those shaking their heads side to side (no motion) overall wanted the tuition to be lowered. Those who had not moved their heads didn't really seem to be persuaded one way or the other.[7] In a similar study at the University of Missouri, the researchers found that TV advertisements were more persuasive when the visual display had repetitive vertical movements, for example, a bouncing ball.[8]

Contact

Engaging customers with human contact also works well for retail stores. Human beings are naturally drawn to other human activity.[9] The sight of other humans in motion attracts people—and increases sales. Studies show that the more contact employees make with customers, the greater the average sale.[10] In fact, any contact initiated by a store employee increases the likelihood that a shopper will buy something.[11] A shopper who talks to a salesperson and tries something on is twice as likely to buy as a shopper who does neither. Talking with an employee has a way of drawing a customer in closer and actively involving them.

The Power of "Yes"

Use questions that will create "yeses." As you create your marketing and persuasive presentations, you must engineer the number of times you get your audience to raise their hands, say yes, or nod their heads. How many verbal yeses are you getting? One easy and effective way to get more affirmative responses is to engineer questions that will receive a positive answer. For example, when a word ends in "n't" it will bring a "yes" response. Consider the following phrases:

Wouldn't it?

Isn't it?

Couldn't it?

Doesn't it?

Shouldn't it?

Won't you?

Can't you?

Wasn't it?

Creating Atmosphere

Another way to boost participation is with atmosphere. Atmosphere is really just a state of mind that you can create. Think about the following locations and the atmosphere they purposefully create:

- Hardware stores

- Bookstores

- Malls

- Casinos

- Theme restaurants

- Amusement parks

- Sporting goods stores

- Bars

- Hospitals

- Law offices

Each establishment is vastly different, but when you walk in, you know immediately the atmosphere or feeling that it evokes. In this way, the atmosphere moves you. Antique stores purposefully create an atmosphere of chaos. They appear to be unorganized with everything strewn around or disheveled. This is done so that customers believe they have stumbled upon a great find, a piece of buried treasure. Nike Town is a set of stores, each with an athletic theme. If the customer is successfully seduced by the excitement and energy of the athletic atmosphere, he will want to make himself just a little worthier of it. This means buying a new pair of Nikes.

Music
Music is an important part of atmosphere. In department stores, shoppers who are exposed to music shop 18 percent longer and make 17 percent more purchases than shoppers in stores not playing music. There are even rhythms, pitches, and styles of music that are best for different shoppers. Grocery shoppers respond best to slow tempos. Fast food restaurants need a higher number of beats per minute. For the use of music to be effective, customers can't really be aware of it—the music should not be overpowering, rather it should be merely an atmospheric presence.

Aroma
Aromas are commonly used as a participation device. We know that our sense of smell can evoke memories quicker (see the Law of Association) and more intensely than any other method. We see many examples of the use of aromas to create the proper atmosphere. Victoria's Secret uses potpourri scents to augment their customers' feelings of femininity. Pizza stores use the smell of freshly baked pizza. Car dealers use the new car smell, even on

used cars. In the Kajima Cooperation in Japan, management uses aromas to increase productivity throughout the day. Their formula is citrus in the morning, for its rousing effects; floral scents in the afternoon, to encourage concentration; and woodland scents before lunch and at the end of the day, to help relax employees.[12] One study showed that people were more than twice as likely to provide a stranger with change for a dollar when they were within smelling range of a Cinnabon store.[13] The right smells can make a persuasive atmosphere.

Rushed vs. Relaxed

Atmosphere can also include the tension in the air. Is there a rush, or are customers relaxed? What type of climate are you trying to create? Do you want a quick, fast decision, or do you want your customers to feel comfortable enough to stay for a while? An interesting study on what happens when you create an atmosphere of being rushed can be seen in the following example:

Princeton University psychologists John Darley and Daniel Batson wanted to see how students would respond if they were in a situation replicating the biblical account of the Good Samaritan.[14] As the story goes, a band of thieves beat, robbed, and left a man traveling alone by the roadside to die. A devout priest and a reputable Levite passed by. Neither of the men stopped to help the dying man. Finally, a Samaritan, loathed and despised by society, stopped to help him. The Samaritan bound up his wounds, took him to an inn, and even paid the innkeeper to care for him until he returned.

Darley and Batson asked seminarians on a one-on-one basis to prepare and present a short speech on an assigned biblical topic. The test was set up so that on their way to the location where they would deliver their speech, each student would cross a man slumped over, coughing and groaning. Which students would actually stop and help? Before preparing their speeches, the students filled out a questionnaire asking why they had chosen to study theology. Then a variety of speech topics were assigned, including the story of the Good Samaritan. As the students were leaving to deliver their speeches, some were told, "You'd better hurry. They were expecting you about three minutes ago." Others were told, "They won't be ready for a few minutes, but you may as well head over now."

Now, most people would assume that seminarians stating on their questionnaires that they had chosen to study theology so they could help people and who were then assigned to speak on the Good Samaritan would be the ones most likely to stop and help the ailing man on their way. Interestingly, neither of those two factors seemed to make much of a difference. In fact, Darley and Batson stated, "Indeed, on several occasions, a seminary student going to give his talk on the parable of the Good Samaritan literally stepped over the victim as he hurried on his way." The element that seemed to be most influential was whether or not the student was rushed. Of the students who were told they were already a little late, only 10 percent stopped to help. Of the students who were told they had a little bit more time, 63 percent stopped to help.[15]

We can learn from this example that we can create atmospheres where people are so involved and feel so much pressure to be sufficiently involved that they ignore other factors they normally would not ignore.

Hands-on Experience

Another good way to get people involved is to get your product into their hands. If they can begin to use it, chances are they will continue. That is why car dealers encourage test drives. You will even see car dealerships give their loyal customers a car to drive for a few days. How can you go back to your old car after driving around in a new car? By that point, neighbors and coworkers have already seen you in the car and have commented about your new vehicle. You're thoroughly involved and the new car is yours. You want people to experience your product for free. Free trials are really what made the Internet company AOL (America Online) successful. Who doesn't have free CDs from AOL?

Many TV advertisers offer a free one-month trial before you have to pay for their product. After the month is up, most consumers will keep the product, even if they didn't use it. The trial period has created a sense of ownership in the product, and consumers don't like to relinquish ownership. This is also why so many companies use introductory offers. Credit card issuers are known for tempting customers with introductory deals that give very low interest rates.

To get your product in your prospects' hands, get them to open the box and play with the object, give them the feeling of ownership, make them feel as if they already bought it, and suggest how the product can be used in their home. There are many other examples of the Law of Involvement. Think about the listening stations in the music stores, the comfortable chairs where you can kick back and read in the bookstores, booths set up at the malls where you can try and test products and equipment, CD clubs where you get so many free CDs, frequent user programs, coupons, contests, and the variety of services offering free estimates.

The 3M Company certainly discovered the value of putting product into customers' hands. At their outset, Post-it Notes were not very successful. 3M was going to discontinue the whole line until the brand manager sent a case of Post-it Notes to 499 of the Fortune 500 Companies. Because of their trial run, the Fortune 500 companies loved the efficiency of Post-it Notes, and the rest is history.[16]

Another common way for businesses to cash in on the Law of Involvement is to use the "magic" of written declarations. This occurs through the use of an innocent-looking promotional device. You're probably familiar with company-sponsored essay contests, you know, the ones that ask you to write a 100-word essay beginning with the statement, "I love this product because . . ."? Well, is there any better way to get a commitment from someone than to have them put it in writing? What about those Crayola drawing contests, where kids had to submit their artwork created with Crayola's crayons? It's the same principle.

Usually we are more inclined to favor our own ideas over the ideas of others, right? Knowing that people do not typically resist their own ideas can be key when trying to influence others. Always seek to get your prospects to think your ideas are their own. An example of this strategy in action is when companies have the customers fill out a sales agreement. Cancellations are amazingly low when customers have filled out their agreements on their own. It's a double whammy: Not only are your prospects agreeing to what you want, but they are also putting it in writing!

Maintaining Attention

It is common sense to realize you have to keep your audience's attention in order to persuade them. If you lose them, you lose your chance for them to understand and accept your proposal. We know from our own personal experience that we tend to let our minds naturally drift when we are listening to other people. We cannot focus on one item for too long unless we are forced to do so. Master Persuaders can make a person want to pay attention and stay focused. You may lose your audience's attention from time to time but it is your job to bring them back to full attention status. You can help your prospect lose track of time.

Some estimate that the average adult attention span is about eighteen minutes. What's more, studies indicate that attention spans have been decreasing steadily over the past decade. The blame seems to be put on the media, on lack of circumstances that require concentration, and of course on the MTV generation always wanting to be entertained or tuning out. After our attention span has lapsed, we become bored and no longer listen. You have to be creative to maintain the mental involvement that is required to persuade a mind. One way to keep the mind harnessed is to give your audience enough time to process what you are telling them. You can tell by the look in their eyes if you have lost them. I'm sure you have taken seminars or college classes where you have been completely lost. When the professor asks questions, you don't raise your hand because you have no idea what is going on. Give your listeners enough time to absorb what you're saying, but obviously not so long that they become totally bored and detached.

Some more ideas on ways to help people choose to pay attention:

- Use questions
- Present new and innovative ideas
- Use quotes
- Make startling statements
- Provide relevant examples
- Change mediums
- Speak in the first person
- Make them feel important
- Give them shortcuts or tips
- Keep your body moving
- Avoid excessive detail
- Make sure your transitions flow

You can see that these techniques are used to grab back the attention of your listeners when their minds have started wandering. Employed properly they will bring your audience's attention back to you.

Thousands of sales are lost each day simply because the salesperson talks too much. Salespeople tend to oversell by making a laundry list of reasons why people should buy their product. This is not what people want to hear. As a result, they will always find one reason or another not to buy. The more benefits you list, the greater the chances that your prospect will find a reason not to buy. Overselling will also kill the emotions of the prospect.

Movement is another common technique for grabbing attention. It causes us to be alert. Stores utilizing movement-oriented end-caps (displays at the end of the aisle) always have more shoppers around than those using end-caps without movement. This strategy can be used to your advantage when doing a presentation. When your movements are purposeful and well timed, your audience will be more tuned in to your message.

Using the Art of Questioning

Of all the tools in your persuasion toolbox, questioning is probably the one most often used by Master Persuaders. Questions gain immediate involvement. Questions are used in the persuasion process to create mental involvement, to guide the conversation, to set the pace of conversation, to clarify statements and objections, to determine beliefs, attitudes, and values, to force you to slow down, to find out what your prospect needs, and to show your sincerity. Questioning is a very diverse and useful tool. Negotiation experts Neil Rackham and John Carlisle observed hundreds of negotiators in action in an attempt to discover what it takes to be a top negotiator. Their key finding was that skilled negotiators ask more than twice as many questions as average negotiators.[17]

Much like movement, questions elicit an automatic response from our brains. We are taught to answer a question when it is posed to us. We automatically think of a response when asked a question. Even if we don't verbalize the answer, we think about it in our head. Most people want to be cooperative. We don't want to be considered rude because we don't answer the questions. In this way, a question stimulates our thinking response.

Let's look a little bit at how to form good questions. First, design your questions ahead of time. The structure of your questions dictates how your listener will answer them. When asked to estimate a person's height, people will answer differently depending on whether the question asked is "How tall is he?" versus "How short is he?" In one study, when asking how tall versus how short a basketball player was, researchers received dramatically different results. The "how tall" question received the guess of 79 inches whereas the "how short" question received the guess of 69 inches.[18] Words have a definite effect on how people respond. "How fast was the car going?" suggests a high speed, but "At what speed was the car traveling?" suggests a moderate speed. "How far was the intersection?" suggests the intersection was far away.

If you are probing for lots of information, it is best to keep your questions unstructured. The more unstructured the question, the more information you are likely to get. In a conversation in which you are asking many unstructured questions, the other person is likely to be doing most of the talking. Along this vein, it is a good idea to ask open-ended questions. It is too easy to respond to a question that can be answered with a simple "yes" or "no." For example, instead of saying, "Do you wish you had decided differently?" ask, "How did you feel after you made that decision?" Then the person's answer can be used as a device to lead into your more detailed questions—"Why did you make that decision?" or "What do you wish you could change about your decision?"— without your seeming intrusive.

A good rule of thumb is to start with the easiest questions first. You want to draw your audience into the conversation and help them feel relaxed and comfortable. People are encouraged by answers they know are right. Begin the conversation by starting with a general topic instead of a specific subject. You need to get the wheels in your listeners' minds rolling before you ask them to answer the more specific questions.

One facet of questioning is the use of leading questions. Leading questions are questions that give a semi-interpretation to your audience. The best trial lawyers are experts at using leading questions to cross-examine and influence witnesses. Stanford professor Elizabeth Loftus researched how leading questions influenced eyewitness testimonies. In one project, her subjects watched a one-minute multiple-car accident. One group was asked, "About how fast were the cars going when they smashed into each other?" The second group was asked, "How fast were the cars going when they hit?" The third group was asked, "How fast were they going when they contacted?" The first group estimated that the cars were going about 40.8 miles an hour, the second group estimated 34 miles an hour, and the third group estimated 31.8 miles an hour.[19] The same question led to three different answers just by using alternative phrasing.

Leading questions not only alter the way we interpret facts, but they also influence what we remember. In another study conducted by Loftus, study subjects who were asked, "Did you see *the* broken headlight?" were two or three times more likely to answer yes than subjects who were asked, "Did you see *a* broken headlight?"[20]

A Two-Way Street

Questioning can also measure the level of receptivity in your prospects. How receptive your audience is correlates with how many questions or statements arise. So what if there are no questions? What do you do? If there are no questions, it could be because the audience needs time to think about what you have just said, they could be afraid to ask because of what others might think, or they just might not be able to think of a good question to ask. Maybe you went on too long or stepped on a sensitive issue. Perhaps the audience has already made up their minds, or maybe they don't speak English.

The best questions draw a person into a conversation and out of being unreceptive. So, it is to your advantage to direct questions at your prospects that will reel them in:

What do you think about . . . ?

Have you ever thought about . . . ?

How do you feel about . . . ?

When did you start . . . ?

Where did you find . . . ?

Be prepared to field questions that the audience will ask and want to know. Brainstorm ahead of time for possible questions, scenarios, and answers. There will always be someone who asks the tough questions. If you are the expert, you are expected to know the answers. Obviously, if you don't know the answer, you should not make one up. If the question is way out of line, you can say you don't know the answer. But what do you do when your audience expects you to know the answer and you don't? How do you save yourself from losing credibility?

One way is to throw the question back to the audience and ask for the audience's help or opinions. Another strategy is asking to have the question repeated. This gives you more time to think of a response. Restate the question and ask if that is correct. This also helps you make sure you understand the question. You can request that the person asking the question consult with you later: "Get with me at the break so we can talk about that." It is better to tell one person you don't know than admitting it to the whole audience. Alternatively, you can ask the person posing the question whether they have any of their own insights into the subject.

Handling Objections

When you get people involved in the process, you will get some objections. The way you handle objections will correlate with how mentally involved people become with your message. The better you become at handling objections, the more persuasive you will become.

When you become a Master Persuader, you will learn to love objections. You will come to understand that when people voice their objections, it actually indicates interest and shows that they are paying attention to what you are saying. The key to persuasion is anticipating all objections before you hear them. Fielding questions and handling objections can make or break you as a persuader. Such skills will help you in every aspect of your life.

Here are some tips on how to handle objections:

1. *The first thing is to find out if the objection is something you can solve.* Suppose you are negotiating a large office furniture order and the objection comes up about not being able to afford your furniture. You then find out your prospect just declared bankruptcy. Obviously there is nothing you can do or say that will resolve such an objection.

2. *Let your prospect state his objection:* Hear him out completely, without interruption. Wait until he is finished before you say anything. Hold your response until the other person is receptive to what you are about to say. This is the first time your prospect has voiced his objection; he will not listen until he has said what is on his mind.

3. *Always ask your prospect to restate or repeat his key points.* Every time he replays his objection it becomes clearer in both your minds. Letting him speak, particularly if he is upset, drains emotion from his objection. Allowing him to voice his concerns also gives you time to think about a response and helps you determine his intent in bringing up the objection in the first place.

4. *Always compliment your prospect on her objection.* As a Master Persuader, you can appreciate a good objection; it dictates the direction in

which you should take your presentation. You don't have to prove you are right 100 percent of the time. Skillful persuaders will always find some point of agreement. It's important to recognize the apprehension or objections people have instead of ignoring them.

5. *Stay calm*. Scientific tests have proven that calmly stated facts are more effective in getting people to change their minds than are threats and force.

6. *Don't be arrogant or condescending*. Show empathy with your prospect's objection. Let him know others have felt this way. Talk in the third person; use a disinterested party to prove your point. This is why we often use testimonials—to let someone else do the persuading for us.

7. *Give the person room to save face*. People will often change their minds and agree with you later. Unless your prospect has made a strong stand, leave the door open for her to later agree with you and save face at the same time. It could be that she did not have all the facts, that she misunderstood, or that you didn't explain everything correctly.

Quick Note: If you are dealing with a stubborn person who absolutely will not change his mind about anything, don't panic. There are reasons why this person is closed-minded and always saying "no" to everything. He might not have a clear idea about what you are proposing, he may have been hurt in the past, he may be afraid of being judged, or he may feel his ideas are not appreciated. Don't take it personally; it will happen from time to time.

Telling Mesmerizing Stories

Stories are powerful tools for persuaders. Compelling storytelling automatically creates attention and involvement with your audience. We can all think of a time when we were in an audience and not paying attention to the speaker. We were off in our own world when all of a sudden we perked up and started to listen because the speaker had begun to tell a story. We sat up, listened attentively, took note of what was being said, and wanted to know what would happen next. Whenever you sense your audience is starting to wander, you should have a relevant story ready.

Notice I said "relevant." You can capture attention by telling a story but you will lose long-term persuasiveness if your story does not relate to you or your topic. When your stories work well to underscore your main points, your presentation will hold greater impact. Remember, facts presented alone will not persuade as powerfully as they will when coupled with stories that strike a chord within your listeners. By tapping into inspiration, faith, and a person's innermost feelings, you will cause your prospects to be moved by your story.

Stories can be effectively used to do any or all of the following:

- Grab attention and create involvement

- Simplify complex ideas

- Create memorable hooks

- Trigger emotions

- Tap into existing beliefs

- Persuade without detection

- Bypass existing resistance to you or to your ideas

- Demonstrate who you are

- Build interest

- Encourage participation

Stories answer questions in the audience's mind about who you are and what you represent. If you don't answer these questions for your listeners, they will make up the answers themselves. Your audience members can tell from a story whether you are funny, honest, or even whether you want to be with them. Remember, building rapport is a key ingredient for persuasion. Since you usually don't have time to build trust based on personal experience, the best you can do is tell your prospects a story that simulates an experience of your trustworthiness. Hearing your story is as close as they can get to the firsthand experience of watching you in action.

Your goal is for the listeners to arrive at your conclusions of their own free will. Your story needs to take them on a step-by-step tour of your message. A persuasive story simplifies your concepts so your audience can understand what you are talking about and what you want them to do. We love stories to give us answers to our problems. We accept the answers a story gives us more than if someone were to just provide us with those answers.

Courtroom lawyers often create reenactments of events. They make the stories so rich in sensory detail that the jury literally sees, hears, and feels the event as it unfolded. The trial lawyer's goal is to make the description so vivid that the jurors feel the client's distress as their own and as such are moved by it. The more concrete and specific your descriptive details, the more persuasive your story telling will be. Using specific details pulls the listener into the story, making it real, making it believable.

Pack your stories with authenticity, passion, and humor. Make sure they are straightforward and that the timeline or character development is not confusing. A story that confuses will not convince. Use your body, voice, props, music, or costumes if necessary. These methods intensify your message because they reach all the senses. Engaging the senses of your listeners will make your story more effective. If you can get your listeners to see, hear, smell, feel, and taste the elements of your story, their imaginations will drive them to the point of experiencing without actually being there.

As you learn to incorporate the senses, you will find that their effects can persuade faster than your words. For example, smells and tastes can be very powerful. Both can evoke strong emotional memories and even physiological reactions in your listeners. Invite them to imagine the smell of freshly baked chocolate chip cookies and you will see noses flare and faces relax with the feeling associated with that special aroma. Such sensation will fill their minds with feeling. Or describe in full detail the sensation of biting into a fresh orange. You want the experience to come alive in their mind as if it is happening to them. Paint the picture in such a way that it becomes so real that your audience feels a part of it. People will participate in your stories when you let them.

Repeating and Repackaging

The more you expose someone to a particular concept or idea, the more that concept or idea will become favorable to them. Things do grow on us. Have you ever heard a song on the radio that you didn't like until it started to grow on you? This is also true with people. You may not like some people at first, but after awhile you grow to like them, and sometimes you even become their friend. Ever wonder why politicians want signs and posters with their names and faces all over everyone's yards, street corners, bumpers, and windows? The use of repetition can be very effective. It is often said that repetition is the mother of all learning, but it is also the mother of effective persuasion. Repetition increases awareness, understanding, and retention.

You have to be careful to use repetition wisely, however. My motto is, "Repackage; Don't Repeat." This means you can use the power of repetition, but you don't always have to say the words exactly the same way. You can make the same point with a story, a fact, a statistic, an analogy, or a testimony and never have to repeat yourself. You know how you feel when you hear the exact same joke for the second or even third time—it doesn't carry the same punch as it did the first time, so you usually tune out.

Even when repackaging, keep it to no more than three times. If you present your message less than three times, it will not have a very strong effect. If you present your message more than three times, it becomes "worn out" and loses its potency. For example, in a study where children were shown the same ice cream commercial over and over while watching a cartoon, the children who saw the commercial three times actually wanted the ice cream more than those who had seen the commercial five times.[21] In another study, students were told they were to judge the sound quality of audiocassettes. What the researchers were really searching for, however, was the varying responses after having heard the recorded message one, three, or five times. The message discussed support of an increase in university spending via visitor luxury tax or increased student tuition. Students actually favored the argument for the luxury tax with up to three repetitions, but at five repetitions, their favor for this argument declined.[22]

Another aspect of repetition is persistence. If you have ever been in sales, you know that the most successful salespeople are the most persistent; they keep nudging until the sale is made. Most sales reps try to close the sale only once or twice, but we know the average person has to be asked five to six times before a sale takes place. Many people are afraid to ask again and again. We tend to think that if we ask someone to do something and they say they'll think about, that they will. Well, I hate to break the news to you, but they don't. We forget. Our lives are busy. That is why repetition and persistence increase your involvement and your ability to persuade.

Master Persuaders can feel the fine line between persistence and annoyance. My general rule is that if you detect even the slightest of interest, keep up your persistence. I was in Mexico recently with a friend. We were enjoying a nice walk through the town, looking at all the shops and buildings. Out of nowhere, a vendor selling bracelets and necklaces approached and disrupted our nice stroll. "No, thank you" did little to deter the pesky vendor. He followed us through the town and through the streets. When we went into a shop hoping he'd leave, he even waited outside the store for us. Again, we told him "no, thank you" and that we had no need for his gold and silver bracelets. "But I have a special deal," he kept telling us! Well, he was persistent (or we could say a pain in the butt) but it finally paid off. We bought a bracelet and he went home happy.

Persistence is a state of mind, which means it can be cultivated. Most people do not lack desire; they lack persistence. As Calvin Coolidge said:

Successful people always have high levels of persistence, and don't give up until they have reached their objective. Nothing in the world can take the place of persistence. Talent will not. Nothing is more common than unsuccessful men with talent. Genius will not. Unrewarded genius is almost a proverb. Education will not. The world is full of educated derelicts. Persistence, determination and hard work make the difference.

Remember, you can have the best product and it might even be a perfect fit for the person you are trying to persuade. They might even feel it is a perfect fit and want it, but they will say no just because it's human nature. Good persuaders don't take "no" for an answer. If they know their product is what the prospect needs and is looking for, they keep pursuing. Persuasion is getting the other person to want what you want and to like it. This can only happen with honorable persistence.

Building Suspense and Distraction

The element of mystery can be effectively employed to involve your audience. We are all naturally curious about the unknown. When we feel we've been left hanging, it drives us crazy! We want to know the end of the story. We want our tasks to be completed so we can check them off our list. This is also known as the "Zeigarnik Effect," named after Bluma Zeigarnik, a Russian psychologist. This effect is the tendency we have to remember uncompleted thoughts, ideas, or tasks more than completed ones.

We see the Zeigarnik Effect on the television news and other programs. Right before a commercial break, the newscasters announce some interesting tidbit that will come later in the hour. This piques your interest and, rather than flipping the channel, you stay tuned. Movies and dramas on television also leave you hanging in suspense. By leaving something uncompleted right before the commercial break, the programs draw our attention, keep us involved, and motivate us to continue watching. We don't feel satisfaction until we receive finality, closure, or resolution to the message, our goals, or any aspect of our life.

You also see the Zeigarnik Effect in the courtroom. We already know that people feel more confident and impressed with information they discover for themselves over time. This dictates that persuaders slowly dispel information, rather than dumping large volumes of information all at once. A good lawyer does not disclose everything he knows about the case or the plaintiff during his opening statement. As the trial progresses, the jury can fill in the blanks for themselves with the additional information they gradually receive. This works much better than dumping all the information on them in the beginning. It holds the jurors' attention longer and gives the message more validity. The jury discovers the answers for themselves, and is more likely to arrive at the desired conclusion.

Distraction has been proven to increase your ability to persuade. On the flip side, if the distraction is disagreeable, your persuasive ability will diminish. This means, depending on the situation, you can persuade better with a distraction than with total concentration. Social psychologists Leon Festinger and Nathan Maccoby proved this theory with their landmark study on what are the best distracters. They discovered that food and sex appeal worked the best.[23]

In another experiment, the two men attempted to persuade college students that fraternities are bad.[24] Their presentation was not well received by the students, so they did the experiment a second time. This time they used a funny silent movie during the presentation. The results were clear. More of the students who were distracted with the silent movie changed their opinions about fraternities. In this study, distracting the conscious mind increased the persuasiveness of the message.

Generating Competition

Most humans are very competitive. When you package something as a competition, most people will want to be involved. Certainly some personality types shy away from competition, but most people are naturally *competitive*. Master Persuaders must be able to see how the use of competition works within the group they are dealing with. As you introduce competition into your presentation, you can create rivalry between different entities. Maybe you are using a competition where each individual is competing against himself or perhaps you create competition among the individual members of the group. Maybe you are pitting the group against another group or perhaps you are trying to get them to compete against the status quo.

All of these approaches will create involvement, but the most effective way may be to get the whole group working together against a common enemy. When you can create a unity of competition against an enemy, you will see more energy, teamwork, and motivation toward the goal. The fastest way to set up this type of competition within a group is to either create an external threat or to simply set your group against another group.

A group of researchers wanted to test the effectiveness of competition as a motivator at a summer camp for boys. As you might imagine, it was pretty easy to create an atmosphere of competition. In fact, simply separating the boys into two cabins created sentiments of "we versus they." The competitive feelings between the two groups grew as increasingly competitive activities were introduced. For example, as the boys became involved in cabin-against-cabin treasure hunts, tugs-of-war, and other athletic team competitions, name-calling and scuffles grew more common.

The researchers then sought to see whether they could use the competitiveness to create cooperation toward something mutually productive and beneficial. The researchers set conditions so that if the boys didn't work together, they were all at a disadvantage and, conversely, if the boys did work together, all had the advantage. For example, the truck going into town for food was stuck. It required all the boys helping and pushing to get it on the road again. When the boys were told there was a great movie available to rent but no money to rent it, the boys pooled their resources and enjoyed the movie together.[25]

Engaging the Five Senses

We were all born with five senses, each helping us to make generalizations about the world. You should engage all five sensations when trying to persuade an audience. When we learn, 75 percent comes to us visually, 13 percent comes through hearing, and 12 percent comes through smell, taste and touch.[26]

However, keep in mind that there are three dominant senses we gravitate toward. They are sight, hearing, and feeling, or, visual, auditory, and kinesthetic sensations. Most people tend to favor one of these perceptions over the others. As a Master Persuader, you need to identify and use your prospect's dominant perspective on the world. Granted, we generally make use of all three senses, but the point is to find the dominant perception. As you determine the dominant mode, consider the size of your audience. If you are speaking to one person, for example, you would want to pinpoint the one perception that is dominant in that person. If you have an audience of one hundred, on the other hand, you need to use all three styles.

For example, if you were to ask an auditory person to be an eyewitness to a robbery, he would describe the situation something like, "I was walking down First Avenue listening to the singing birds when I heard a scream for help. The yelling got louder, there was another scream, and the thief ran off." A visual person might describe the same situation this way: "I was walking down First Avenue watching the birds playing in the air. I observed this large man coming around the corner. He looked mean and attacked the smaller man. I saw him take his wallet and run from the scene." The kinesthetic person would use this description: "I was walking down First Avenue and I felt a lump in my throat, feeling that something bad was going to happen. There was a scream, there was tension, and I knew that a man was getting robbed. I felt helpless to do anything."

The most commonly prevalent of the senses is sight, or visual perception. One study showed that those who used visual presentation tools (slides, overheads, etc.) were 43 percent more persuasive than subjects who didn't. Also, those using a computer to present their visual aids were considered more professional, interesting, and effective.[27] Visually oriented people understand the world according to how it looks to them. They notice the details, like an object's shape, color, size, and texture. They say things like, "I see what you mean," "From your point of view . . . ," "How does that look to you?" "I can't picture it," and "Do you see what I mean?" They tend to use words like "see," "show," "view," "look," "watch," and "observe."

Auditory people perceive everything according to sound and rhythm. Phrases you would commonly hear would be, "I hear you," "That sounds good to me," "Can you hear what I'm saying?" "It doesn't ring a bell," and "Let's talk about it." They use words such as "hear," "listen," "sounds," "debate," "silence," "harmony," "rings," "say," "speak," "discuss," and "verbalize."

Kinesthetic people go with what they feel, not only in a tactile way, but also internally. They are very into feelings and emotions. A kinesthetic person would say things like, "That feels right to me," "I will be in touch with you," "Do you feel that?" "I understand how you feel," and "I can sense it."

They use words such as "feel," "touch," "hold," "connect," "reach," "unite," "grasp," "tension," "sense," "lift," and "understand."

One last word on visual, auditory, and kinesthetic sensations: A general way to tell which type describes a particular person is to watch the movement of their eyes when they have to think about a question. Ask them a question, watch their eyes, and make sure the question is difficult enough that they have to ponder for a moment. Generally, but not 100 percent of the time, if they look up when they think, they are visual. When they look to either side, they are usually auditory. When they look down, they are kinesthetic. I am simplifying a complicated science, but if you try it, you will be amazed at the accuracy of this technique.

12

The Law of Esteem
How Praise Releases Energy

I can live for two months on a good compliment.
—MARK TWAIN

THE LAW OF ESTEEM recognizes that all humans need and want praise, recognition, and acceptance. Acceptance and praise are two of our deepest cravings; we can never get enough. William James once said, "The deepest principle of human nature is the craving to be appreciated." You can give simple praise to a child and watch them soar to the top of the world. We know how a simple thank you can make our day. Human beings have a psychological need to be respected and accepted. We need affection to satisfy the need to belong, we want praise so we can feel admired, and we want recognition to satisfy our need for personal worth.

In the persuasion process, it is essential to realize that people will act and behave in a certain way in order to validate compliments. If you present your request in a manner that compliments or builds up your listeners, they will be much more inclined not only to follow through, but to do so eagerly. Compliments have the power to change behavior because they make the recipient feel needed and valued. The individual now has a reputation to live up to or an opportunity to prove the validity of the compliment. Besides that, it's hard to not get along and comply with people who admire you, agree with you, and do nice things for you.

To use the Law of Esteem effectively, you must clearly understand the relationships between self-esteem, pride, and ego.

Self-Esteem
Self-esteem is the elusive aspiration of most people. It is a confidence or self-satisfaction in oneself. Where does self-esteem come from? The people who

are truly happy and comfortable with themselves are the ones who are able to live with and achieve what *they* want, not what they think *others* want. When people truly function in this manner, they are more pleasant to be around. They tend to be more generous, upbeat, and open-minded. They fulfill their own needs, but are careful to consider the needs of others.

People who possess self-esteem are strong and secure, meaning they can admit when they are wrong. They are not unraveled by criticism. Their self-confidence permeates into all aspects of their lives: their jobs, their education, their relationships, etc. After an in-depth study, the National Institute for Student Motivation even rated self-confidence as more influential in academic achievement than IQ.[1] Other studies have shown that self-esteem even impacts your income levels.[2]

Unfortunately, several studies show that Americans overall do not enjoy high self-esteem. Two out of three Americans suffer from varying levels of low self-esteem. In one survey of child development, 80 percent of children entering third grade said they felt good about themselves. By fifth grade, the number had dropped to 20 percent. By the last year of high school, only 5 percent of the seniors said that they felt good about themselves. To some degree, we all suffer from low self-esteem in different areas of our lives, whether it's our IQ, our looks, our education, or how we look in a swimsuit. The short list of symptoms attributable to low self-esteem includes: inability to trust others, aggressive behavior, gossiping, resentment of others, criticism of others, inability to take criticism, defensiveness, procrastination, and inability to accept compliments.

There are two reasons why our culture suffers so greatly from low self-worth. First, media and advertising continuously show us how we *should* look, what we *should* drive, what we *should* smell like, etc. The message is that we are never good enough with what we are. We see images of grooming, fashion, popularity, and attractiveness to which we can never measure up. These images constantly remind us that we need to improve ourselves and that there is always someone better than us. Secondly, we judge and measure ourselves not against our own norm, but against some other individual's norm. But because we think, believe, and assume that we should measure up to some other person's norm, we feel miserable and second rate, concluding that there is something wrong with us.

How does self-esteem affect persuasion? Author Elaine Walster Hatfield conducted a study that gives us one example. She found that a woman who is introduced to a man is more likely to find him appealing if her self-esteem has been temporarily injured than a woman whose self-esteem has not been impaired. This explains the good old rebound effect whereby a person quickly finds herself engaged in a new relationship right after one ends, usually with someone whom she wouldn't date under "normal circumstances."[3]

Esteem is definitely among the very top needs on the list of all the human needs. When you're in a persuasive situation and not sure what to do, helping your prospect feel important is a fail-proof place to start.

Pride

Pride is the exact opposite of self-esteem. A prideful person gets no pleasure out of having something, but only out of having more of it, better or bigger than someone else's, or something that no one else has. It is the comparison that makes you proud, the pleasure of being above the rest. Contrary to popular opinion, there is no lasting joy or fulfillment in pride. Peace and satisfaction will never come because the looming possibility of something or someone bigger and better coming along will always exist. One relishing their position at the top of the hill can never rest easy for too long.[4] Pride is a false sense of accomplishment because it is not based on true or pure motives. As C.S. Lewis observed, "Pride is a spiritual cancer; it eats up the very possibility of love, or contentment, or even common sense."

Pride is being secure in and taking pleasure in external things like possessions, degrees, influence, or position. People who have too much pride constantly compare themselves to others in an attempt to help them feel better about themselves. They love to gossip and pull others down. They are always concerned about *who* is right instead of *what* is right. They have a scarcity mentality that there never is enough for everyone. As Stephen R. Covey wrote, "An abundance mentality springs from an internal security, not from external rankings, comparisons, opinions, possessions, or associations."[5]

Self-esteem and pride are actually opposites, even though the terms are commonly thought to be interchangeable. Pride is usually a red flag for *low* self-esteem because people use it to cover their weaknesses and insecurities. People afflicted with pride usually have a low opinion of themselves. They often will bully or berate others to feel and manifest their own self-importance. With self-esteem, there is an internal security about who you are. You are fine with what you are and what you are doing. You like to help others and are not concerned with what people think. You like to lift others up and enjoy an abundance mentality.

Notice the comparisons between the two attributes:

Pride	Self-Esteem
External security	Internal security
Scarcity mentality	Abundance mentality
Comparisons to others	No need to compare
Value in possessions or positions	Value in self
Tears others down	Lifts others up
Concerned with who is right	Concerned with what is right

The Ego

We all have an ego, and at times a very fragile one. We all yearn to feel important. The ego, or the individuality of each person, demands respect, wants approval, and seeks accomplishment. Deep inside every man and woman is a desire for importance and approval. This ego of ours can cause us to act illogically and destructively, or it can cause us to act nobly and bravely. When our ego is starved, we seek nourishment for it in any way we can get it. Feed the hungry ego and it will be more persuadable. This hunger is universal; we need our ego fed on a daily basis. We have to have an affirmation every day that our worth as a human being is still intact and that we are appreciated and noticed. After analyzing many surveys, Researcher J.C. Staehle found that the principal causes of dissatisfied workers stemmed from the actions of their supervisors.[6] Those actions included the following, listed in the order of their importance:

- Failing to give employees credit for suggestions
- Failing to correct grievances
- Failing to encourage employees
- Criticizing employees in front of other people
- Failing to ask employees their opinions
- Failing to inform employees of their progress
- Practicing favoritism

All of these causes are related to a bruised ego. This is unfortunate because studies show that employees are most effective when they are recognized for their efforts. Psychologists at the University of Michigan found that the foreman of a construction crew who is interested in the people working under him gets more work out of them than the bossy type who tries to force them to work harder.[7]

In an interesting study, school administrators sought to find the ratio of positive to negative statements overheard in the schools' faculty lounges. Thirty-two schools throughout the nation were visited. Now would you be more likely to assume that there were more positive or more negative comments? Negative? Well, you're right, but you may not realize *how* right you are. Researchers were shocked to tally up the statements and find that the ratio was 6 percent positive statements to 94 percent negative statements![8] This is certainly a startling result for those of us who find ourselves in positions of leadership.

When you find yourself in a persuasive situation, it is essential that you seek to enhance your prospect's ego in some way. Too often we present ourselves in a manner that instills feelings of threat, competition, jealousy, and mistrust. When enhancing someone's ego, be sure your praise is sincere and genuine. When we solicit someone's *cooperation*, everyone wins. For example, what happens when a sales associate tells a woman she looks great in the dress? The woman changes back into her original outfit and heads straight for the register! She feels great and the associate gets her sale. Or how about when the lady in shipping says she can really tell you've been working out? You do your "Can you tell?" expression, and then the next thing you know, you're helping her carry boxes. You get to bask in the glory of someone announcing that they think you look strong, and then you're extended the opportunity to demonstrate your power and might.

We can all learn from General James Oglethorpe's example. The general desired King George II of England's permission to establish a colony in the New World. Yet none of his arguments or presentations, no matter how carefully crafted, won the king over. At last, the general had a brilliant idea. He proposed that the colonies be named after the king. Suddenly, the general had not only permission, but abundant financial means and even people to help populate the new colony of Georgia.

There is a particular set of ego rules that should be employed when dealing with a superior. If you are trying to impress your boss, you should approach it differently from how you would handle an employee. Always make those above you feel comfortably superior. In your desire to please or impress them, do not go too far in displaying your talents. Otherwise, you might accomplish the opposite of what you hoped for by inspiring fear and insecurity. When a student outshines the master, there is a blow to the ego. The master wants to appear more brilliant than the student.

Challenge to the Ego

Here's another very effective technique. Anytime someone challenges your abilities, especially your abilities to do *your* business, what's your immediate and instinctive reaction? To prove them wrong! Try politely expressing your concerns about your proposal and then watch the results. For example, if you said to a supervisor, "I'm not sure you're able to get those reps of yours producing, so I may hire a consultant." Don't worry, that guy will be on it, pronto! Or when you say, "You probably don't have the authority to pull this off," the prospect will make sure to show you that he does indeed have that power! When employing this technique, however, be careful to avoid damaging the ego. When you cause damage instead of producing a challenge, you will create an air of indifference from your prospect.

Another challenge to someone's ego is commonly used by sports coaches in a team environment. When during football practice a player is not putting in 100 percent, is late for meetings, or keeps making the same mistake, the coach has a perfect ego-based solution. He brings the team together and explains exactly what has happened with that particular player. He then has the whole team, except for the guilty player, run laps. This punishment is a challenge to the ego of this football player. Such a situation only has to happen once to be persuasive for each member of the team. Of course, the technique also works if the player also has to run with the whole team, but having him watch magnifies the results.

There are many challenging messages geared toward our egos. Think of a multilevel marketing meeting, where managers say they are looking for "go-getters" and "people who can take action." Or what about a teacher who tells the student, "I'd like you to do these *advanced* assignments"? I have seen sales representatives make a subtle attack on the prospect's ego when they were not getting the sale. They simply say, "I guess you don't have the authority to make that decision." You should see the egos take action! Another example is giving people credit for things they don't even know. When you give people credit for knowing something they really know nothing about, they generally will say nothing and allow you to believe them to be smarter or more aware than they really are. The catch is that they then will try to live up to the undeserved credit that you have bestowed upon them in order to lead you to believe they really are smart. You have heard such phrases as, "You probably already know. . . ." or "You will soon realize . . ." These are direct challenges to our egos.

Respond Instead of React

In persuasion, we are faced with the difficult task of building the egos of our listeners while placing our own egos on hold. In order to effectively persuade, you have to let go of your ego and focus on your objective. You don't have time to mend a bruised ego. Check your ego at the door and remember your overriding purpose. Focus on persuasion, not on yourself.

Ingratiation: Make Others Feel Important

Ingratiation is gaining favor by deliberate effort. Ingratiation techniques can include compliments, flattery, and agreeableness. Ingratiation can also involve a special recognition of someone such as, "We don't usually do this, but in your case I'm going to make an exception," or "I am personally going to take care of this matter and see that you get what you want." Many people consider ingratiation sucking up or brown-nosing, but it is an effective technique for making others more persuadable. The reason this strategy works is because The Law of Esteem increases likability and promotes an increase in ego.

   Research has demonstrated these conclusions about using ingratiation. In one study, "ingratiators" were perceived as more competent, motivated, and qualified for leadership positions by their supervisors.[9] In another study, subordinates who used ingratiation developed an increased job satisfaction for themselves, their coworkers, and their supervisor.[10] In yet another study, ingratiators enjoyed a 5 percent edge over noningratiators in earning more favorable job evaluations.[11] Ingratiation works even when it is perceived as a deliberate effort to win someone over. Our esteem is so starved that we accept any flattery or praise we can get.

The Leverage of Praise

Sincere praise and compliments can have a powerful effect on people. Praise boosts one's self-esteem. When you genuinely give praise, it releases energy in the other person. You have seen it and experienced it yourself. When you receive sincere compliments or praise, you get a smile on your face, your spirits soar, and you have a new aura about you.

Praise Others Daily

I think of all the funerals I have attended, and how all of them ended with beautiful eulogies. Why do we have to wait until someone is dead to say something nice about them? As Ralph Waldo Emerson put it, "Every man is entitled to be valued by his best moments." Men will sacrifice their lives for praise, honor, and recognition. We crave and yearn for a boost to our esteem. We all wear an imaginary badge that says, "Please make me feel important." It is criminal to withhold our praise when we see someone, especially children, do great and honorable things. Yet then when they do something wrong, we jump down their throats. Have you ever thought about how we would never think of physically harming someone or depriving them of food and water, yet often without reservation we hurt someone emotionally or deprive them of love and appreciation? George Bernard Shaw said, "The worst sin toward our fellow creatures is not to hate them, but to be indifferent to them." We should make it a habit to give genuine praise to someone every day. Don't wait for a reason or for something big to happen. Be generous with your praise. Praise makes others more open to persuasion.

How to Give Sincere Praise

Always be sincere. Even the most cunning flatterer is ultimately detected and discovered. Complimenting someone sincerely for something small is better than complimenting someone insincerely for something big and grand. If, instead of being constantly self-focused, we are attentive to others, we will always find building moments where we can deliver honest and sincere praise. Even Napoleon figured out that men will die for blue ribbons. Men will sacrifice their lives for praise, honor, and recognition.

Often it is more effective to praise the specific act rather than the person. This way, your praise is attached to something distinct and concrete. It is harder to be interpreted as flattery or favoritism when there is a specific and concrete thing you have praised. General compliments may have temporary effect, but can incite jealousy from others and create even more insecurity in the recipient because that person is often not really sure what they did to deserve the compliment. Then they feel pressure to live up to the standard you have set, even though they're not sure how or why it was set. They may even subconsciously fear that you will retract the praise because they don't know how to keep it. Things really backfire when that person feels mistrustful toward you. Did you ever witness coworkers gathering to complain after a "pep rally" with the boss? Instead of feeling inspired and motivated, everyone griped about how the boss was full of it. Of course, during the meeting, everyone played along, because it was their job and they had to listen. When a boss asks you to do something you do it because you have to. When someone has influence or is a leader you do it because you want to.

So how do you effectively give someone a compliment they can live up to without feeling anxiety? Instead of barking at your assistant, "Why haven't you finished these files?" say, "Thank you so much for helping me get these files done! I know I can count on you get them done in a timely manner." Because the latter statement incorporates your assistant's behavior into how you view her, you can be sure she'll follow through. Consciously or subconsciously, she will want to maintain the apparent image you have of her. Consequently she will continue that pattern of behavior so as not to disappoint you.

As a manager or supervisor, your responsibility to praise and recognize your employees is paramount. Regularly communicate the organization's changing objectives and priorities and show employees you feel they are important enough to be aligned with your goals. Invite new ideas from workers, stressing that there are always better ways to do every task. Trust workers by delegating responsibilities that give growth opportunities. Check with employees to determine what extra time or equipment they need, and work to provide them with these requests. Be fair to all. Playing favorites undermines morale. Praise each employee for any job well done; doing so orally is okay, but putting it in writing is even better. Want to know another plus? Sincere praise costs your organization absolutely nothing!

Effects of Praise

You know people are more likely to be persuaded to say "yes" when you make them feel good about themselves, their work, and their accomplishments. People will do almost anything for you when you treat them with respect and dignity and show them that their feelings are important.

I remember going to try on suits at the local mall. I was thinking about buying a suit but I was pretty indifferent about making a purchase that day. Because I knew the sales representative would want to persuade me to buy a suit that same day, I came in prepared for his persuasive techniques. He asked, "What type of suit were you looking for?" I answered, "Blue, double breasted." "What size are you?" he asked. I said, "I'm not sure." He looked at me with a twinkle in his eye and asked, "Do you work out?" I said, "Yes, I do." He said, "I thought so. You will need a suit that has an athletic cut."

I smiled and felt the rush of esteem. I knew he was attempting to sell me a suit, and it worked. I took the bait and he reeled me in. It was something so simple yet so powerful. Yes, I did go home that day with a new suit.

An experiment testing the effects of praise on a group of men in North Carolina was very insightful. The men received different types of comments from someone who needed a favor from them. The comments were either positive, negative, or a mixture of both. As you might expect, the person giving the positive comments was liked the best. Secondly, this conclusion held true even when the men knew their "complimenter" was seeking a favor. Finally, unlike the other types of comments, pure praise did not have to be accurate to work. Positive comments produced just as much liking toward the flatterer when they were untrue as when they were true.[12] Strive to be sincere in your praise, although flattery works even when it is not sincere.

The following example shows the immense strength that praise has. At a small college in Virginia, twenty-four students in a psychology course decided to see whether they could use compliments to change the way the women on campus dressed. For a while, they complimented all the female students who wore blue. The percentage of the female student population wearing blue rose from 25 percent to 38 percent. The researchers then switched to complimenting any woman who wore red. This caused the appearance of red on campus to double, from 11 percent to 22 percent. These results indicate that when you favorably comment on behavior, that behavior will increase.

Praise can also cause people to change their minds. In another study, student essays were randomly given high or low marks. When surveyed, the students who had gotten A's tended to lean even more favorably in the direction of the positions they had advocated in their essays. Students who had received failing marks, however, did not stand behind their previous positions as willingly.

When we show people that they are important, we can persuade them to do many things. In elementary schools, teachers will dub a child to be the king or queen for the day. The king receives a crown and the other students write notes of praise. Children keep these sayings for years to come, proof that no matter our age, we crave praise, recognition, and acceptance. For example, Andrew Carnegie devised a plan to sell his steel to the Pennsylvania Railroad. When he built a new steel mill in Pittsburgh, he named it the J. Edgar Thompson Steel Works, after the president of the Pennsylvania Railroad. Thompson was so flattered by the honor that he thereafter purchased steel exclusively from Carnegie.

The greatest car salesman in the world sends 13,000 former customers a card every month that simply says, "I like you," and then signs his name. You can calculate the expense, but this is the backbone of his business. No one has sold more cars than Joe Girard.

Of course, there is an opposite effect that also lasts a lifetime. I heard a story of a young lady who wanted to learn how to dance. She went to take lessons but she was having a hard time. The dance steps were unfamiliar and awkward for someone who had never danced before. The instructor gave her a few lessons and then unsympathetically said, "You dance like a hippo. You will never be a good dancer." This one comment kept the young lady off the dance floor for the rest of her life.

One negative comment has more power than ten positive comments. I can give a give seminar and have twenty people come up to me and praise me. But it is the one person in the front row, the one who had a sour face the whole time, whom I will remember. Just keep in mind that the use of praise affects the very core of our beings, so use it with caution.

Acceptance

Closely related to praise is acceptance. We all long for acceptance. We want to feel like our actions and contributions help an effort or cause. We want to be noticed by others. We all want to be someone of significance who is held in high regard. Knowing this, you can help your listeners and prospects feel that their help is appreciated, that they are personally accepted, and that their contributions are essential. When they feel accepted unconditionally, with no strings attached, their doubts, fears, and inadequacies will go out the window. Be kind, don't patronize, and be genuine in your acceptance— have it come from your heart. When that sense of belonging is established, you have tapped into a basic human need.

Have you ever watched a politician on the campaign trail? You always see it on television. Amidst the throngs of people, the candidate strives to shake hands and look into the eyes of as many individual people as possible. He wants his supporters to feel that their individual efforts contribute to the cause, that without their help, the cause would be lost. This personal touch boosts morale so that everyone wants to help out and will not rest until the candidate who reached out and shook their hand secures the victory.

Never criticize people you want to persuade or influence. It damages your relationship and destroys the connection you have with them. Instead, use praise and appreciation to increase acceptance and self-confidence. Many times an overly zealous boss destroys any possibility for loyalty and genuine compliance by telling subordinates why their ideas are stupid and will never work. Little does he know that these belittling comments will only make his staff cling to their own ideas and resent his even more.

One way to make people feel accepted is to offer genuine thanks. Seek to make a conscientious and deliberate effort to thank people. Don't assume they know you care and appreciate them. Don't make the mistake of thinking that a paycheck is thanks enough. One of the main reasons people are dissatisfied with their jobs is because they are never thanked or given any recognition for their efforts. It might seem unnatural to use thanks and gratitude, since most people were not raised in an environment where doing so was commonplace, but it's worth the effort to learn how to dole out thanks effectively.

Often individuals increase their feelings of acceptance by building their association with certain people, places, or things. This has been referred to as the Social Identity Theory.[13] For example, a sports fan may increase his self-esteem by plastering his walls with his favorite team's sports paraphernalia. Even though no one on that team has any clue who this Joe Schmo is, he feels better about himself anyway, just because of the association and identity he has created for himself with the team. Thinking back, why was it such a life-or-death situation to belong to social groups in high school? A sense of belonging is even more important to us as adults. Whom you know and what you have are in direct correlation to your self-esteem and acceptance.

13

The Law of Association
Create the Climate

It's not the situation. It's your reaction to the situation.
—BOB CONKLIN

TO MAINTAIN ORDER OF THE WORLD, our brains link objects, gestures, and symbols with our feelings, memories, and life experiences. We mentally associate ourselves with such things as endorsements, sights, sounds, colors, music, and symbols, just to name a few. This association allows us to make judgment calls when we don't have the required time to do thorough research.

Master Persuaders take advantage of association to evoke positive feelings and thoughts that correspond with the message they are trying to convey. In this sense, you, as a persuader, can actually arouse a certain feeling in your audience by finding the right association key to unlock the door. Associations are not the same for all people—obviously, each person has their own set of triggers. However, once you understand the general rules, you can find the right associations to match any prospect. And of course, some associations are universal for an entire culture.

The Law of Association is constantly at work. If an audience likes a picture, a logo, or a musical jingle that appears in an advertisement for a product, they also tend to like the product. Why is it we must dress up for a job interview? It is because we know a slovenly appearance will bring into bearing certain unwanted assumptions or associations about us. Have you ever heard about past cultures where the messenger was actually killed when he brought back bad news? Why do you think it is that restaurants decorate a certain way, have their lighting a certain way, and play certain types of music? All these things are defined in the Law of Association.

I remember having a corporate credit card when I was working for a certain unnamed corporation. The company had a nasty habit of not paying their bills. One day I got a phone call from a collection agency claiming that because my name was on the credit card, I was responsible for making the payments due. I informed the representative of the situation, but he was quite persistent. Of course, I was not responsible, but the interesting association was that the representative's name was Thor, the god of thunder (or so he said). The point is that if you want to create the feeling of a tough, persistent, strong person, then Thor is the perfect name to go by. Suppose his name had been Stanley or Herbert or Shannon instead? Not quite as threatening, are they?

The Amazing Power of Endorsements

We all know what endorsements are: Companies use famous people to pitch their products so we'll associate that individual and their success with the product. For example, Bill Cosby endorses Jell-O and Kodak, Michael Jordan pitches for Nike and Hanes underwear, and Tiger Woods does ads for Nike golf balls and Buick automobiles. We tend to like products, services, and ideas that are endorsed by people we like, regardless of the quality of the product. Sometimes, we will even buy a product for the first time simply based on a celebrity endorsement.

We naturally want to be associated with fame, fortune, and success. That is why we follow the lead of celebrities we admire, respect, and like. It's also why we use the products they endorse. It is amazing to see teenagers ignore their parents' warnings about drugs, but when their favorite star or professional athlete says it's not cool, they stop. This is the power of association.

All in all, the use of celebrities to endorse products is one of the most popular and effective associations marketers and advertisers use. Why do corporations spend tremendous resources to find the right spokesperson to bring the right association to their products? We hold our beliefs and attitudes to define and make sense of who we are. By shaving with the right razor or eating the right cereal, we are saying, "I am just like that ball player; I am part of the attractive "in group." By purchasing the "right stuff," we enhance our own egos. We rationalize away our inadequacies as we become just like our favorite celebrity."[1]

The critical factor in using a celebrity endorsement is creating an emotional tie or association between the consumer and the athlete/celebrity. The athlete or celebrity's positive associations have been transferred to the product or service.[2] Wearing the same shoes or driving the same car as their hero allows consumers to identify and associate with their idols.

There is a downside to using celebrities to promote products and services, however. Anytime a celebrity gets negative press, that association also tends to carry over to the products and companies they promote. In such cases, depending on the severity of the circumstances, the celebrities are usually dropped like hot potatoes. Michael Jackson was once an endorser for Pepsi until he was accused of child molestation. The company was quick to pair its product with someone else. Tonya Harding, the Olympic figure skater, was a Nike endorser until she was convicted of assault on fellow skater Nancy Kerrigan. Mike Tyson was also an endorser for Pepsi until he was convicted of rape. O.J. Simpson was once the spokesman for Hertz car rentals until he went on trial for a double murder.

Anchors: Capture the Feeling

Anchoring is a technique that captures the feelings, memories, and emotions of certain events, places, or things. The psychology behind the technique lies in the use of elements from a previous situation or circumstance to replay the emotions and feelings of that experience. An anchor can be anything that brings up a thought or feeling and reminds you of something you have previously experienced. It will usually reproduce the exact emotion or feeling you experienced at the time. Remember the experiment of Pavlov's dog? It's the same idea: You use a certain stimulus to create an association that will bring about a particular response.

An anchor can be produced either externally or internally. Anchors don't have to be conditioned over a period of several years to be established. They can be learned in a single event. The more powerful the experience, the stronger the anchor will be. Phobias are an excellent example: Most phobias are established after one single, intense experience. Here we'll talk about three different sets of anchors: smells, music, and symbols. There are other elements (sights and taste) that can be used as anchors, but these three anchors are the most powerful stimuli in evoking memories in our minds.

Smells: The Aroma of Persuasion

Our sense of smell is so powerful that it can quickly trigger associations with memories and emotions. Our olfactory system is a primitive sense that is wired directly to the center of our brain. By four to six weeks, infants can tell the difference between their own mother's scent and that of a stranger.[3]

Almost everyone has experienced situations in which a smell evoked a nostalgic (or not so nostalgic) memory. Think of the smells that take you back to your childhood. For some it is the smell of fresh baked bread, of freshly cut grass, or of the neighborhood swimming pool, etc. You can go back fifty years in a matter of seconds with the sense of smell.

Fragrances, aromas, and odors trigger memories, feelings, and attitudes in our minds. Smell can enhance or reinforce desired responses as well as positive and negative moods. There are multiple examples of this. Supermarkets with bakeries fill the air with the warm aroma of breads and coffee. Some children's stores send baby powder through the air ducts. When you walk through the mall, the food merchants will make sure you smell their cookies, cinnamon rolls, and Chinese food. Real estate agents are famous for having homeowners bake bread before they have interested buyers tour the house. Large amusement parks will pipe in certain scents at certain times of the day to trigger responses and get immediate reaction. The use of smell in these instances is an attempt to link the seller's products and services with a positive attitude, thereby inducing the shopper to buy. In the same way, you can link positive smells with your message to create a positive attitude in your prospects.

There have been numerous studies conducted on the bearing scent and fragrance have on association. A 1983 study conducted among undergraduate students found that female students wearing perfume were rated as more attractive by male students.[4] Scents were even found to improve scores on job evaluations in a study published by the *Journal of Applied Psychology*.[5] Of course, offensive odors can also be used (and actually have been used) to evoke a negative response. This technique was once used while campaign committees were rating and appraising political slogans. Not surprisingly, ratings for the slogans went down.[6]

Music: Feel the Beat

Music is much like smells in that our brains link music with attitudes and experiences from our past. Music is closely tied to our emotions. Think of the theme music from *Rocky* and then think of *Jaws*; the two movie themes evoke different emotions, don't they? Local gyms pipe upbeat music outside to get passersby to associate it with high energy and good times inside. In one case, a local convenience store had problems with teenagers loitering outside. The store owners wanted the teenagers business, but didn't want the drugs and fights that seemed to go with it. They decided to play a Frank

Sinatra song outside the store and soon found that the teenagers voluntarily stopped loitering.[7] You may still remember the particular song that played during the dance with your high school flame. Music has a powerful pull on us and triggers instant memories.

Because music is so powerful, persuaders need to carefully select the music they're going to use. Advertisers often use a popular song or a catchy jingle. Notice the next time you watch television how many songs you recognize from all the commercials—you will be surprised. Every time the ad is played, the tune reinforces the product's appeal. Music is universal because it has the power to evoke the emotions shared by all of humanity. We know music can soothe the savage beast or create instant energy and excitement.

The Might of Symbols

We live in an especially symbolic world. Symbols bypass our thoughts and our logic and they affect our perceptions and behaviors. Take gold, for example. As one of the world's most precious metals, gold is very symbolic of wealth and success. Countless stories are told of the search for gold. But, if you stop and think about it, there are other precious metals that are harder to find and far more precious. Gold, however, just holds a certain symbolism; it denotes success and wealth.

Symbols can also help us understand and feel a message without actually having to undergo the experience. For example, a skull and crossbones on poison says it all—we don't have to ingest the poison to know of the fatal experience. The simple symbol of a red stop sign triggers an automatic response. For many, the sight of a police car on the highway will also trigger the automatic braking response.

Think of these symbols as you read the list and pay attention to the feelings, memories, attitudes, and experiences they trigger in your mind:

- Crucifix

- Star of David

- Statue of Liberty

- World Trade Center

- American flag

- Swastika

- Military uniform
- Olympic symbols
- Wedding dress
- Christmas tree

When you are trying to mold attitude as a persuader, it is useful to know how symbols shape the attitudes of your audience. Make careful study and research of the symbols you want to use before you employ them. If used well, they will influence your audience's feelings and behavior to your benefit. Marketing and advertising executives use symbols in a very sophisticated way to manipulate consumers. For example, did you know that the average child recognizes McDonald's' arches before he or she is even twenty months old?[8] There are symbols of freedom, symbols of success, and symbols of poverty. Find and use the symbols you need to create the proper association with your prospect.

Affiliation: Create the Link

Another aspect of the Law of Association is the use of affiliation. Persuaders want you to affiliate their company with positive images, feelings, and attitudes. We tend to affiliate our feelings with our surroundings and environment and then transfer our feelings to those we are with. For example, one frequently used technique is to take the prospect to lunch. Why? Because people like whom they are with and what they experience while they are eating (if the food and company are good). The idea is to link something positive in the environment with your message.

For example, a good game of golf, a weekend at the beach, NFL tickets, or an exotic cruise would all typically build positive associations and feelings in your prospects. Do you remember ever noticing how, after a crushing victory, sweatshirts sporting the university's logo were seen all over the place? People want to be associated with winners. In fact, a study showed that when a university football team won, more students would wear that college's sweatshirts. The bigger the victory, the more college sweatshirts become visible. When you bring positive stimuli into the situation, you will be associated with the pleasant feeling you have created.

We are now going to discuss the four different affiliation techniques that are most often used: advertising, sponsorships, images, and color. Each of these has a unique role in affiliation.

Advertising: The Billion Dollar Persuasive Industry

Advertisers and marketers use affiliation to evoke valuable associations in the minds of their prospects. They know that babies and puppy dogs automatically carry great associations of warmth and comfort in the minds of their audience. Consequently, we see tire commercials with babies and car commercials with puppies, even though cars and tires aren't really warm and cuddly. These warm appeals grab our attention and create positive associations in our mind.

Want some other examples? Consider some of the popular slogans: "Like a good neighbor," "The same as home-style cooking," "Like a rock," and "The breakfast of champions." Using slogans in this way, marketers are able to readily create positive feelings and associations without having to create a new image. They simply create even stronger and more positive associations with what already exists.

One of the most common examples of advertising affiliation occurs in the alcohol and cigarette industries. How often do you see a lung cancer patient in a cigarette ad? Instead, advertisers in these industries use young vibrant people who are in the prime of their lives. The beer companies want you to associate drinking beer with having fun and attracting the opposite sex. Their ads portray images of men and women having fun, while surrounded by beer. Their message is, "If you aren't drinking, you aren't having fun." On an intellectual level, we all know that these are just advertisements, but the associations they arouse in us stick in our minds.

When companies need to change their image, they usually find a good cause to latch on to. They will typically find a good social or environmental issue they can tap into. For example, an ice cream company advertises their support for an environmental movement, or yogurt companies start a campaign to stop breast cancer. You also see patriotic endorsements being employed to create a positive association in your mind. The simple sight of the American flag, or the phrases "Buy American" and "Made in America," can trigger instant positive associations.

In the 1970s, the big American car still dominated the U.S. automobile scene. American carmakers had no fear of imported automobiles. There was a tradition in most families to always buy the same make of car. Imports were associated with being cheap, unreliable, and a waste of money. When the baby boomers came along, however, they became better educated and they refused to blindly follow the guidelines laid out by their parents. They viewed imports as having better gas mileage, greater reliability, and lower prices. During the oil crisis of the 1970s, the negative association shifted suddenly from foreign cars to gas-guzzling American-made cars, and the rest is history. American carmakers were almost put out of business by this shift, and they, still to this day, lose big market share to imported cars. As the tide turned, American car companies had to learn to make new associations with their cars.

Sponsorship: Lasting Impact

Closely related to advertising is the notion of sponsorship. Companies and organizations sponsor events that they believe will produce a positive association in the eyes of the public. They hope this positive association will transfer over to their company. The Olympic Games pull huge sponsorships—companies pay big money to get their name and products associated with the Olympics. What company wouldn't want to be associated with peace, unity, perseverance, determination, success, and winning the gold? The affiliations that companies create for us are very strong and memorable.

Let's try an experiment: Think about the following beverages and pay attention to the images that come to your mind while you do so.

- Dr. Pepper

- Pepsi

- Budweiser

- Schlitz

- Heineken

- 7-up

- Coke

- Coors

Try doing the same thing with the following cars:

- Volvo

- Toyota

- Mercedes

- Rolls Royce

- Hyundai

- Chevy

- Ford

- Porsche

Now try it with these companies and institutions:

- Welfare Department

- IRS

- American Red Cross

- Microsoft

- Enron

- DMV

- Exxon

- FBI

The companies themselves created these images and aroused feelings in you. Of course, we are affected by our environment and our experience, but we are also affected by the images these companies create for themselves and their products. Everything we buy symbolizes something.

Images: How to Get Through Their Guard

The images we see create attitudes within us. It is no random accident that most U.S. presidents have pet dogs in the White House. Consciously and unconsciously, we believe a loving, obedient, trusting dog creates a positive image of its owner. Voters would be more likely to reject a politician who preferred cats, hamsters, snakes, ferrets, or tarantulas.

It really isn't a secret that we are abundantly influenced by imagery when making everyday decisions. We are much more likely to donate to someone wearing a Santa Claus suit than to someone in street attire. We are more trusting of a sales rep wearing a gold cross around his neck. Sports bars decorate their walls with jerseys and other sports paraphernalia.

Credit card companies are among the greatest users of imagery and association. Because credit cards give us immediate gratification without us having to face the negative consequences until weeks later, we often think of the perceived positive associations before the negative ones. Consumer researcher Richard Feinberg conducted several different studies testing the effects credit cards had on our spending habits. He came across some very interesting results. For example, he found that restaurant patrons gave higher tips when using a credit card as opposed to cash. In another case, consumers were found to show a 29 percent increase in their willingness to spend when the merchandise was examined in a room displaying MasterCard signs. More interesting still was the fact that the subjects were unaware that the MasterCard signs were an intentional and calculated part of the experiment.

Feinberg discovered the same results when subjects were asked to donate to a charity. When the room contained the MasterCard insignias, 87 percent donated, as compared to only 33 percent donating when the room did not contain such signs. Ironically, credit cards were not accepted for making donations. The study produced startling evidence of how associations can be used to create greater compliance. A simple image, with its related associations, caused the subjects to be more liberal with the cash they had on hand.[9]

Color Triggers

Countless hours of research indicate that color does matter. Notice how fast food restaurants, schools, and professional sports teams all choose certain colors that "represent" them. You already know that colors can suggest a mood or attitude, but did you also know that color accounts for 60 percent of the acceptance or rejection of an object or a person?[10] These impressions don't change overnight. We all have automatic color triggers and hidden associations about various colors. Color impacts our thinking, our actions, and our reactions. Armed with this knowledge, we must take into account the association of colors in our persuasion and marketing efforts.

Color is a great persuasive device. Since we don't perceive what is happening, we don't develop a resistance to persuasive color techniques. This process happens at a completely subconscious level. Color is critical in marketing, in advertising, and in product packaging. Colors are not just for appearance—they have significance. The favorite food colors are red, yellow, orange, and brown.[11] These colors trigger automatic responses in our nervous system and stimulate our appetite. Fast food restaurants decorate with shades of red, yellow, and orange. These hues are known as "arousal colors" because they stimulate the appetite and encourage you to eat faster. Compare these bright colors to the calming colors found in fine restaurants. These restaurants tend to use greens and blues in their design schemes, colors which encourage you to stay and linger.

Colors can also be used to attract our attention. The shades that grab our attention are reds and oranges. The challenge is that each color has multiple meanings; one person might draw one meaning while another person might conclude an entirely different meaning. Red can be exciting to one group and mean "unprofitable" to another. To others it could signal "stop" or "danger." Red can denote boldness, aggressiveness, and extroversion, but it also represents anger, danger, sin, and blood. Yellow is known as a fast color and is the first color to register in the brain. Yellow causes you to be alert and watchful. The results of such research explain why new fire trucks and fire hydrants are being painted yellow.

An interesting study on the use of color occurred at the U.S. Naval Correctional Center in Seattle, Washington. The entire holding cell was painted pink, except for the floor. Many inmates at this stage of confinement were hostile and violent. The cell was painted pink to see whether the color would have a calming effect on the prisoners. Each person was only held ten to fifteen minutes a day in these pink cells. After 156 days of constant use, there were no incidents of erratic behavior in the inmates.[12]

What about the color of the pills you take? Research has shown that the color of medicine can change the perception or association of the pill. When scientists studied the drugs people took and the associations they formed of them based on their colors, they found that most people felt white pills were weak while black ones were strong. In another study, researchers gave blue and pink placebos to medical students, who were told the pills were either stimulants or sedatives. The students taking the pink pills felt more energy while the students taking the blue pills felt drowsy.

Color even enhances the perceived flavor and desirability of the food we eat. For example, orange juice with enhanced orange hue was preferred over naturally colored orange juice and was thought to be sweeter. This was also true for strawberries, raspberries, and tomatoes. The redder they looked, the more they were preferred.[13]

In one experiment, the flavor of coffee was manipulated by the color of the serving container. Two hundred people were asked to judge coffee served out of four different containers—red, blue, brown, and yellow. All containers contained the same brand of coffee, yet the coffee in the yellow container was found to be "too weak." The blue container coffee was dubbed "too mild." Seventy-five percent of respondents found the coffee in the brown container to be "too strong" while 85 percent found the red container coffee to be "rich and full-bodied."[14] A similar experiment was also done with women and facial creams. Subjects were given pink and white face creams, which were identical except for their color. One hundred percent of the women surveyed said that the pink cream was more effective and milder on sensitive skin.[15]

In another experiment, researchers gave subjects laundry detergent to test for quality. Of course, all of the boxes contained the exact same detergent, but the outsides of the boxes were different colors. The test colors were yellow, blue, and a combination of both. After a two-week testing period, the test groups reported that the soap in the yellow boxes was "too harsh" and the detergent in the blue boxes was "too weak." The detergent in the combination yellow and blue boxes was "just right." The findings indicated that the yellow represented strength while the blue represented antiseptic power.[16]

Original research into Cheer laundry detergent produced similar results. Louis Cheskin conducted research on three different color flecks in Cheer: red, blue, and yellow. Again, the detergent was the same, but the colors were different. As the research unfolded, subjects determined that the yellow flecks did not clean clothes enough, the red flecks were too strong, and the blue flecks were best for cleaning clothes. Colors play a large role in the success of a product, its packaging, or its persuasive ability. Color communicates and triggers emotions, moods, thoughts, and actions, all without words.[18]

Explore the following list to see some common color associations:

■ *Red:* strength, power, anger, danger, aggression, excitement

■ *Blue:* coolness, truth, loyalty, harmony, devotion, serenity, relaxation

■ *Yellow:* brightness, intelligence, hostility, wiseness, cheerfulness, loudness

■ *Green:* peacefulness, tranquility, youthfulness, prosperity, money, endurance, growth, hopefulness

■ *Orange:* brightness, unpleasantness, sun, warmth, bravery, invigoration, radiation, communication

■ *Purple:* royalty, passion, authority, stateliness, integrity, mysticalness, dignity

■ **White:** plainness, purity, coldness, cleanliness, innocence, hygiene

■ *Black:* desperation, wickedness, futility, mysteriousness, death, evilness

■ *Gray:* neutrality, nothingness, indecision, depression, dullness, technology, impersonality

Use Association to Persuade and Influence

The Law of Association is a powerful tool in helping you influence and persuade your audience. If used correctly, you will be able to create the desired feelings, emotions, and behavior in your prospects. It is in this way that you can use association to bring about the best experiences and create a persuasive environment. Whatever your subject is drawn to, impressed by, or desirous of, seek to incorporate it into your message, your product, or your service.

14

The Law of Balance
Logical Mind vs. Emotional Heart

When dealing with people, remember you are not dealing with creatures
of logic, but with creatures of emotion, creatures bristling with prejudice
and motivated by pride and vanity.
—DALE CARNEGIE

IN PERSUASION, your message has to focus on emotions, all the while maintaining a balance between logic and feelings. Logic and emotion are the two elements that make for perfect persuasion. We can be persuasive using only logic or only emotion, but the effect will be short-term and unbalanced.

Emotions create movement and action. They generate energy during the presentation and get prospects to act on the proposal being presented. The challenge with relying exclusively on emotion to persuade your prospect is that after she has left the persuasive situation, her emotions fade, leaving her with nothing concrete to fall back on. Logic plays the role of creating a foundation for emotion. This balance between logic and emotion could be called the twin engines of persuasion and influence. Master Persuaders know that each audience and individual has a different balance between logic and emotion. Your analytical type personalities need more logic than emotion. Your amiable personalities require more emotion and less logic. Always remember, you have to have both elements present in your message, regardless of the personality types listening.

In most persuasive situations, people react based on emotions, then justify their actions with logic and fact. A message that is completely based on emotion will often set off alarm bells on the logical side. On the other hand, a logical message with no appeal to emotion doesn't create a strong enough response in the audience. A Master Persuader will create a proper balance between logic and emotion in order to create the perfect persuasive message.

We are persuaded by reason, but we are moved by emotion. Several studies conclude that up to 90 percent of the decisions we make are based on emotion. We use logic to justify our actions to ourselves and to others. Take note that emotion will always win over logic and that imagination will always win over reality. Think about talking to children about their fear of the dark, or to someone about their phobia of snakes. You know it is useless to use logic to persuade them that their thoughts and actions don't make sense. They are still convinced that there is a problem.

This emotional pattern can also be seen in the way we buy and even in the way we convince ourselves of something. Our heads see the numbers and tell us to stick with a car that's more modestly priced, while our hearts see the gleaming sports car, telling us to go home with a Jaguar. Our heads tell us it's ridiculous to buy another pair of shoes since we already have fourteen pairs. We may even realize that no one is going to notice or care about the new shoes as much as we will. But our hearts win out, thinking of all the stunning new outfits these shoes will go with, and we go home with the new shoebox tucked under our arms. Our heads tell us not to believe everything we hear, that politicians are a bunch of liars, but our hearts are won over by their impassioned speeches.

Logic: What Stirs an Audience

Are we rational human beings? Do we follow all forms of logic? Do we only act if it feels right? Do we even want the facts all the time? Have you ever tried to persuade an emotional person with logic? We generally think we make decisions based on facts, but truly this is not the case. It has been found that when people agree with a particular message, they tend to perceive it as being more logical or rational. On the other hand, when people disagree with the message, they perceive it as an emotional plea.[1] The truth is that that our decision-making process relies on a mixture between emotion and its partner, logic. However, we cannot rely entirely on emotion until our logical side has been engaged.

In one study, twenty-one students prepared speeches that were written from either a logical or an emotional standpoint. The speeches were presented, filmed, and then evaluated by other college students. Interestingly, there was no real consistency in the findings except that speeches bearing a message that the evaluator agreed with were rated as more rational (even if they were intended to be emotional), while those the evaluator did not agree with were considered to be more emotional (even though some of those were intended to be logical). It seemed that whether a speech was considered logical or emotional depended on the listener. Researchers also concluded that, as a general rule, people seem unable to consistently distinguish between logical and emotional appeals.[2]

The logical side of an argument appeals to our reason. Reasoning is the process of drawing a conclusion based on evidence. For an argument to be legitimate, it has to be true and valid, and logical reasoning must be used to back it up. Many persuaders and marketers use faulty forms of logic, leaving gaping holes that require the audience to make assumptions and fill in the blanks. These are called logical fallacies. A fallacy is, very generally, an error in reasoning. It differs from a factual error, which is simply being wrong about the facts. In other words, a fallacy is an "argument" in which the premises don't completely support the conclusion. In the next section, some of the most common logical fallacies are outlined.

Common Logical Fallacies

1. *Faulty Cause*: assumes that because one thing follows another, the second thing was definitively caused by the first—also known as the *post hoc, ergo propter hoc* fallacy. *Example*: Shawn broke his mother's mirror, and sure enough, he was in a car wreck the next week.

2. *Sweeping Generalization*: assumes that what is true in most cases must be true in all cases. *Example*: We can't hire this candidate because he's an ex-felon, and studies show that most ex-felons experience relapses.

3. *Hasty Generalization*: assumes that a small piece of information is soundly representative of the whole situation. *Example*: I don't like Thai food at all. The food I tried at this one Thai restaurant just was terrible and I was sick for days.

4. *Faulty Analogy*: assumes that if two things are alike in some ways, they must be alike in all ways. *Example*: Britney Spears and Christina Aguilera dress the same and sing the same type of music, so they must have very similar personalities.

5. *Faulty Sign*: assumes that one event is a reliable predictor of another. *Example*: That guy is wearing a big Starter jacket, has a tattoo, and wears baggy pants. He's probably a gang member.

6. *Tautology*: defines an argument in a manner that makes it impossible to disprove. *Example*: You are a disagreeable person and, if you disagree with me, it will just prove even more how disagreeable you are.

7. *Appeal to Authority*: justifies an argument by citing a famous or popular person who also supports the argument. *Example*: Those shoes are great for Michael Jordan, so they'll be great for me.

8. *Slippery Slope*: assumes that a particular step invariably leads to similar steps, culminating with a negative outcome. *Example*: If I let one student hand in their paper late, then I'll have to let others hand theirs in late, too, and before you know it, everyone will be begging for an extension.

9. *Red Herring*: attempts to divert attention away from the real issue. *Example*: When accused by his wife of cheating at cards, Frank says, "Nothing I do ever pleases you. I spent a whole week cleaning out the garage, and then all you did was complain about how I'd reorganized it."

10. *Appeal to Ignorance*: uses a person's inability to disprove a claim as proof that the claim is right. *Example*: We know there are people living on other planets in other galaxies because no one can prove that there are not.

Evidence and Logic

Reasoning is a powerful tool for the mind, but strong, concrete evidence should be the cornerstone of a logical speech. Evidence not only makes an argument ring true in persuasive situations, but it also substantially enhances your credibility. There are four major types of evidence: testimony, statistics, analogies, and examples. You will strengthen your position when you use elements of all four forms, rather than depending on only one. When you provide proof in this manner, you remove doubts that may linger in your audience's mind.

Testimony

Your audience wants to know what the experts say about you or your topic. Testimony is the judgment or opinions of others considered experts in the particular field or area of interest. A testimony can be a quote, an interview, or an endorsement from a credible person. It can be implied with someone's presence (attending your event), picture (on your product), or signature (on your product).

Statistics

Statistics are numerical proofs of your claims. For example, "this demographic uses . . ." or "four out of five dentists recommend. . . ." Using graphs and charts makes statistics more memorable and leaves a greater impression on the listener.

Some people are suspicious of statistical proof, so make sure your statistics are credible and sound. Know where you got them and who did the research. People know you can arrange statistics to say just about anything. Use statistics sparingly and only in conjunction with other forms of evidence. Besides, a roll of statistics can be very boring.

Analogies

Analogies have a great impact in the mind of the receiver. They enable you to make your points quickly and easily in a way that prospects will understand immediately. ("Installing our new home security system is like having a police officer standing guard on your front porch twenty-four hours a day.") Analogies allow you to present a new and foreign idea and compare it with something similar that your prospects can relate to in their own lives. Analogies can also give us a new perspective on an old concept.

Examples

Examples can really make your evidence come alive. We love to relate to examples that bridge the gap between logic and our personal lives. Your prospects understand examples at a deeper level because they are based on common experiences and interpretations of meaning. Examples can be real or hypothetical and can include quotations, personal accounts, physical evidence, empirical studies, or published reports.

Compelling Evidence

As you prepare your message, understand that we humans aren't capable of absorbing all of the information you can gather. We are hit with data all day long and most of the time we don't absorb it. In fact, we are very selective in what we allow ourselves to retain. When we hit information overload, we turn our minds off and retain nothing.

A study on comprehension of television messages produced very revealing results. After watching commercials and other forms of messages, an amazing 97 percent of viewers misunderstood some part of *every* message they saw. On average, viewers misunderstood about 30 percent of the overall content they viewed.[3] Information is just poured out too fast. The evidence that you choose must be selective, precise, and powerful. You can't afford to bombard your audience with too much information.

When creating the logical side of your message, you have to understand the concept of the number seven. This is also known as channel capacity, which is the amount of room in our brains capable of storing various kinds of information. George Miller, professor of psychology at Princeton University, wrote, "There seems to be some limitation built into us either by learning or by the design of our nervous systems, a limit that keeps our channel capacities in this general range."[4] There is only so much room in your prospect's brain to absorb logical numbers and information. This is why phone numbers only have seven digits.

Spend the time necessary to fully research the types of evidence you want to use to strengthen your arguments. You already know that using the *right* evidence from the right sources greatly increases the credibility of your message. However, the opposite is also true; poor or irrelevant evidence undermines the credibility of your message. When compiling evidence, consider the following:

1. Use evidence supported by an independent expert rather than facts presented alone.

2. Statistical evidence will be more persuasive when paired with individual case studies.

3. Document the sources of all testimonials.

4. Use new information. Updated data with new facts or research is often more convincing than old data.

5. Use evidence consistent with your audience's beliefs. It will be more persuasive because they'll evaluate everything from their own perspectives and attitudes.

6. Build credibility by also acknowledging and even including the other side of the argument. A two-way discussion will bear far more weight than a one-sided lecture.[5]

Evidence works best when it is suited to the audience and their experience. Consider the following presentation points:[6]

1. Referring to evidence as fact increases its weight.

2. Evidence that is verifiable will always be more persuasive.

3. Evidence that is specific will always be more persuasive.

4. Unbiased testimony is more persuasive than a biased one.

5. Personal experience is more persuasive than not having any personal experience.

6. Presenters who have not yet established their credibility will benefit more from the use of evidence than those with established credibility.

7. Evidence is especially important when the audience is unfamiliar with the topic.

8. Factual evidence is particularly persuasive when the audience consists of highly intelligent people.

9. Evidence is more persuasive when you provide not only the sources, but also their qualifications.

10. Evidence is more persuasive when you confirm an audience's beliefs.

Emotion: Winning People's Hearts

Whereas logic is the language of the conscious mind, emotion is the language of the unconscious mind. We know that emotions are reactions to perceived and imagined stimuli, not based on logic, but on one's own personal experiences. Emotions often outweigh our logic. Imagine placing a plank of wood on the ground and walking its length a few times. Easy enough, right? But suppose you placed it a hundred feet in the air between two buildings. You *know* you can walk that plank—you just did it over and over again. Yet now, emotions and fears outweigh logic. Your "what-ifs" and your imagination supersede the concrete knowledge of your ability to walk the plank.

In his book *Emotional Intelligence,* Daniel Goleman asserts that understanding emotions is more pertinent to leading a successful life than having a high intelligence. Often people of high IQ struggle at work because of their weaknesses in fundamental human relation skills. Goleman calls this skill "emotional intelligence." He emphasizes that emotional intelligence largely determines our success in relationships, work, and even physical wellness. Emotional intelligence "is a type of social intelligence that involves the ability to monitor one's own and others' emotions, to discriminate among them, and to use the information to guide one's thinking and actions."[7] Emotional intelligence includes emotional management, personal motivation, empathy, self-awareness, and social skills.

When you are persuading someone, emotions provide the springboard for a successful execution of your argument. In fact, I would even say emotions are the energy and very fuel of the persuasion process. Without tapping into your audience's emotions, there is no strength or energy in your message. Emotion is a power you can harness and use in practically every aspect of persuasion. Remember, logic is important, but emotion helps you catapult an otherwise dull or flat exchange to the next level.

Consider the following advantages of emotion over logic:

1. Arousing the emotions of your audience engages your listeners and distracts them from your intention to influence and persuade.

2. Emotion requires less effort than logic. Logic solicits cognitive effort, whereas emotion is automatic.

3. Presentations aimed at engaging the audience's emotions are usually more interesting than logical ones.

4. Emotion-based arguments are often easier to recall than logic-based arguments.

5. Emotion almost always leads more quickly to change than logic does.[8]

You must know when to create positive or negative emotions and when to dispel negative emotions. You have to find ways to tap into your prospects' emotions, such as hope, love, pride, gratitude, and excitement. If you can do this, you can inspire anyone. Decide ahead of time what emotional climate you want to create, capture those emotions within yourself, and you'll be surprised how you can transfer those emotions to your audience.

Types of Emotions: Emotional Mastery

Over the centuries, philosophers have tried to categorize the very many complex emotions of humanity—no easy task. Aristotle came up with fourteen emotions:

- Anger

- Patience

- Friendship

- Enmity

- Fear

- Confidence

- Shame

- Shamelessness

- Emulation

- Contempt

- Kindness

- Pity

- Indignation

- Envy

Other philosophers argued that emotions are largely influenced by one's time period and culture. We will focus on a few major, elemental emotions, both positive and negative. In the persuasive process, you want to control negative emotions while constructing positive emotions. You don't want your message to end with negative feelings.

Worry

When your prospect is worried or preoccupied with something occurring now or that is about to happen in the future, your ability to persuade declines. Worry is feeling anxious, uneasy, or concerned about something that may or will happen, or has already happened. I have heard worry referred to as "negative goal setting." Anxiety creates tension—a fear that occupies our thoughts, which if encouraged will grow and continue to dominate our thoughts.

You can combat worry in your prospects by modifying their anxiety into thoughts of reality. Bring them back to reality by having them realize we can't change many things in life. Stress that most of the things we worry about are those very things we can't change and which won't likely ever happen in the first place. Help your prospects replace their negative mental images with positive ones.

Fear

Fear is anxiety or tension caused by danger, apprehension, harm, pain, or destruction. The possibility of harm can be real or imagined. Fear motivates and moves us away from unpleasant circumstances or potential destruction. Fear persuades us to do many things we might not otherwise do. Out of fear we buy life insurance, air bags, home alarms, and guns.

Fear does not work in every circumstance, however; if we were solely motivated by fear, we would never speed or start smoking. The proper dose of fear is essential in persuasion. If the dose is too small, it will not stimulate action. If the fear is too large, it will trigger resistance and acceptance will decrease.[9] For fear to stick and create action and persuasion, it must include the following steps:

1. The image of fear must be unpleasant, such as threat of pain, destruction, or grief.

2. It must be imminent. Your prospects must feel not only that the fearful event is likely to happen, but also that they could be victimized by its occurrence. They must feel vulnerable.

3. You must provide a solution to the fear. Give your prospects a recommended action to suspend or eliminate the fear.

4. Your prospects must believe they are capable of doing what is asked of them and that doing so will work for them.

Anger

Anger is a secondary emotion. A prospect's anger is usually an indicator that something else is askew and/or that he needs and wants attention. You can assist in diminishing his anger by determining the key issue he is upset about. It is also often effective to ask for his help, opinions, or advice. This will usually diffuse his anger or even change his attitude and demeanor completely. In some circumstances, you may want to use anger to make a certain point or to evoke a certain reaction.

Sympathy and Compassion

You can generate action for your cause by creating sympathy for it. When we see others victimized by misfortune that was beyond their control, we feel more sympathetic toward them and more motivated to help them. You've probably seen this technique used by marketers when they show you pictures of starving children, battered women, abandoned animals, and disabled adults.

Jealousy

Jealousy is the pain caused by seeing others' good fortune, not because we want what they have, but because we resent them for having it. The cause of jealousy is the false perception that one's worth lies in the possession of those goods.

Shame

Shame is pain and disrespect felt in connection to regrettable behaviors, experiences, or events. It often involves disgrace or loss of respect for oneself because we feel we have fallen in the eyes of our family, friends, or loved ones. We feel shame because of our vices, our abuses, or any of our perceived failures.

Pity

Pity is empathy we feel toward someone who has been unjustly trespassed against. We often feel pity for others due to death, injury, sickness, calamity, natural disaster, accidents, and so on. We can feel pity for people who are close to us as well as toward people we don't know at all.

Your Emotional Radar

When using emotions in persuasion, remember to pay attention to the circumstances that surround your presentation. Aristotle highlighted three aspects you should consider:

1. The nature of the actual experience (funeral, party, sporting event, fundraiser, or business meeting)

2. Those toward whom the message will be directed (blue or white collar, male or female, religion, race, common interests, or hobbies)

3. The likely emotion that will be created in participants (what is going to happen?)

Tip the Scale

As a Master Persuader you know how to use the dual engine of *Balance*. This dual engine allows you to fly straight and true in any persuasive situation; become a student of both logic and emotion and develop the ability to articulate logic that rings true to your audience; and learn how to use your human emotion radar. It will help you determine important aspects of your audience, such as what your prospects are feeling, what emotions they are trying to hide, and how you can use each of these emotions in the persuasive process. As a Master Persuader you know what emotion to use, when to use it, how to trigger specific emotions, and how to balance the audience's emotion with logic. Engineer your persuasive message with Balance.

15

Your Pre-Persuasion Checklist

The Inside Secrets of Maximum Influence

Before anything else, getting ready is the secret to success.
—HENRY FORD

TO BE AN EFFECTIVE PERSUADER, you cannot use the same techniques for all people all the time. You have to customize your message to fit the demographics, interests, and values of your audience. This chapter presents what I call the Pre-Persuasion Checklist. It will help you to effectively adapt your persuasive techniques to your target audience. The foundation of the Pre-Persuasion Checklist is rooted in a solid understanding of human psychology, the ways to handle resistance, and the methods of effectively structuring a persuasive argument. This is the knowledge necessary to make the Pre-Persuasion Checklist work in any persuasive situation.

All battles are first won in the mind. You have to be mentally ready to persuade. Prepare yourself by knowing as much about your audience as possible. The persuasion process can be thought of as "persuasion engineering." You have to draw up the blueprint for your persuasive techniques instead of "flying by the seat of your pants." It's like reading the roadmap before you drive. You need to understand where you are going, what route you should take, what the driving conditions will be, etc. Pre-persuasion operates the same way. Just remember the three D's: discover, design, and deliver:

Discover what your prospects want and need to hear.

Design and structure a winning persuasive argument.

Deliver the message with passion, compassion, and purpose.

We all have our own "personal code." As a Master Persuader, you must unlock your prospects' codes. Most of this code is hidden from the untrained eye, so you'll have to know what to look for. Consider how code is used in designing Web pages. We have all surfed the Internet and seen hundreds, even thousands, of different Web pages. Underlying each page is HTML code. This code makes each page look and act differently. Many pages have hidden code that is difficult to find and understand. Similarly, we each have code that is apparent and some other code that is *not* apparent. Our code is the sum of our beliefs, experiences, motivations, thoughts, attitudes, values, personality, and so on, that makes us who we are. The key for you as a Master Persuader is to decode the situation or the prospect, so you can know how to most effectively persuade your audience.

Finding and interpreting code comes with knowledge and experience, and the more knowledge and more experience you have, the easier it becomes to find and crack the code.

The following items make up the Pre-Persuasion Checklist:

1. Beliefs and Values

2. Change

3. Acceptance

4. Listening

5. Personality Directions

6. Persuasion Structure and Engineering

Monitoring Mindset: The Mental Game of Persuasion

Beliefs

Understanding your audience's beliefs will help you know what approach to take. Beliefs are those things we accept as truth, consciously or subconsciously, proven or unproven. Beliefs come from our environment, our culture, our education, our experience, or even through osmosis from our friends and family. One of the most common sources of our beliefs comes from being a part of a group, such as a family or a type of tight-knit community. People often take on the beliefs and rules of the groups to which they belong and then behave in accordance with those beliefs and rules.

Values

A value is more ingrained than a belief because it is more deeply and consciously committed to. A value is typically something that has been very thoroughly contemplated and accepted. It is for this reason that values are much harder to change than beliefs. Usually, a true value will not be changed, not even by wealth, acceptance, or pressure. Be sure when you are in a persuasive situation that your audience doesn't feel like you're trying to attack their values. This will only make them feel defensive toward you. As Walt Disney wisely stated, "When values are clear, decisions are easy."

Indifference

People who are indifferent most likely have never even thought about the issue, or they have had no reason to care about it. Indifferent people come across as greatly apathetic because the topic you are presenting is something they've never had to cognitively process before. People who are indifferent don't want to be bothered. These people usually don't care about you or your message. Often they're only there because they have to be, or their indifference is just a general lack of interest or boredom in general. An indifferent audience needs attention, empathy, and a reason to care.

Monitoring the Ability to Change: Getting Inside the Closed Mind

Life is change; persuasion is change. As a Master Persuader, you must be able to create and motivate change. Understanding human nature is knowing that most people will resist change and burrow into their comfort zones. We tend to follow the path of least resistance. However, change is the only thing that can lift us up from where we currently lie. Oliver Wendell Holmes said, "Man's mind, stretched to a new idea, never goes back to its original dimensions." We all want to become a better person and to be "stretched" to accomplish more things, but we are stuck in our daily patterns.

As you go through the Pre-Persuasion Checklist, find out how resistant to change your audience is likely to be. Will persuading them be like breaking through a brick wall or a cardboard box? Are they ready to make changes because of their circumstances and surroundings? Are they already trying to change? Some of your prospects will oppose you and blatantly resist your persuasive message. This is great news—this means they are listening and it's a sign of involvement. If the audience gives no feedback, then they are not involved in your message.

There are three ways people make changes in their life. One is through *drastic change*. This could be a heart attack, a personal tragedy, or losing a job. These events force people to change their lives. They did not feel a need to change until threatening, life-changing events occurred. The second is through *gradual change*. This is a process that evolves from events or personal relationships. Gradual change happens over time, so much so that you usually don't notice that it is happening. The third way people change their lives is through *internal change*. This can come from inspiration or desperation, but either way, you have consciously decided you are going to make changes in your life.

To get change to stick, you must make sure three things occur, whether within yourself or your audience. First, there must be a long-term, enthusiastic commitment to change. You have to decide there is no other option. The second thing is that you must be willing to pay the price, persisting even when you feel weak. Third, you have to know where the change is taking them. How is this going to affect their lives? What are the end results?

The biggest obstacles to change are lack of motivation, lack of knowledge, and fear. People will not change if they don't know where that change is taking them. We naturally watch out for our own future and want to prevent harm from reaching us. As a persuader, you need to create a vision for your audience, one that shows them what they will be like in the future. If you can get people to see themselves in the future and witness where that change will take them, they will be more willing to embrace change. Understand that people will resist change unless sufficient reinforcement and tools are provided to assist them. Without having this knowledge, their attitudes won't change, and if their attitudes won't change, then their actions won't change.

Monitoring the Acceptance Level: Determine Where the Audience Stands

An important part of the Pre-Persuasion Checklist is determining what the audience's current acceptance level is for the subject you want to present. Ask yourself the following questions when making this determination:

1. *Knowledge*: What does my audience know about the topic I want to talk about?

2. *Interest*: How interested is the audience in my subject?

3. *Background*: What are the common demographics of my audience?

4. *Support*: How much support already exists for my views?

5. *Beliefs*: What are my audience's common beliefs?

Understanding different types of audiences will also help you determine their acceptance level. Following are some different categories of audiences and how to deal with each of them.

The Hostile Audience

This group disagrees with you and may even actively work against you. For a hostile audience, use these techniques:

■ Find common beliefs and values.

■ Use humor to break the ice.

■ Don't start the presentation with an attack on their position.

■ You are only trying to persuade on one point; don't talk about anything else that could be considered hostile.

■ Because of your differences, they will question your credibility. Increase your credibility with studies from experts or anything that will support your claim.

■ They will try to find reasons to not like you; don't give them any.

■ Don't tell them you are going to try to persuade them.

■ Express that you are looking for a win-win outcome rather than a win-lose situation.

■ If possible, meet with the audience more than once before confronting them on areas of disagreement.

- Show them you've done your homework.

- Respect their feelings, values, and integrity.

- Use logical reasoning as clearly and as carefully as possible.

- Use the Law of Connectivity and the Law of Balance.

The Neutral or Indifferent Audience

This audience understands your position but doesn't care about the outcome. The key to dealing with this group is creating motivation and energy—be dynamic. To persuade the indifferent audience:

- Spell out the benefits to them or the things around them.

- Point out the downside of not accepting your proposals.

- Grab their attention by using a story. Make them care by showing them how the topic affects them.

- Get them to feel connected to your issues.

- Avoid complex arguments.

- Use concrete examples with familiar situations or events.

- Identify why they should care.

- Use the Law of Involvement and the Law of Social Validation.

The Uninformed Audience

An uninformed audience lacks the information they need to be convinced. To persuade them, you should employ the following tactics:

- Encourage them to ask questions throughout the presentation.

- Keep the facts simple and straightforward.

- Find out why they are uninformed.

- Use examples and simple statistics.

- Quote experts the audience respects.

- Stress your credibility, such as degrees, special expertise, and experience.

- Make your message interesting in order to keep their attention.

- Use the Law of Dissonance and the Law of Scarcity.

The Supportive Audience

A supportive audience already agrees with you. You may think that persuading these people is easy, but remember that your goal is to get them to take action, not necessarily to just agree with you. These techniques should be used with a supportive audience:

- Increase energy and enthusiasm with inspiration.

- Prepare them for future attacks by inoculating them against other arguments.

- Get them to take action and to support your cause.

- Let them know what needs to be done.

- Use testimonials to intensify the commitment.

- Use the Law of Esteem and the Law of Expectation.

Most audiences are a mix of all four of these types. Find out the dominant audience type that will be present and tailor your remarks accordingly. Of course, mix in some techniques from the other three areas since your prospects will always be a blend of all four.

The Persuasion Pitfall

Understand your audience and what laws of persuasion you are going to use on them. There are times and situations where certain persuasive laws or techniques are not appropriate. You cannot treat every person or every audience the same way. If you take persuasion too far, you will run into what I call the Persuasion Pitfall.

People are persuaded and influenced until they feel cheated, misled, or taken advantage of, and then they never tell you about their feelings or do business with you again.

In sales and marketing, we have a tendency push the envelope a little too hard when trying to persuade others. This could be in a personal one-on-

one encounter with a friend or in a visit to the local furniture store. Persuaders who do not possess the ability to read others or who do not have the skills necessary to persuade typically fall victim to the Persuasion Pitfall. They will take persuasion a little too far, using extreme pressure or trying to sell you a product you don't need or want. Use persuasion, influence, or power the wrong way and people lose all trust in you, never to be persuaded by you again. When over-persuading, you do or say something that sets off silent alarms in you prospects' minds. It could be a feeling of uneasiness, or a bad feeling toward you, your store, or your product.

This pitfall also includes selling a faulty product. The challenge with this pitfall is that 99 percent of the people in the world will say nothing to you about the defective item or about your over-persuading. They simply will never go into your store again. They will never want to associate with your product. Or, if you are a friend or member of the family, they will never trust or listen to your point of view again. This pitfall is a silent killer because most persuaders don't even realize the mistake was ever made. The duped person will never come back to the store and will probably tell others not to go back too. You have probably had this happen to you many times, at a car dealership, in retail stores, and on the phone. You have to have a sixth sense in persuasion and know how hard you can push.

We hate to feel manipulated or pressured. We have all been burned or taken advantage of, and when we see signs of such behavior we start to run. Many uneducated persuaders can be offensive, condescending, obnoxious, and insulting. Some people will need to have space, some will have to talk to a spouse, and still others will have to come back later before making a decision. You have to sense and know via knowledge and experience and nonverbal cues how many tools of persuasion you can use without running up against this pitfall. You have to sense your limits before you cross the line.

Monitoring Your Listening Skills: Crack the Code

Fortune 500 companies commonly require listening training, even though many employees think it's a waste of time. The truth is, poor listening skills account for the majority of communication problems. Dale Carnegie asserted many years ago that listening is one of the most crucial human relations skills. Listening is how we find out people's code, preferences, desires, wants, and needs. It is how we learn to customize our message to our prospects. Of all the skills one could master, listening is probably the one that will pay you back the most.

Good listening is not just looking at someone and nodding your head in agreement. You have to acknowledge what is being said and let the other person know that you understand. The more you can acknowledge what is being said, the greater ability you have to persuade and influence. Why? Because the person speaking with you will feel important and understood (Law of Esteem). Why is listening so difficult for most of us? Why is it that when two people get together and talk, they both walk away with two completely different views about the conversation?

Top Five Challenges to Listening Effectively

■ *Thinking About Our Response.* Instead of thinking about what the other person is saying, we often think about what *we* personally want to say next or where *we* want the conversation to lead. We are mentally planning our own agenda and game plan. In effect, we patiently wait our turn to talk but we never have give and take between the two parties.

■ *Not Concentrating.* We talk at a rate of 120 to 150 words per minute, but we can think 400 to 800 words per minute. This allows us time to think in between words that are being said. We can pretend to listen while really thinking of something else.

■ *Jumping to Conclusions.* Sometimes we assume we know exactly what the other person is going to say next and we begin forming reactions based on those assumptions. We start putting words into the other speaker's mouth because we are so sure of what they mean.

■ *Prejudging Speakers on Their Delivery and Personal Appearance.* We often judge people by the way they look or speak instead of listening to what they say. Some people are so put off by personal appearance, regional accents, speech defects, and mannerisms that they don't even try to listen to the message.

■ *Lack of Training.* Some people just honestly and truly don't know *how* to listen effectively, even if they want to. If they haven't ever had any training or guidance in how to listen effectively, they may not be accustomed to or even realize the mental effort or level of involvement really required to do so.

If you know how to listen, you'll always know what someone is thinking and what they want from you. Listed below are the insider secrets for effective listening. Follow these guidelines, and you'll always be able to get below the surface of your audience:

1. *Give them your undivided attention.* They are the most important people in the world to you at this time—make them feel that way. Don't get distracted by your surroundings. Stop talking and concentrate on them.

2. *Look them directly in the face while they are talking.* Lean forward to indicate interest and concern. Listen calmly like you have all the time in the world.

3. *Show sincere interest in them.* There is no need to talk. Just nod your head and agree with verbal sounds like "uh huh." Don't interrupt and listen for main points.

4. *Keep the conversation going by asking questions.* Prompt more information from them by repeating their phrases.

5. *Use silence to encourage them to talk.* You have heard that silence is golden. Being silent encourages your prospects to talk about themselves and reveal truths that will help you in the persuasion process. Pausing for silence shows you are interested in your audience and stimulates interest in the conversation.

6. *Pause before replying or continuing.* Wait three to five seconds and reply thoughtfully. Don't leap in, even if you know the answer. When you pause, it shows the other person you consider what they are saying is valuable.

If you apply your listening skills, you will be able to glean golden nuggets of information from your audience. Because you must adapt your message to the person you are talking to, there is nothing more crucial than listening.

Monitoring Personality Directions: Fine-Tune Your Persuasion Radar

The more we understand personality directions and personality types, the better we will be able to customize our persuasive presentations. A personality direction is the way we lean most of the time in terms of the way we act and react to most stimuli. We hate to be put in a box and categorized, but the reality is that (most of the time) we are predictable. Sure, people can never be 100 percent predictable, but you will be amazed at how predictable they actually are as you become a student of human nature.

Each personality direction will dictate how you customize your message. When you analyze personality directions, ask yourself the following questions:

A. Are your audience or prospects mostly logical or emotional?

Logical
__ Use their heads
__ Go with what makes sense
__ Are persuaded by facts, figures, and statistics
__ Rely on past history
__ Use their five senses

Emotional
__ Use their heart
__ Go with what feels right
__ Are persuaded by emotions
__ Rely on intuition
__ Use their "sixth sense"

B. Are your audience or prospects introverted or extroverted?

Extroverts
__ Love to communicate
__ Are talkative
__ Involve others
__ Tend to be public people
__ Want face-to-face contact

Introverts
__ Keep feelings inside
__ Listen more than they talk
__ Like to work solo
__ Tend to be private
__ Use memos and e-mails

C. Are your audience or prospects motivated more by inspiration or desperation?

Desperation
___ Try to get away from the problem
___ Are stuck in the past, don't want to repeat prior mistakes
___ Avoid pain
___ Want to get away from something

Inspiration
___ Work towards a solution
___ See a better future
___ Are motivated by pleasure
___ Want to move forward (have a vision)

D. Are your audience or prospects assertive or amiable?

Assertive
___ Consider results more important than relationships
___ Make decisions quickly
___ Want to be in control
___ Are task-oriented
___ Don't waste time
___ Are independent

Amiable
___ Consider relationships more important than results
___ Are friendly and loyal
___ Like to build relationships
___ Are great listeners
___ Avoid contention
___ Are nonassertive and agreeable

It is important to note that, when it comes to persuasion, personality directions most like our own personality type create a feeling of comfort and safety for us. Styles that differ from our own create tension and defensiveness. Master Persuaders can match all personality directions.

Structuring Winning Arguments

Why should we be concerned with the structure of an argument? Well, persuasive messages have several pieces that must be included. Just as Plato stated that every message should have a structure like an animal (head, body, and feet), so must our arguments follow an understandable pattern.

There are two basic elements to any persuasive message. These are the *substance* (arguments, facts, and content) and the *form* (pattern of arrangement). If you make up the form and pattern of your presentation as it comes into your head, it will be a detriment to long-term persuasion. A confused mind says "no." If the audience can't follow your facts or the substance of your message, their brains will not accept your message—there is no clear message to accept.

At one time or another, you have probably been in a classroom where the teacher has completely lost you. You had no idea where the topic was going or where it had been. When this happens, your mind stalls and the learning process stops. Confusion is a state of mind that creates tension. We hate to be confused. When we *create* this mental confusion as persuaders, we are shooting ourselves in the foot. Most uneducated "one-note persuaders" follow Harry Truman's advice: "If you can't convince 'em, confuse 'em."

Before we jump into the meat of this topic, remember as you prepare your persuasive message that you want to focus on one defined issue. You are not there to persuade on ten different points. Stay focused and steer clear of sensitive issues that aren't on your original agenda. In other words, don't inadvertently offend your audience on one issue when your focus in on another. The structure of your persuasive message should follow the pattern discussed below.

1. Create Interest

You have to generate an interest about your chosen topic. Your audience needs a reason to listen: Why should they care? What's in it for them? How can you help them? A message that starts with a really good reason to listen will grab the attention of the audience, enabling you to continue with the message. Without this attention, there is no hope of getting your message across.

2. State the Problem

You must clearly define the problem you are trying to solve. The best pattern for a persuasive speech is to find a problem and relate how it affects the audience. In this way, you show them a problem they have and why it is of concern to them. Why is this a problem to your audience? How does this problem affect them?

3. Offer Evidence

This is the support you give to your argument. Evidence validates your claims and offers proof that your argument is right. It allows your audience to rely on other sources besides you. Evidence can include examples, statistics, stories, testimonies, analogies, and any other supporting material used to enhance the integrity and congruency of your message.

4. Present a Solution

You have gained your audience's interest and provided evidence in support of your message; now you must solve their problem. You present the argument you want them to believe and satisfy the need you have identified or created. You have created dissonance and now you are providing the solution. How can your product meet their needs and wants and help them achieve their goals?

5. Call to Action

A persuasive message is not true persuasion if your audience does not know exactly what they need to do. Be specific and precise. In order to complete the solution to their problem, they must take action. This is the climax, the peak of your logic and emotion. The prescribed actions must be feasible. Make your call to action as easy as possible.

Using this type of structure facilitates people's acceptance of your message and clarifies what you want them to do. We all have a logical side to our mind, which results in our need for order and arrangement. If we don't sense some sort of structure, we tend to become confused and create our own organizational flow—thus creating our own solution. If you can't be clear, concise, and orderly, your prospect will find someone else who is.

In order to create a good structure for your argument and to reach your audience, it may be helpful to consider the following set of questions.

Ask yourself these questions in regard to yourself and your message:

What do I want to accomplish?

What will make my message clear to my audience?

What will increase my credibility and trust?

What Laws of Persuasion am I going to use?

What do I want my prospects to do?

Ask yourself these questions in regard to your audience:

Who is listening to my message? (Audience demographics)

What is their initial mindset? (What are they thinking and feeling now?)

When will the call to action work? (What do you want them to do and when do you want them to do it?)

Why should they care? (What is in it for them?)

In what areas of their lives does this affect them? (Health, money, relationships, etc.)

How will they benefit? (What will they gain?)

These questions should help you create effective arguments in each of the key areas: interest, problem, evidence, solution, and action. The remainder of this chapter will present a variety of techniques that will be helpful in structuring your arguments.

Giving a Call to Action

The call to action is the most important part of your presentation. This is where your audience understands exactly what you want them to do. It's where you define yourself as a persuader instead of a presenter. This conclusion should not come as a shock to your audience. Throughout your presentation, you should have gently led them to the same conclusion that you are now giving them. You should have already prompted them to want to do what you are about to tell them to do.

Some people hate this part of persuasion because they are asking their prospects to do something. This should really be the best part—the action is the only reason you are giving the presentation in the first place; your audience is going to understand that. If you become tense and uneasy, so will your prospect. The whole presentation should be structured to make the call to action smooth and seamless. In fact, the prospects should not even see or feel your call to action coming.

You should prepare your audience for this conclusion before you even start on the rest of the presentation. Your entire presentation should be built around the call to action. I mean, write out the call to action word for word beforehand. From the outset of your message, you must be eager to get to this point. Be positive and enthusiastic. In your preparation, make sure your conclusion is explicit and that the audience is not left on their own to make sense of and understand your message. You need to tell them what to believe; you draw the conclusion for them. Make the call to action easy for them to follow and simple for them to do. There should be no doubt in your prospects' minds about exactly what you want them to do.

There is a story of an old man who goes to a dentist because he has a tooth that is killing him. He has been putting it off for months and finally he has to get the tooth taken care of. Once there, the dentist agrees that the tooth needs to come out. The man asks the dentist how much it will cost. The dentist replies that it will be about $250. The old man yelps and yells, "$250 to pull out a tooth?!!" Then he asks how long the procedure will take. He is told it will take about five minutes. "$250 for five minutes of work? That is highway robbery!" the old man protests. "How can you live with yourself charging people that kind of money?" The dentist smiles and says, "If it's the time you are worried about, I can take as long as you want."

When planning and preparing your call to action, remember that the process does not have to be long and painful. Be short, brief, and to the point.

Structure Points

Once the call to action has taken place, your audience needs to remember, retain, and respond to your message. They have to keep doing what you want them to do. Have your points been memorable, easy to understand, and simple to follow? Remember, your message will boil down *not* to what you say and do, but to what the other person remembers. The following critical items must be included in your persuasive presentation.

1. Repetition

The use of repetition is very effective. We have heard that repetition is the mother of all learning; it is also the mother of effective persuasion. Repetition creates familiarity toward your ideas, and that leads to a positive association. When something gets repeated, it gets stuck in your memory. It improves your comprehension. You need to repeat your message several times so your audience understands precisely what you are talking about and comprehends exactly what you want them to do. You can repeat the message several times without saying the same thing over and over again.

My motto is: When you repeat, repackage how you say it. Each time you express your point, use new evidence and new words, so you don't sound like a broken record. When you use repetition too much, it might result in diminishing returns. You know how you feel about someone telling you a joke or a story you've already heard or about that commercial you've seen one too many times. If you've heard it a million times before, you tune out and quit listening. Keep your repetitions about each point to approximately three references, and definitely no more than five.

2. Theme

We see general themes in commercials and advertisements. A theme is easily remembered and easily retained. Attorney Gerry Spence uses themes during his court cases. For example, when a small ice cream manufacturer sued McDonald's for breach of oral contract, Spence centered his whole argument and position around the theme, "Let's put honor back into the handshake." The jury was won over and Spence's client was awarded $52 million. In another case, Spence's client was suing an insurance company for quadriplegic fraud. This time, Spence's theme was: "Human need versus corporate greed." The insurance company ended up having to shell out $33.5 million *plus* the interest on $10 million.

Having a theme will give your presentation flow, order, and presence in the minds of your audience members. Themes provide an easy way for people to remember the heart of your message. If you have strong and well-organized themes, you can be sure your audience will understand and remember your message more clearly and more strongly.

3. Brevity and Simplicity

Keep your message short and simple. Boring an audience to tears has never yet worked as an effective persuasive technique. If the message is short and simple, it will most likely be clearer and therefore easier to remember. Consider the profundity of Abraham Lincoln's historical Gettysburg Address. The whole speech, from start to finish, was only 269 words. He presented it in less than three minutes.

The Gettysburg Address

Four score and seven years ago our fathers brought forth on this continent a new nation, conceived in liberty and dedicated to the proposition that all men are created equal. Now we are engaged in a great civil war, testing whether that nation or any nation so conceived and so dedicated can long endure. We are met on a great battlefield of that war. We have come to dedicate a portion of that field as a final resting-place for those who here gave their lives that that nation might live. It is altogether fitting and proper that we should do this. But in a larger sense, we cannot dedicate, we cannot consecrate, we cannot hallow this ground. The brave men, living and dead who struggled here have consecrated it far above our poor power to add or detract. The world will little note nor long remember what we say here, but it can never forget what they did here. It is for us the living rather to be dedicated here to the unfinished work, which they who fought here have thus far so nobly advanced. It is rather for us to be here dedicated to the great task remaining before us—that from these honored dead we take increased devotion to that cause for which they gave the last full measure of devotion—that we here highly resolve that these dead shall not have died in vain, that this nation under God shall have a new birth of freedom, and that government of the people, by the people, for the people shall not perish from the earth.

How about Winston Churchill's "blood, sweat, and tears" speech? He read it in less than two and a half minutes. Even Nelson Mandela's famous speech signaling the end of apartheid—a speech he gave after twenty-seven years of imprisonment—lasted only five minutes.

Make sure your speech is articulate and intelligent, but be careful not to use esoteric language. Use simple terms and jargon that are familiar to your audience. Complexity will not impress them; rather it will muddle your message. Make your points simple, clear, and direct. Avoid facts, figures, examples, questions, or anything else that—if used ineffectively—might complicate your message.

Conversely, if you are trying to *dissuade*, use all the complexity you want. If a person feels confused, perplexed, bewildered, etc., well, as they say, a confused mind says, "No!"

4. Primacy and Recency Effects

Timing is everything. The Primacy and Recency Effects refer to timing your message so it will have its greatest impact. The "Primacy Effect" refers to the impact of points made at the beginning of a presentation, and the "Recency Effect" refers to the impact of information presented at the end of a presentation. These effects can be powerful presentation tools since it is typically the very first and very last parts of your presentation that bear the strongest weight in your audience's overall impression. These impressions will linger longer than anything else about the presentation. Your first and final words determine how you will be remembered and thought of long after your speech has ended. Be sure you carefully craft your opening and closing statements, placing your strongest points at those times.

5. Offer Choices

There is a strange psychological phenomenon in regard to drawing conclusions. If someone tells us exactly what to do, our tendency is to reject that dictated choice when we feel it is our only option. The solution is to offer your prospects a few options so that they can make the choice for themselves. People feel the need to have freedom and make their own choices. If forced to choose something against their will, they experience psychological resistance and feel a need to restore their freedom.

We all need options. Recently, I saw a young moose get surrounded by people who wanted a picture of it. Feeling trapped, this moose charged at the people in an attempt to escape. This type of scenario can also present itself in your persuasive efforts. If you don't offer options to your audience, they could attempt to charge and escape.

The strategy is that you have control over your prospects' options. As a Master Persuader, you only give them options that will satisfy your situation. We have all done this with children: Do you want to finish your dinner or go to bed early? In sales, they call this strategy the alternative close. For example, have you heard the line, "Do you want regular or deluxe?" Or what about, "Do you want it in blue or green?" or "Do you want to meet Monday afternoon or Tuesday evening?" The person has options, but both options meet the persuader's goals.

Even if it is just something simple, people need to have options. I heard a story of one lady who desperately needed to take her medication or she would die. Her doctor, nurse, son, and husband all tried to get her to take her medication but to no avail. The doctor insisted she take her medication first thing when she arose in the morning, but she just wouldn't do it. Distraught, the family took her to a new doctor. This doctor immediately saw the situation and talked to the patient. He explained the benefits of taking the drugs and how it could help her. Then, he gave her an option. He said, "You need to take this once a day. Would you like to take it with your breakfast or your dinner?" The patient smiled and said she would like to take it with her dinner. After she made that decision, she no longer gave people a hard time about taking her medication. The key is that both options the doctor gave her were fixed to achieve the same goal.

If you absolutely have to limit your audience's choice to one thing, you must explain to them why there are limitations on their options. If the audience understands why a limit has been put on their freedom, they are more likely to accept it without feeling undermined.

On the flip side, try not to give your prospects more than two or three choices. If you give too many alternatives, your audience will be less likely to choose any of them. Structured choices give the audience the impression of control. As a result, they increase cooperation and commitment.

Offering choices is also called "binds." Each option offered gives the persuader what he wants without making him appear as if he is restricting freedoms. When you use the word "or," the very opposite is implied, so try to structure your choices with the word "or." For example, "Would you like to make an appointment now, or should we meet next week? I know today you will become involved in our product or make the decision to take it home with you."

Inoculation: Defend Against the Attack

During the Korean War, Americans were shocked at the number of captured soldiers who willingly cooperated with the enemy. Initially they wondered whether the soldiers had been tortured and beaten into submission. Investigation revealed that the soldiers had not been tortured, but rather that they had been subjected to brainwashing sessions led by a skillful questioner. Soldiers were questioned about American ideologies such as freedom, democracy, and equality. Surprisingly, many of the soldiers had great difficulty defending their beliefs. The captors persisted in attacking beliefs the soldiers couldn't explain until the soldiers began to question and doubt the validity of those beliefs. If the captors could get the soldiers that far, getting them to commit treason became much easier. New soldiers from that point on began receiving more extensive political training in addition to the typical military instruction. No soldier would ever again hold vaguely defined beliefs or be unable to defend America verbally or militarily.

How did the military train their soldiers to withstand the potential verbal attacks as had been perpetrated against them in the Korean War? What would keep them strong in the face of such adversity, preventing them from crumbling? It is a method called "inoculation." The term "inoculation" comes from the medical field: Injecting a weak dose of a virus into a patient inoculates or prevents the patient from actually getting the disease. The body's immune system fights off this weak form of the disease and then is prepared when the full disease attacks.

Likewise, when you are presenting and you know that there is an opposing viewpoint standing in the wing, you have to "inoculate" the audience with a weakened form of the other side's argument. If you know someone is going to attack your viewpoint, you prepare your audience in advance.

The idea is to address the issues that your opponent will bring up and then directly refute them. The point to understand is that the inoculation must be a weak form of the "virus." If you inoculated a human body with the strong strain of a disease, it could become sick or even die. The dose must be weak enough to prepare the body for the stronger virus but not so strong that it overpowers the body. In persuasion, you don't want to give strong doses. You don't want to give your prospects all the ammunition from the other side of the persuasive message. On the other hand, if you don't prepare your audience for what they are about to hear, the sting of your opponent's words, logic, or testimony might be too much for them to handle and they could switch sides.

We are surrounded by countless examples of inoculation, many of which can be seen used in the courtroom. The attorney stands up and says, "The prosecution will call my client mean, evil, a terrible husband, and a poor member of society, but this is not true, as I will show you over the next couple of weeks. . . ." So, when the prosecutor stands up and states anything close to what the defense attorney has claimed she will, the jury is prepared, thinking she is acting exactly the way the defense said she would. This gives the jurors a way to ignore or even discount the prosecutor's arguments.

Street gangs also use this inoculation tool. When they are attempting to convert someone to their beliefs and to join the gang, they will inoculate and prepare the future gang member by telling him his parents, teachers, and cops will encourage him not to join a gang. They will tell him all the reasons his opponents will give, fueling him with ammunition for the impending attack. This preparation enables him to handle the oncoming assault from parents, teachers, etc.

Society needs to understand the importance of inoculation in regards to smoking, drugs, teenage pregnancy, and others issues we know our children will come in contact with. Who should be the first contact with your children—you or the drug dealer? When you inoculate people, they can mentally prepare arguments supporting their stance. This reinforcement prevents them from switching teams. The more prepared they are, the more they'll hold fast to their attitudes and beliefs. The more deeply this reinforcement is ingrained, the more difficult it will become for them to be swayed.

When do you use inoculation? The correct answer depends on the composition and attitude of your audience. If they already agree with your position, you only need to present one side. If they disagree with you, you need to present both sides. If an opposing speaker is going to follow you, you definitely need to inoculate. Giving both sides of the argument works better with audience members who already know something about the opposition's strength. Inoculation works better with knowledgeable prospects because it communicates respect for your opponent's intelligence. If the audience is full of committed believers, you win points by acknowledging there is another position.

Inoculation increases your credibility and your ability to persuade. By presenting them with the other side of the argument, you show the audience that you know how they feel and think. You are not afraid of the truth and have done your research. You prepare your audience in advance about the negative things someone could say about you or your product. You will win a great deal of respect and power when you answer someone's questions before they even ask them.

When you know your audience, not only can you prepare for pending attacks, but you can also answer questions in advance with inoculation. This gives your listeners a solution in their minds. Imagine persuading prospects about the need to use your product. The competition will call your product the most expensive product on the market. You know this so you inoculate. You tell your prospects upfront that this is the highest quality, longest lasting, most expensive product on the market. You let them know why you are the best and the most expensive. Your product has won most of the industry's awards, lasts the longest, and gives the most value for the money. These arguments, strategically planted in the mind of your prospects, will enable them to access these facts when the competition belittles you or your product.

Preparation Is the Key to Influence

Pre-persuasion is everything. Prepare your mind, know your audience, know their code, and structure a winning persuasive argument accordingly. Know who, what, when, where, and why about your message and your audience. Master Persuaders know that information and structure are the seeds for perfect persuasion.

Epilogue

WHEN YOU FOLLOW THE PRINCIPLES, techniques, and strategies outlined in this book, your life will change forever. Get ready to find yourself in the driver's seat of life. Prepare to find yourself in a winning situation—all the time—no matter what your challenges are. Look forward to finding yourself among the 1 percent of the population who know how to control their destiny. You will be included among those elite few who can help and teach others to control their destinies.

Persuasion: The Gas to Your Engine of Success

The ability to persuade is powerful. Master Persuaders make the world turn. Remember the following guidelines as you to step up to your new place in the world:

- Persuasion makes things happen.

- Persuaders are the motivating force in our communities.

- Persuaders are the gas to the engine of our economy.

- Use these persuasion and influence tools to evoke good.

- Treat yourself like a do-it-yourself project.

- Continue to learn, apply, and use these principles.

- Become the person you want to be.

- Make the laws and principles you have learned in this book a part of you, so you don't have to think about them.

- Join the top 1 percent of persuaders.

- Make the world a better place.

- Influence others with integrity.

- Develop a rock-solid character.

- Learn to build trust and exude life-long influence.

- Persuade others with honor.

- Reread this book every year.

Find a product, service, idea, or cause you can believe in. When you know you can help someone with your product or service, you have a moral and ethical obligation to persuade that person to get involved with what you are offering.

Notes

Chapter 1

1. Amanda Bennett, "Economist plus meeting equals a zillion causes and effects," *Wall Street Journal*, January 10, 1995.

2. F. Roselli, J. J. Skelly, and D. M. Mackie, "Processing Rational and Emotional Messages: The Cognitive and Affective Mediation of Persuasion," *Journal of Experimental Applied Social Psychology* 163 (1995).

3. Aristotle, *The Art of Rhetoric*, translation by H. C. Lawson-Tancred (New York: Penguin Books, 1991).

4. Ibid.

5. Carl Hovland and I. Weiss, "The Influence of Source Credibility on Communication Effectiveness," *Walter Public Opinion Quarterly* 15 (1951): 635–650.

6. Aristotle, *The Art of Rhetoric*.

7. *Wall Street Journal*, December 29, 1998.

Chapter 3

1. R. E. Knox and J. A. Inkster, "Postdecision Dissonance at Posttime," *Journal of Personality and Social Psychology* 18 (1968): 319–323.

2. J. C. Younger, L. Walker, and A. S. Arrowood, "Postdecision Dissonance at the Fair," *Personality and Social Psychology Bulletin* 3 (1977): 284–287.

3. David Mitchie, *Invisible Persuaders* (New York: Bantam Books, 1988), p. 95.

4. C. I. Hovland, "Reconciling Conflicting Results Derived from Experimental and Survey Studies of Attitude-Change," *American Psychologist* 14, 1 (1959): 8–17.

5. J. Brockner and J. Z. Rubin, *Entrapment in Escalating Conflicts: A Social Psychological Analysis* (New York: Springer Verlag, 1985).

6. M. Deutsch and H. B. Gerard, "A Study of Normative and Informational Social Influence upon Judgment," *Journal of Abnormal Psychology* 51 (1955): 629–636.

7. E. Aronson and J. Mills, "The Effect of Severity of Initiation on Liking for the Group," *Journal of Abnormal and Social Psychology* 59 (1959): 177–181.

8. H. B. Gerard and G. C. Mathewson, "The Effects of Severity of Initiation

on Liking for a Group: A Replication," *Journal of Experimental Social Psychology* 2 (1966): 278–287.

9. F. W. Young, *Initiation Ceremonies* (New York: Bobbs-Merrill, 1965).

10. M. S. Pallak, D.A. Cook, and J.J. Sullivan, "Commitment and Energy Conservation," *Applied Social Psychology Annual* 1(1980): 235–253.

11. J. L. Freedman and S. C. Fraser, "Compliance Without Pressure: The Foot-in-the-Door Technique," *Journal of Personality and Social Psychology* (1966): 195–203.

12. R. B. Cialdini, J. T. Cacioppo, R. Bassett, and J. A. Miller, "Low-Ball Procedure for Producing Compliance: Commitment Then Cost," *Journal of Personality and Social Psychology* (1978): 463–476.

13. S. J. Sherman, "On the Self-Erasing Nature of Prediction," *Journal of Personality and Social Psychology* (1980): 211–221.

14. C. Seligman, M. Bush, and K. Kirsch, "Relationship Between Compliance in the Foot-in-the-Door Paradigm and Size of First Request," *Journal of Personality and Social Psychology* 33 (1976): 517–520.

15. J. P. Dillard, J. E. Hunter, and M. Burgoon, "Sequential-Request Persuasive Strategies: Meta-Analysis of Foot-in-the-Door and Door-in-the-Face," *Human Communication Research* 10 (1984): 461–488.

Chapter 4

1. I. Eibl-Eibesfeldt, *Ethology: The Biology of Behavior,* 2nd edition (New York: Holt, Rinehart & Winston, 1975).

2. B. M. Depaulo, A. Nadler, and J. D. Fisher, *New Directions in Helping. Volume 2: Help Seeking* (New York: Academic Press, 1984).

3. K. Gergen, P. Ellsworth, C. Maslach, and M. Seipel, "Obligation, Donor Resources, and Reactions to Aid in Three Cultures," *Journal of Personality and Social Psychology* (1975): 390–400.

4. P. R. Kunz and M. Wolcott, "Seasons Greetings: From My Status to Yours," *Social Science Research* (1976): 269–278.

5. Dennis Regan, "Effects of a Favor on Liking and Compliance," *Journal of Experimental Social Psychology* (1971): 627–639.

6. M. S. Greenburg, "A Theory of Indebtedness," *Social Exchange: Advances in Theory and Research* 3 (1980): 26.

7. Bob Stone, *Successful Direct Marketing Methods* (Lincolnwood, Ill.: NTC Business Books, 1994), p. 92.

8. S. H. Berry and D. E. Kanouse, "Physician Response to a Mailed Survey: An Experiment in Timing of Payment," *Public Opinion Quarterly* (1987): 102–114.

9. Ibid.

10. R. M. Groves, R. B. Cialdini, and M. P. Couper, "Understanding the

Decision to Participate in a Survey," *Public Opinion Quarterly* 56 (1992): 475–495.

11. D. Broeder, "The University of Chicago Jury Project," *Nebraska Law Review* (1959): 744–760.

Chapter 5

1. A. H. Eagley, R. D. Ashmore, M. G. Makhijani, and L. C. Longo, "What Is Beautiful Is Good, But . . . : A Meta-Analytical Review of Research on the Physical Attractiveness Stereotype," *Psychological Bulletin* (1990): 109–128.

2. R. A. Kulka and J. R. Kessler, "Is Justice Really Blind? The Effect of Litigant Physical Attractiveness on Judicial Judgment," *Journal of Applied Social Psychology* (1978): 336–381.

3. M. G. Efran and E. W. J. Patterson, "The Politics of Appearance," unpublished manuscript, University of Toronto, 1976.

4. J. Rich, "Effects of Children's Physical Attractiveness on Teachers' Evaluations," *Journal of Educational Psychology* (1975): 599–609.

5. G. H. Smith and R. Engel, "Influence of a Female Model on Perceived Characteristics of an Automobile," *Proceedings of the 76th Annual Convention of the American Psychological Association* (1968): 681–682.

6. M. L. Knapp and J. A. Hall, *Nonverbal Communication in Human Interaction*, 3rd edition (New York: Holt, Rinehart and Winston, 1992).

7. D. Mack and D. Rainey, "Female Applicants' Grooming and Personnel Selection," *Journal of Social Behavior and Personality* (1990): 399–407.

8. P. Suedfeld, S. Bocher, and C. Matas, "Petitioner's Attire and Petition Signing by Peace Demonstrators: A Field Experiment," *Journal of Applied Social Psychology* (1971): 278–283.

9. T. Emswiller, K. Deaux, and J. E. Willits, "Similarity, Sex and Requests for Small Favors," *Journal of Applied Psychology* (1971): 284–291.

10. H. A. Hornstein, E. Fisch, and M. Holmes, "Influence of a Model's Feeling About His Behavior and His Relevance as a Comparison Other on Observers' Helping Behavior," *Journal of Personality and Social Psychology* (1968): 222–226.

11. H. Russell Bernard and Peter Killworth, "The Search for Social Physics," *Connections* 20, 1 (1997): 16–34.

12. J. C. McCroskey, V. P. Richmond, and J. A. Daly, "The Development of a Measure of Perceived Homophily in Interpersonal Communication," *Human Communication Research* (1975): 323–332.

13. Bernard Asbell, with Karen Wynn, *What They Know About You* (New York: Random House, 1991), pp. 28–33.

14. D. J. O'Keefe, *Persuasion: Theory and Research* (Newbury Park, Calif.: Sage, 1990).

15. L. Zunin and N. Zunin, *Contact: The First Four Minutes* (New York: Ballantine Books, 1986).

16. Dale Carnegie, *How to Win Friends and Influence People* (New York: Simon & Schuster / Pocket Books, 1936), p.139.

17. Malcom L. Kushner, *The Light Touch* (New York: Simon & Schuster, 1991) p. 18.

18. Albert Mehrabian, *Silent Messages* (Belmont, Calif.: Wadsworth, 1971).

19. T. G. Hegstrom, "Message Impact: What Percentage Is Nonverbal?" *Western Journal of Speech Communication* (1979): 134–142.

20. Simon Ungar, Mark Blades, and Christopher Spencer, "Mental Rotation of a Tactile Layout by Young Visually Impaired Children," *Perception* 24 (1995): 898–900.

21. John Carton, "Nonverbal Decoding Skills and Relationship Well-Being in Adults," *Journal of Non-Verbal Behavior* 23 (Spring 1999): 91–100.

22. J. Kellerman, J. Lewis, and J.D. Laird, "Looking and Loving: The Effects of Mutual Gaze on Feelings of Romantic Love," *Journal of Research and Personality* (1989): 23.

23. J. D. Robinson, J. Seiter, and L. Acharya, "*I Just Put My Head Down and Society Does the Rest: An Examination of Influence Strategies Among Beggar,*" paper presented to the Western Speech Communication Association, Boise, Idaho (1992).

24. J. K. Burgoon, D. B. Buller, and W. G. Woodall, *Nonverbal Communication: The Unspoken Dialogue* (New York: Harper and Row, 1989).

25. J. K. Burgoon, J. B. Walther, and E. J. Baesler, "Interpretations, Evaluations, and Consequences of Interpersonal Touch," *Human Communication Research* 19 (1992): 237–263.

26. J. D. Fisher, M. Rytting, and R. Heslin, "Hands Touching Hands: Affective and Evaluative Effects of an Interpersonal Touch," *Sociometry* 39 (1976): 416–421.

27. J. Hornick, "Tactile Stimulation and Consumer Response," *Journal of Consumer Research* (1992): 449–458.

28. Ibid.

Chapter 6

1. Sharon Brehm, Saul Kassin, and Steven Fein, *Social Psychology* (New York: Houghton Mifflin, 1999), p. 213.

2. Douglas Rushkoff, *Coercion: Why We Listen to What They Say* (New York: Riverhead Books, 1999), p. 123.

3. M. Sherif, *The Psychology of Social Norms* (New York: Harper, 1936).

4. A. Tesser, J. Campbell, and S. Mickler, "The Role of Social Pressure, Atten-

tion to the Stimulus, and Self-Doubt in Conformity," *European Journal of Social Psychology*, (1983): 217–233.

5. D. L. Altheide and J. M. Johnson, "Counting Souls: A Study of Counseling at Evangelical Crusades," *Pacific Sociological Review* (1977): 323–348.

6. Craig Soderholm, *How 10% of the People Get 90% of the Pie* (New York: St. Martin, 1997), p. 69.

7. I. Sarason, G. Sarason, E. Pierce, B. Sherin, and M. Sayers, "A Social Learning Approach to Increasing Blood Donations," *Journal of Applied Social Psychology* (1991): 21.

8. A. Bandura, J. E. Grusec, and F. L. Menlove, "Vicarious Extinction of Avoidance Behavior," *Journal of Personality and Social Psychology* 5 (1967): 16–23.

9. A. Bandura and F. L. Menlove, "Factors Determining Vicarious Extinction of Avoidance Behavior Through Symbolic Modeling," *Journal of Personality and Social Psychology* 8 (1968): 99–108.

10. S. Asch, "Forming Impression of Personality," *Journal of Abnormal and Social Psychology* (1946): 258–290.

11. R. Fuller and A. Sheehy-Skeffington, "Effects of Group Laughter on Responses to Humorous Materials: A Replication and Extension," *Psychological Reports* (1974): 531–534.

12. T. Nosanchuk and J. Lightstone, "Canned Laughter and Public and Private Conformity," *Journal of Personality and Social Psychology* (1974): 153–156.

13. S. Milgram, L. Bickman, and L. Berkowitz, "Note on the Drawing Power of Crowds of Different Size," *Journal of Personality and Social Psychology* (1969): 79–82.

14. S. Fein, G. R. Goethals, S. M. Kassin, and J. Cross, "Social Influence and Presidential Debates," American Psychological Association, Toronto, Canada, 1993.

15. Kurt Lewin, "Forces Behind Food Habits and Methods of Change," *Bulletin of the National Research Council* 108 (1943): 35–65.

16. M. Gansberg, "37 Who Saw Murder Didn't Call the Police," *New York Times*, March 27, 1964, p. 1.

17. B. Latane and J. Rodin, "A Lady in Distress: Inhibiting Effects of Friends and Strangers on Bystander Intervention," *Journal of Experimental Social Psychology* (1969):189–202.

18. L. Festinger, A. Pepitone, and T. Newcomb, "Some Consequences of Deindividuation in a Group," *Journal of Abnormal Social Psychology* (1952): 382–389.

19. E. Diener, "Deindividuation: The Absence of Self-Awareness and Self-Regulation in Group Members," in *The Psychology of Group Influence*, P. B. Paulus, editor (Hillsdale, N.J.: Erlbaum, 1980), pp. 209–242.

20. E. Diener, S. C. Fraser, A. L. Beaman, and R. T. Kelem, "Effects of Dein-

dividuation Variables on Stealing Among Halloween Trick-or-Treaters," *Journal of Personality and Social Psychology* (1976): 178–183.

21. M. Cody, J. Seiter, and Y. Montague-Miller, *Men and Woman in the Marketplace: Gender Power and Communication in Human Relationships* (Hillsdale, N.J.: Erlbaum, 1995), pp. 305–329.

22. Cavett Robert, *Personal Development Course* (Englewood Cliffs, N.J.: Prentice Hall, 1966).

23. Festinger, Pepitone, and Newcomb, "Some Consequences of Deindividuation."

Chapter 7

1. See http://www.usatoday.com/life/special/jackie/ljack000.htm

2. A. Pratkanis and E. Aronson, *Age of Propaganda* (New York: W. H. Freeman, 1991), p. 188.

3. S. Brehm and J. Brehm, *Psychological Reactance: A Theory of Freedom and Control* (New York: Academic Press, 1981).

4. F. Rhodewalt and J. Davison, "Reactance and the Coronary-Prone Behavior Pattern: The Role of Self-Attribution in Response to Reduced Behavioral Freedom," *Journal of Personality and Social Psychology* (1983): 44.

5. J. Brehm and M. Weintraub, "Physical Barriers and Psychological Reactance: Two-Year-Olds Response to Threats to Freedom," *Journal of Personality and Social Psychology* 35 (1977): 830–836.

6. Thomas Hammock and Jack W. Brehm, "The Attractiveness of Choice Alternatives When Freedom to Choose Is Eliminated by a Social Agent," *Journal of Personality* 34 (1966): 546–554.

7. A. Tversky and D. Kahneman, "The Framing of Decisions and the Psychology of Choice," *Science* (1981): 453–-458.

8. M. Gonzales, E. Aronson, and M. Costanzo, "Increasing the Effectiveness of Energy Auditors: A Field Experiment," *Journal of Applied Social Psychology* (1988): 1046–1066.

9. S. Worchel, J. Lee, and A. Adewole, "Effects of Supply and Demand on Ratings of Object Value," *Journal of Personality and Social Psychology* (1975): 906–914.

10. M. Mazis, "Antipollution Measures and Psychological Reactance Theory: A Field Experiment," *Journal of Personality and Social Psychology* (1975): 654-666.

11. "The Beanie Baby Prices Are Insane," *U.S. News & World Report*, July 28, 1998.

12. B. Nalebuff and A. Brandenburger, *Competition* (New York: HarperCollins, 1996), p. 114.

13. A. Knishinsky, "The Effects of Scarcity of Material and Exclusivity of In-

formation on Industrial Buyer Perceiver Risk in Provoking a Purchase Decision," unpublished doctoral dissertation, Arizona State University, 1982.

14. D. Zellinger, H. Fromkin, D. Speller, and C. A. Kohn, "A Commodity Theory Analysis of the Effects of Age Restrictions on Pornographic Materials," Paper No. 440 (Lafayette, Ind.: Institute for Research in the Behavioral, Economic and Management Sciences, Purdue University, 1974).

15. S. Worchel, S. Arnold, and M. Baker, "The Effect of Censorship on Attitude Change: The Influence of Censor and Communicator Characteristics," *Journal of Applied Social Psychology* (1975): 222–239.

16. D. Broeder, "The University of Chicago Jury Project," *Nebraska Law Review* (1959): 744–760.

17. Worchel, Arnold, and Baker, "The Effect of Censorship on Attitude Change."

Chapter 8

1. H. H. Kelley, "The Warm-Cold Variable in First Impressions of Persons," *Journal of Personality* 18 (1950): 431–439.

2. E. Loftus, "Reconstructing Memory: The Incredible Eyewitness," *Psychology Today* 8, 1 (1974): 116.

3. Aaron Delwiche, "Examples: How Newt Gingrich Uses These Techniques," Institute for Propaganda Analysis, World Wide Web.

4. A. Pratkanis and E. Aronson, *Age of Propaganda* (New York: W. H. Freeman, 1992), p. 43.

5. Ibid, p. 128.

6. Gerry Spence, *How to Argue and Win Every Time* (New York: St. Martin's Press, 1995), pp. 130–131.

7. E. Langer, A. Blank, and B. Chanowitz, "The Mindlessness of Ostensibly Thoughtful Action: The Role of 'Placebic' Information in Interpersonal Interaction," *Journal of Personality and Social Psychology* (1978): 635–642.

8. R. N. Bostrom, J. R. Baseheart, and C. M. Rossiter, "The Effects of Three Types of Profane Language in Persuasive Messages," *Journal of Communication* (1973): 461–475.

9. John Caples, *Tested Advertising Methods*, 5th edition (Englewood Cliffs, N.J.: Prentice Hall, 1997), p. 31.

10. Bob Stone, *Successful Direct Marketing Methods* (Lincolnwood, Ill.: NTC Business Books, 1994), p. 4.

11. Steven Beebe and Susan Beebe, *Public Speaking* (New York: Allyn and Bacon, 1997), p. 293.

12. A. Mehrabian and M. Williams, "Nonverbal Concomitants of Perceived and Intended Persuasiveness," *Journal of Personality and Social Psychology* 13 (1969): 37–58.

Chapter 9

1. David E. Kanouse and Hanson L. Reid, Jr., "Negativity in Evaluations," in *Attribution: Perceiving the Causes of Behavior,* E. E. Jones et al., editors (Morristown, N.J.: General Learning Press, 1972).

2. J. M. Burger, "Increasing Compliance by Improving the Deal: The That's-Not-All Technique," *Journal of Personality and Social Psychology* (1986): 277–283.

3. I. P. Levin and G. J. Gaeth, "How Consumers Are Affected by the Framing of Attribute Information Before and After Consuming the Product," *Journal of Consumer Research,* December 1988, pp. 374–378.

4. A. Tversky and D. Kahneman, "Choices, Values, and Frames," *American Psychologist* 39 (1984): 341–350.

5. R. Cialdini and K. Ascani, "Test of Concession Procedure for Inducing Verbal Behavioral and Further Compliance with a Request to Give Blood," *Journal of Applied Psychology* (1976): 295–300.

6. Alan N. Schoonmaker, *Negotiate to Win: Gaining the Psychological Edge* (Englewood Cliffs, N.J.: Prentice Hall, 1999), p. 236.

7. John Mowen, *Consumer Behavior* (New York: Macmillan, 1993), pp. 81–84.

8. D. Kenrick and S. Gutierres, "Contrast Effects in Judgments of Attractiveness: When Beauty Becomes a Social Problem," *Journal of Personality and Social Psychology,* (1980): 131–140.

9. J. Freedman and S. Fraser, "Compliance Without Pressure: The Foot-in-the-Door Technique," *Journal of Personality and Social Psychology* (1966): 195–203.

10. J. Dillard, J. Hunter, and M. Burgoon, "Sequential-Request Persuasive Strategies: Meta-Analysis of Foot-in-the-Door and Door-in-the-Face," *Human Communication Research* (1984): 461–488.

11. E. Fern, K. Monroe, and R. Avila, "Effectiveness of Multiple Requests Strategies: A Synthesis of Research Results," *Journal of Marketing Research* 23 (1986): 144–152.

12. Daniel Howard, "The Influence of Verbal Responses to Common Greetings on Compliance Behavior: The Foot-in-the-Mouth Effect," *Journal of Applied Social Psychology* 20 (1990): 58–59.

Chapter 10

1. John Maxwell and Jim Dornan, *Becoming a Person of Influence* (Nashville: Thomas Nelson Publishers, 1997), p. 64.

2. R. L. Miller, P. Brickman, and D. Bolen, "Attribution vs. Persuasion As a Means for Modifying Behavior," *Journal of Personality and Social Psychology* 3 (1975): 430–441.

3. R. E. Kraut, "Effects of Social Labeling on Giving to Charity," *Journal of Experimental Social Psychology* 9 (1973): 551–562.

4. Kenneth Erickson, *The Power of Praise* (St. Louis: Concordia Publishing House, 1984), p. 56.

5. Miller, Brickman, and Bolen, "Attribution vs. Persuasion."

6. Maxwell and Dornan, *Becoming a Person of Influence*, p. 63.

7. Robert Cialdini, *The Psychology of Influence* (New York: Quill, 1984), p. 7.

8. Roger Dawson, *The Secrets of Power Persuasion* (Englewood Cliffs, N.J.: Prentice Hall, 1992), p. 29.

9. Wilson Bryan, *The Age of Manipulation* (Lanham, Md.: Madison Books, 1989), p. 189.

10. Milton Erickson, Ernest Rossi, and Sheila Rossi, *Hypnotic Realities* (New York: Irvington Publishers, 1976).

11. Milton Erickson and Ernest Rossi, *Hypnotherapy: An Exploratory Casebook* (New York: Irvington Publishers, 1979).

12. C. A. Mace, *Incentives: Some Experimental Studies* (London: Industrial Health Research Board, Report No. 72, 1935).

13. Mortimer R. Feinberg, *Effective Psychology for Managers* (Englewood Cliffs, N.J.: Prentice Hall, 1986).

14. George Kelling and Catherine Coles, *Fixing Broken Windows* (New York: Touchstone, 1996).

15. Malcolm Gladwell, *The Tipping Point* (New York: Little Brown, 2000), p. 142.

16. Maxwell and Dornan, *Becoming a Person of Influence*, pp. 71–72.

17. P. Zimbardo, C. Banks, and C. Haney, "Interpersonal Dynamics in a Simulated Prison," *International Journal of Criminology and Penology* (1973): 73.

Chapter 11

1. David Sears, J. Freedman, and L. Peplau, *Social Psychology* (Englewood Cliffs, N.J.: Prentice Hall, 1985), p.154.

2. A. C. Elms, "Influence of Fantasy Ability on Attitude Change Through Role Playing," *Journal of Personality and Social Psychology* 4 (1966): 36–43.

3. A. Pratkanis and E. Aronson, *Age of Propaganda* (New York: W. H. Freeman, 1992), pp. 123–124.

4. Les Giblin, *How to Have Confidence and Power in Dealing with People* (Englewood Cliffs, N.J.: Prentice Hall, 1956), p.120.

5. W. L. Gregory, R. B. Cialdini, and K. M. Carpenter, "Mediators of Likelihood Estimates and Compliance: Does Imagining Make It So?" *Journal of Personality and Social Psychology* (1982): 89–99

6. N. Christensen, *The Art of Persuasion and Selling* (New York: Parker Publishing, 1970), p. 20.

7. G. Wells and R. Petty, "The Effects of Overt Head Movements on Persuasion," *Basic and Applied Social Psychology* 1, 3 (1980): 219–230.

8. Ibid.

9. P. Underhill, *Why We Buy: The Science of Shopping* (New York: Simon & Schuster, 1999), p. 37.

10. Ibid.

11. Ibid.

12. Des Dearlove, "A Breath of Lemon-Scented Air," *The London Times,* April 3, 1997.

13. Matt Crenson, "Scent of Cookies Brings Out Best in Shoppers," *Las Vegas Review Journal,* October 14, 1996.

14 Luke 10:30–37.

15. J. Darley and D. Batson, "From Jerusalem to Jericho: A Study of Situational and Situational and Dispositional Variables in Helping Behavior," *Journal of Personality and Social Psychology* 27 (1973): 100–119.

16. S. Godin and M. Gladwell, *Unleashing the Idea Virus* (New York: Hyperion, 2001).

17. N. Rackham, *Account Strategies for Major Sales* (New York: McGraw-Hill, 1989), p. 143.

18. E. Loftus, "Reconstructing Memory: The Incredible Eyewitness," *Psychology Today* 8 (1974): 116.

19. L. Wrightsman, M. Nietzel, and W. Fortune, *Psychology and the Legal System* (Pacific Grove, Calif.: Brooks/Cole Publishing, 1994), p. 147.

20. Ibid.

21. G. Gorn and M. Goldberg, "Children's Responses to Repetitive TV Commercials," *Journal of Consumer Research* (1980): 421–425.

22. R. E. Petty and J. T. Cacioppo, "Effects of Forewarning of Persuasive Intent and Involvement on Cognitive Responses and Persuasion," *Personality and Social Psychology Bulletin* (1979):173–176.

23. L. A. Festinger and N. Maccoby, "On Resistance to Persuasive Communication," *Journal of Abnormal and Social Psychology* 68 (1964): 359–366.

24. Ibid.

25. M. Sherif, O. Harvey, B. White, W. Hood, and C. Sherif, *Intergroup Conflict and Cooperation: The Robbers' Cave Experience.* (Norman, Okla.: University of Oklahoma Institute of Intergroup Relations, 1961).

26. D. Peoples, *Presentations Plus* (New York: John Wiley and Sons, 1988), p. 66.

27. The 3M Meeting Management Team, *How to Run Better Business Meetings* (New York: McGraw-Hill, 1987), pp. 114–115.

Chapter 12

1. J. Maxwell and J. Dornan, *Becoming a Person of Influence* (Nashville: Thomas Nelson, 1997), p. 50.

2. Maxwell Maltz, *Psycho-Cybernetics* (Los Angeles: Wilshire Book Company, 1960).

3. E. Walster Hatfield, "The Effect of Self-Esteem on Romantic Liking," *Journal of Experimental Social Psychology* (1965): 1.

4. Stephen R. Covey, *Principle-Centered Leadership* (New York: Simon & Schuster, 1990).

5. Ibid.

6. Maxwell and Dornan, *Becoming a Person of Influence*, p. 43.

7. *Science* Newsletter, April 16, 1949.

8. K. Erickson, *The Power of Praise* (St. Louis: Concordia Publishing House, 1984), pp. 79–80.

9. J. D. Watt, "The Impact of Frequency of Ingratiation on the Performance Evaluation of Bank Personnel," *Journal of Psychology* 127, 2 (1993): 171–177.

10. S. J. Wayne and R. C. Liden, "Effects of Impression Management on Performance Ratings: A Longitudinal Study," *Academy of Management Journal* 38, 1 (1995): 232–260.

11. R. J. Deluga, "Supervisor Trust Building, Leader-Member Exchange and Organizational Citizenship Behaviour," *Journal of Occupational and Organizational Psychology* 67 (1994): 315–326.

12. D. Drachman, A. DeCarufel, and C. Insko, "The Extra Credit Effect in Inter-Personal Attraction," *Journal of Experimental Social Psychology* (1978): 458–467.

13. M. Tesser, *Advanced Social Psychology* (New York: McGraw-Hill, 1995).

Chapter 13

1. A. Pratkanis and E. Aronson, *Age of Propaganda* (New York: W. H. Freeman and Company, 1992), p. 93.

2. G. E. Belch and M. A. Belch, *Advertising and Promotion: An Integrated Marketing Communications Perspective* (New York: McGraw-Hill, 1998).

3. M. Schleidt and B. Hold, "Human Odour and Identity," in *Olfaction and Endocrine Regulation*, W. Breipohl, editor (London: IRL Press, 1982), pp. 181–194.

4. Robert A. Baron, "Sweet Smell of Success: The Impact of Pleasant Artificial Scents on Evaluations of Job Applicants," *Journal of Applied Psychology* 68 (1983): 709–713.

5. Ibid.

6. G. H. S. Razran, "Conditioned Response Changes in Rating and Appraising Sociopolitical Slogans," *Psychological Bulletin* 37 (1940): 481.

7. Doug Murphy. See: www.ahwatukee.com/afn/community/articles/010704b .html

8. David Leonhardt, with Kathleen Kerwin, "Hey Kid, Buy This!" *Business Week,* June 30, 1997.

9. R. Feinberg, "Credit Cards As Spending Facilitation Stimuli," *Journal of Consumer Research* (1986): 348–356.

10. K. Fehrman and C. Fehrman, *Color: The Secret Influence* (Englewood Cliffs, N.J.: Prentice Hall, 2000), 141.

11. Ibid, p. 142.

12. Ibid, pp. 12-13.

13. Ibid, p. 84.

14. Ibid, p. 144.

15. Ibid, p. 144.

16. Ibid, p. 145.

17. Ibid, p. 145.

Chapter 14

1. Arthur Lefford, "The Influence of Emotional Subject Matter on Logical Reading," *Journal of General Psychology* 34 (1946): 127–151.

2. Randall Reuchelle, "An Experimental Study of Audience Recognition of Emotional and Intellectual Appeals in Persuasion," *Speech Monographs* 25, 1 (1958): 49–57.

3. Gerard Tellis, *Advertising and Sales Promotion Strategy* (Reading, Mass.: Addison-Wesley, 1998), p. 138.

4. George Miller, "The Magical Number of Seven," *Psychological Review* 63, 2 (1956).

5. Charles Larson, *Persuasion* (Belmont, Calif.: Wadsworth,1995), pp. 222–225.

6. J. C. McCroskey, "A Summary of Experimental Research on the Effects of Evidence in Persuasive Communication," *Quarterly Journal of Speech* 55 (1969): 169–176.

7. P. Salovey and J. D. Mayer, "Emotional Intelligence: Imagination, Cognition, and Personality," reprinted in *Human Emotions,* J. M. Jenkins, K. Oatley, and N. L. Stein, editors (Oxford: Blackwell Publishers, 1998), pp. 313–319.

8. Tellis, *Advertising and Sales Promotion Strategy*, pp. 160–161.

9. L. Janis and S. Feshbach, "Effects of Fear-Arousing Communications," *Journal of Abnormal and Social Psychology* (1953): 78–92.

Index

About the Author

Kurt Mortensen is founder and CEO of The Persuasion Institute, and one of America's leading authorities on persuasion, motivation, and influence. Through his highly acclaimed speaking, training, and consulting programs, Kurt has helped thousands of people achieve unprecedented success in both their business and personal lives. His Maximum Influence Mastery Course is dramatically changing the way people achieve their most treasured goals.

Contact information:
Visit Kurt Mortensen at:
www.maximuminfluence.com

Persuasion Institute
3214 North University Avenue #613
Provo, Utah 84604
801-434-4022